LAW&BANKING

Applications

CRAIG W. SMITH

EDUCATION POLICY & DEVELOPMENT

 AMERICAN
BANKERS
ASSOCIATION

1120 Connecticut Avenue, N.W.
Washington, D.C. 20036

Printed in the United States of America

Library of Congress Cataloging-in-Publication data

Smith, Craig W.
    Law & banking : applications / Craig W. Smith.
        p.   cm.
    ISBN 0-89982-361-0
    1. Banking law—United States.   I. Title.   II. Title: Law and banking.
KF974.S64   1990
346.73'082—dc20
[347.30682]   90-30969
                                                                    CIP

Contents

List of Figures

Preface

This edition of *Law and Banking: Applications* incorporates changes in the law governing commercial transactions that have transpired since its publication in 1986. For example, a substantial portion of chapter 4, "Bank Collections," is dedicated to a discussion of the Expedited Funds Availability Act (EFAA), which was passed by Congress and signed into law on August 10, 1987. The purpose of this act is twofold: to provide bank customers with quicker access to deposits made into their accounts and to expedite the return of unpaid items to the depositary institution.

Law and Banking: Applications has been designed to be used either independently or in conjunction with *Law and Banking: Principles*, which sets forth the basic concepts of commercial law that underlie banking transactions, and which provides a foundation for mastery of the following specific areas of banking law presented in *Law and Banking: Applications*—negotiable instruments, letters of credit, and secured transactions. Although useful, a course in *Law and Banking: Principles* is not a necessary prerequisite to the study of *Law and Banking: Applications*.

The primary objective of this textbook is to serve as a classroom reference, and its secondary objective is to serve as a general reference. As a study aid, this textbook will enable the reader to recognize problems that commonly arise under the law of negotiable instruments, letters of credit, and secured transactions. If those problems are recognized, then this book's secondary purpose as a general reference can be realized.

This book does not attempt to deal with every legal issue that might arise, and it is not intended as a legal treatise. Consequently, it is of the utmost importance that all legal questions be referred to a bank's counsel for advice and guidance.

Many individuals have contributed to the development of this book. First, I would like to acknowledge the help given by the members of the review committee, who spent long hours reviewing the text. They are

Donna Cook-Lewis
Lending Officer
Sovran Bank/Central South
Nashville, Tennessee

James B. Curtis
Senior Attorney
California Federal Bank
Los Angeles, California

Dinah Bogart Engel
Assistant Counsel
Germantown Savings Bank
Bala Cynwyd, Pennsylvania

Keith R. Fisher
Of Counsel
Hogan & Hartson
Washington, D.C.

Tom Greco
Associate General Counsel
American Bankers Association
Washington, D.C.

Johnny A. Ioanou
Attorney-at-Law
Southfield, Michigan

David W. Johnson
Group Vice President
Trust Company Bank of
   Northwest Georgia
Rome, Georgia

Randy L. Kalmbach
Attorney
Look, Kalmbach and Look,
   P.C.
Wyandotte, Michigan

Brian E. Sullivan
Vice President and General
   Counsel
First National Bank
   in Wichita
Wichita, Kansas

Next, I would like to thank my secretary, Holly J. Watson, for her long hours spent typing and retyping the manuscript. Last, my special thanks for the support and patience of my wife, Heather, and my daughter, Lindsay, and to my parents for their constant support and example.

1

Negotiable Instruments

After studying this chapter, you will be able to

- list the four types of negotiable instruments
- explain the principal differences between order and promissory instruments and list the parties to both
- define drafts, checks, notes, and certificates of deposit
- explain the concept of negotiability
- describe the five essential elements of a negotiable instrument
- discuss the rules of interpretation

WHAT ARE NEGOTIABLE INSTRUMENTS?

Originally, negotiable instruments were developed to serve as meaningful substitutes for money. Experts disagree on whether the Romans, Greeks, Florentines, Jews, or merchants of Lombard originated negotiable instruments. Historically, however, Lombardian merchants used negotiable instruments in the early fourteenth century to avoid the perils of transporting gold to foreign countries. The concept of negotiability is what distinguishes negotiable instruments from other agreements to pay money. This concept protects holders of negotiable instruments from other claims of ownership and certain defenses against their payment and thus makes them a meaningful substitute for money.

The two types of negotiable instruments are **order instruments** and **promissory instruments**. Order instruments take two forms—drafts and checks—and are called order instruments since they contain the drawer's order or direction to the drawee to pay the payee. Promissory instruments also take two forms—notes and certificates of deposit—and are called promissory instruments since they contain the maker's promise to pay the payee.

Order Instruments

An order instrument principally serves as a payment device and thus functions as a substitute for money. Drafts and checks are order instruments that involve three parties.

Drafts

A **draft** is an order by one person (the **drawer**) to another person (the **drawee**) to pay money to a third person (the **payee**). A draft may also be called a bill of exchange. Figure 1.1 shows an example of a draft. The parties to this draft are the payee (John Doe and Co.), the drawer (John Doe and Co.), and the drawee (Richard Roe, Inc.).

```
No.  410               Somewhere, U.S.A.  January 15,  19 ___

       AT      SIGHT

Pay to the
order of _____ John Doe and Co. (PAYEE) ____ $ 500.00 _____

_____ Five Hundred and no 100 _____ DOLLARS

TO  Richard Roe, Inc. _____
      Main St. _____          John Doe and Co. (DRAWER)
      Anywhere, U.S.A. _____      John Doe, Pres.
     (DRAWEE)
```

Figure 1.1 Sample Draft

The parties to this draft have made the following agreement: the drawer (John Doe and Co.) orders the drawee (Richard Roe, Inc.) to pay the amount of the draft ($500) to the payee (John Doe and Co.) when the draft is presented to the drawee for payment. Thus, to be negotiable, a draft generally contains an order to pay. The order is the drawer's specific direction to the drawee to pay the draft when presented by the holder.

A draft and a bill of exchange do not differ except in the way the terms are applied. In U.S. domestic trade, the instrument is called a draft. In foreign transactions, the same instrument is usually called a bill of exchange.

The payee and the drawer are the same entity in figure 1.1, which is a situation common to draft instruments because a draft is frequently used as a payment device for the sale of goods. For example, in exchange for the goods sold, the buyer and seller agree that the seller may prepare (draw) a draft payable to the seller's order for the amount of the goods. The draft is drawn on the buyer who is then obligated to pay for it when presented by the seller.

Finally, drafts are typically classified as either sight or time drafts. A **sight draft** (shown in figure 1.1) is payable on demand. A **time draft** is payable at a fixed future date. That date may be specified in either of two ways: on a definite day stated in the instrument or at a fixed time after sight or demand. For instance, a time draft may be dated January 15, 1995, and state, "on April 15, 1995, pay to the order of . . . ." Alternatively, it may be payable at a fixed time after sight or demand when it states, "90 days after sight, pay to the order of . . . ."

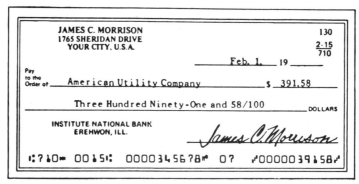

Figure 1.2   Sample Check

Checks   A **check** is a draft drawn on a financial institution and payable on demand. It too is an agreement between three parties for the payment of money. Figure 1.2 is an example of a check. This check is an instrument drawn by a checking-account depositor, the drawer (James C. Morrison), on his bank, the drawee (Institute National Bank). The instrument directs the bank to pay the sum specified ($391.38) from the available funds in the drawer's checking account on demand by the payee (American Utility Company). What distinguishes a check from other drafts is that it is always drawn on a bank and payable on demand.

Promissory Instruments

Notes and certificates of deposit are promissory instruments. A promissory instrument principally serves as a credit device, that is, a means of borrowing money to be repaid in the future. Unlike order instruments, which involve three parties, promissory instruments involve two—a maker and a payee.

Notes

A **note** is a promise by one person (the **maker**) to pay money to another person (the payee). Figure 1.3 is an example of a promissory note. The parties to this note are the maker (David Debtor) and the payee (The Commerce Bank).

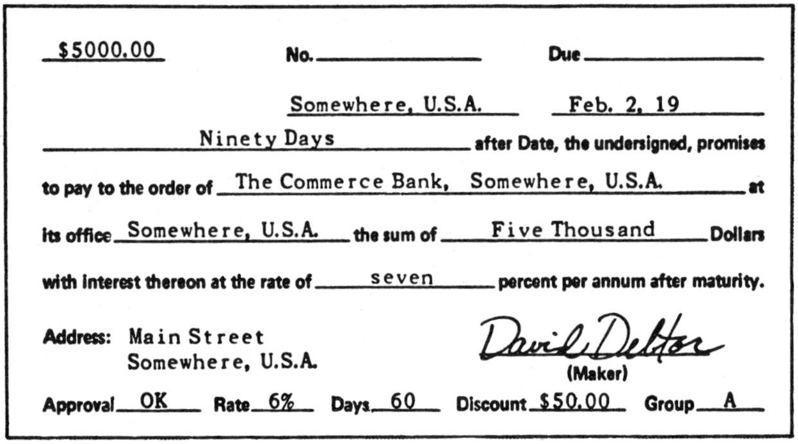

Figure 1.3 Promissory Note

The parties to the note in figure 1.3 have made the following agreement: the maker (David Debtor) promises to pay the amount of the note ($5,000) to the payee (The Commerce Bank) 90 days after its date. Commonly, a maker signs a note to evidence a debt owed to the payee.

Notes may be payable at either a definite time, as shown in figure 1.3 ("90 days after date"), or on demand. A demand note generally will read, "On demand, I promise to pay . . . ." In addition, time notes can be paid in installments. For example, a car loan might be payable in 36 monthly installments.

People use promissory instruments frequently in today's society. Businesses use them, for example, to borrow money to build plants and to buy equipment and inventory, while consumers use them to borrow money to buy homes, cars, furniture, and clothes.

Certificates of Deposit Like a note, a certificate of deposit (CD) is an agreement between two parties for the payment of money. Figure 1.4 is an example of a certificate of deposit. A CD is a financial institution's written acknowledgment of the receipt of money from its depositor, with an agreement to repay it with interest on a specified date.

_____Bank

_____, (State) _____, 19___ NO. 000000
Issued at Office   City   Date

This certifies that there has been deposited in this bank the sum of

_____ Dollars $_____

Payable to _____, depositor

or order on_____, 19____, together with interest   Total Payable $_____

(Computed for the actual number of days from date hereof to maturity at _____% per annum on the basis of a 360-day year) and only upon presentation and surrender of this Certificate, properly endorsed, at the above office. No interest hereon shall accrue after maturity. Neither the deposit evidenced hereby nor the interest thereon may be withdrawn prior to maturity.

Figure 1.4   Certificate of Deposit

CONCEPT OF NEGOTIABILITY

For a negotiable instrument to serve as a meaningful substitute for money, it must freely circulate in the marketplace and carry with it a reasonable expectation of payment. Under specific conditions, the law of negotiable instruments insulates the takers (holders) of such instruments against (1) another person's claim to ownership of the instruments, and (2) either the drawer's or maker's attempt to deny or avoid the obligation to pay the instruments.

EXAMPLES ■ Allen draws a check payable to the order of cash and gives it to Williams as payment for services performed. Williams later loses the check. Jones finds the check and cashes it at his bank, which is unaware that the check was lost. In this situation, the law of negotiable instruments may insulate the bank from Williams's competing claim to ownership of the check.

■ Lopez draws a check payable to Wilson's order for the purchase of a car. Wilson then cashes the check at his bank but fails to deliver the car to Lopez, so Lopez stops payment on the check. When the bank receives the check back unpaid, it sues Lopez. Lopez claims the right to deny payment, since he never received the car. The law of negotiable instruments may insulate the bank from Lopez's defense that he never received the car (failure of consideration) because the bank gave value.

This insulation against competing claims of ownership and certain defenses to avoid payment of an instrument are comprised in the concept of **negotiability**. Thus, negotiability provides for the free circulation of instruments accompanied by a reasonable expectation that they will be paid, resulting in their use as a meaningful substitute for money.

Article 3 of the Uniform Commercial Code (UCC) determines whether an instrument is negotiable. The UCC unites into one text commercial law for both commercial and financial transactions. Its 11 articles cover such topics as sales, commercial paper, bank deposits and collections, letters of credit, investment securities, and secured transactions. The UCC is a codification of rules of commercial law that has been adopted by the legislatures of each of the fifty states. The UCC is not federal law, which as a general rule is uniformly applied in each state jurisdiction. Instead, it is state law and thus its provisions vary somewhat from one state to another.

ELEMENTS OF A NEGOTIABLE INSTRUMENT

When is a note, draft, check, or certificate of deposit considered a negotiable instrument? The answer to this question is determined solely from the face of the instrument. For an instrument to be negotiable under the UCC (section 3–104), it must be

- in writing

- signed by either the maker of a note or the drawer of a draft

- an unconditional promise or order to pay a sum certain in money

- payable on demand or at a definite time

- payable to the order or bearer of the instrument

A Writing   A negotiable instrument must be in writing. An oral agreement cannot be negotiable. Obviously, a person cannot transfer an oral contract to another person and thus it cannot possibly serve as a meaningful substitute for money.

While the writing for a negotiable instrument is usually on paper, any tangible medium may be used (U.C.C. § 1–201(46)). For instance, a negotiable instrument may be written on wood, metal, or plastic, although such an instrument might be regarded with suspicion. In fact, banks have occasionally honored negotiable instruments written on watermelons, pumpkins, and shirts.

Further, the writing for a negotiable instrument may also be made by any type of instrument, including a pencil, pen, or stylus. The use of a pencil, however, is not recommended since it invites alteration of the instrument. Finally, a message transmitted by any medium, such as radio, fax, wire, teletype, or cable, and reduced to printed form may also be considered a writing.

EXAMPLE   Olsen wrote a note in pencil payable to the order of Lattimore for $50. When Lattimore received the note, he erased the $50 and wrote in $1,000. Lattimore then transferred the note to Michaels, a holder in due course (this term will be discussed in chapter 2). When the note matured, Michaels demanded $1,000 from Olsen. Olsen refused to pay, so Michaels sued him. In this case, Michaels probably would win. This is because the UCC (section 3–406) holds a person responsible for an alteration caused by his own carelessness. Certainly, using a pencil to write a note is a careless act that invites alteration.

Although a writing does not have to be on paper, in its checking account rules, a bank normally requires its customers to use checks in a form it has approved. This rule facilitates the bank's use of high-speed check-processing machinery that promptly and accurately processes checks for collection.

A Signature

The second element essential to the formation of a negotiable instrument is a maker's or drawer's signature. Unless and until an instrument is signed, no person is obligated to pay it.

A signature does not have to be a full, written name. The maker or drawer may use any name (including a trade or assumed name), word, or mark to make the signature. In addition, the name, word, or mark serving as a signature may be handwritten, typed, printed, or made in any other manner, such as with a rubber stamp.

However, the drawer or maker must intend such name, word, or mark to operate as his or her signature before an obligation to pay the instrument arises (U.C.C. § 3–401). For example, the appearance of a drawer's name printed on the upper left-hand corner of a check does not mean that the drawer has signed the check. The printing only identifies the drawer and does not serve as his or her signature.

Finally, although it normally appears there, a drawer's or maker's signature does not need to be placed in the lower right-hand corner of an instrument. A signature may instead appear, for example, in the body of an instrument, as in "I, Carolyn Perrin, promise to pay . . . ."

EXAMPLES ■ Sam Jones cannot write, so he signs his checks with the mark "X." In this case, the "X" is a valid signature since Jones intends it to operate as his signature.

- Judson Lewis writes "I, Judson Lewis, promise to pay to the order of Lindsay Smith, $2,500." In this case, Lewis's name in the body of the instrument is sufficient to serve as a valid signature.

- Consolidated Services, Inc., signs its checks with the trade name "Rent-It-All." In this case, the trade name serves as a valid signature.

- Lisa Bellamy, an entertainer, uses the stage name "Eva." She carries out all her business transactions, including the signing of checks, under her stage name. In this case, the stage or fictitious name "Eva" operates as a valid signature.

Unconditional Promise or Order to Pay a Sum Certain in Money

The third element essential to the formation of a negotiable instrument is a promise or order to pay a sum certain in money that is not subject to the terms of another agreement, transaction, or event. In other words, to be negotiable, an instrument must contain a promise or order to pay that is

- unconditional

- payable in a sum certain

- payable in money

Promise to Pay

Recall that the maker of a note must promise to pay the sum specified to the holder. The promise in a note usually states, "I promise to pay . . . ." However, when a note does not use the usual statement of a promise, determining whether certain words form an actual promise or just an acknowledgment of debt is sometimes difficult.

To ascertain whether certain language amounts to a promise, the following question should be asked: "Does the language contain a commitment to pay or does it merely acknowledge a debt?" If the language contains a commitment to pay, it is a promise. For example, if a note states, "I owe you $10," that language does not constitute a commitment to pay and thus is not a promise. Thus, phrases like "I owe you" and "due to" merely acknowledge the existence of a debt.

■ A note reads, "I owe you $200, which I agree to pay you on demand." The words "which I agree to pay" accompany the words "I owe you." This makes the instrument an acknowledgment of the debt and a specific commitment to pay it.

■ A note states "Due to Jackson Ford $25." The phrase "due to" like the phrase "I owe you" is merely an acknowledgment of debt and not a promise to pay.

■ A note states "Due to Jackson Ford $25," but also contains the phrase "by me and on his demand." The addition of the words "by me and on his demand" may transform a writing that formerly only acknowledged a debt into an instrument that now promises to pay that debt. The language in this instrument is not perfectly clear, however, and illustrates the advantage of using the simpler phrase, "I promise to pay" to form a promise. These words eliminate any doubt as to whether the instrument contains a promise.

Thus, for clarity and uniform interpretation, a promissory instrument should always include the words "promise to pay."

Order to Pay   Just as a note must contain a promise to pay, a check or draft must contain an "order to pay" before it can become a negotiable instrument. An order to pay is the drawer's specific direction to the drawee to pay the instrument when presented by the holder.

The usual—but not required—wording of the order in a check or draft is "pay to the order of . . . ." However, any words that express an order to pay will meet the UCC requirement that a negotiable draft contain an order. But again, when the usual form of an order is not used, determining whether certain words form an order or just a request to pay is sometimes difficult. For example, a check that states, "I wish you would pay . . ." is merely a request to pay and not an order.

Therefore, to ascertain whether certain language amounts to an order, the following question should be asked: "Does the language contain a direction or merely a request to pay?" If the language contains a direction, it is an order. In addition, for clarity and uniform interpretation, an order instrument should always include the words "pay to the order of . . . ."

EXAMPLES ■ A draft states, "I direct you to pay . . . ." Although the word "order" does not appear in the instrument, this language is sufficient to constitute an order since it is a direction by the drawer to pay the drawee.

■ A draft states, "Please pay to . . . ." It is questionable whether this language constitutes an order. Some courts have ruled that such language is an order, while others have ruled that the language is only a request. These conflicting viewpoints show the advantage in using the language "pay to the order of. . . ." to form an order since it eliminates any question about whether the instrument contains an order.

Unconditional Promise or Order

A negotiable instrument must also contain a promise or order to pay that is not based on any other promise, agreement, event, or transaction.

EXAMPLE ■ A note reads, "I promise to pay Grant $100 on his wedding day." Although Grant may be engaged and the wedding day set, he may never get married. Accordingly, since the promise is conditioned upon an event, the note is nonnegotiable. Similarly, a note reading, "I promise to pay Grant $100 on my 30th birthday," is nonnegotiable since the maker may die before reaching age 30.

Payable in a Sum Certain

For an instrument to be negotiable, the order or promise to pay must not only be unconditional but generally must also be payable in a definite amount or **sum certain** that can be calculated from the face of the instrument. Consequently, a promissory note bearing interest at a variable rate that is ascertainable from a recognized index, such as the U.S. prime rate published in the *Wall Street Journal*, is not negotiable. This is because a holder of the note is unable to calculate the exact amount due at maturity solely from the face of the instrument. However, since the use of variable rate interest notes is widespread, several states recently have amended their statutes to make variable rate notes negotiable under the provisions of the UCC. For instance, these amendments to the UCC generally provide that a variable rate interest note is negotiable as long as the interest rate is readily ascertainable by a reference in the instrument to an announced rate of a named financial institution or some other recognized interest rate index.

In addition, the UCC (section 3–106) provides that the amount payable is a sum certain, even though the amount is payable with interest, in installments, with a penalty if paid late, or with costs of collection including attorney's fees upon nonpayment.

EXAMPLES ■ A note has a clause that states, "Late charge on each installment in default shall be $5.00." The sum stated on the face of the instrument is still a sum certain because the UCC permits the inclusion of a penalty clause without affecting the negotiability of an instrument.

■ A note states, "I agree to pay all costs, expenses, and attorney's fees in any proceedings for the collection of this note." The sum stated on the face of the instrument is still a sum certain since the UCC permits the inclusion of collection clauses without affecting the negotiability of an instrument.

■ A note states, "Twenty days after date, I promise to pay to the order of Ralph King $25, together with interest at the current bank rates." In this situation, the sum stated is probably not a sum certain because the interest rate is not a fixed rate. As a result, at maturity of the note, the holder cannot calculate the exact amount due solely from the face of the instrument. This result would probably be the same even in a jurisdiction that provides that variable rate notes are negotiable. This is because the note used in this example does not refer to a named financial institution or some other recognized index to accurately ascertain the interest rate in the note. However, even though the note may not be negotiable, it is still a legally enforceable contract between the parties.

Payable in Money

Finally, a promise or order to pay must also be payable in money or the instrument is not negotiable. Section 1–201 of the UCC defines money as a medium of exchange that a domestic or foreign government authorizes or adopts as a part of its currency. This definition of money does not include gold, silver, or any other metal or object used as a medium of exchange. If an instrument states, for example, that it is "payable in 12 ounces of gold," it is not payable in money and so is nonnegotiable. Likewise, if an instrument is payable in silver, platinum, tobacco, or beads, it is not payable in money and thus is nonnegotiable.

EXAMPLE ■ Albert Vaughn promises to pay 250 marks to the order of Jennifer Carter. Since Germany recognizes marks as currency, the note is payable in money and thus negotiable.

Payable on Demand or at a Definite Time

The fourth element essential to the formation of a negotiable instrument is that it be payable either on demand or at a definite time. If a holder cannot determine from the face of an instrument when payment is due, then the instrument is nonnegotiable.

Payable on Demand

A holder of a demand instrument can require its payment at any time. The UCC (section 3–108) provides that an instrument is payable on demand if it states that it is payable on demand, it is payable at sight, or it does not state a time for payment.

EXAMPLES ■ The parties to a note left the due date blank: "_____ after date, the undersigned promises to pay . . . ." Since the note does not state a time for payment, it is due on demand.

■ A standard form "demand" note states that the maker has the option to pay it in four monthly installments. This note is not a true demand note. The option to pay it in monthly installments converts the note to one that is payable for a fixed period of time.

Payable at a Definite Time

If the date on which an instrument is to be paid can be determined exactly from the face of the instrument, then it is payable at a definite time and negotiable. However, if the date on which the instrument is to be paid depends on a future act or event, then the instrument is not payable at a definite time and is not negotiable. For example, an instrument states that it is payable "20 days after the project's completion." This instrument is not payable at a definite time because payment depends on a future event.

EXAMPLE ■ A note, dated May 1, states, "Ninety days after date, I promise to pay to the order . . . ." The time of payment is definite since it can be determined from the face of the note. Payment is due 90 days after May 1, or on July 30, and thus is due at a fixed date.

Payable to Order or Bearer

The fifth and final element essential to the formation of a negotiable instrument is that it be payable either to the order or bearer of the instrument. The words "pay to the order of," "pay to bearer," and their equivalents are frequently called words of negotiability. Only with such words is an instrument negotiable. The precise words "pay to order of" or "pay to bearer" are not absolutely necessary to make an instrument negotiable. However, several courts have refused to recognize an instrument as negotiable unless it contains the word "order" or is payable to bearer. Thus, to ensure negotiability, the use of these precise words is recommended.

Payable to Order　　The UCC defines an order as a direction to pay (U.C.C. § 3–102). That direction must be more than a mere authorization or request, and it must also identify with reasonable certainty the person to be paid. For instance, an instrument that states, "pay to the order of the grocer," probably does not sufficiently describe the payee to qualify as an order instrument.

Further, an order instrument may be payable to the order of any of the following:

- the maker or drawer

- the drawee

- two or more payees

- an estate, trust, or fund

- an office or an officer by his or her title

- a partnership or unincorporated association (See U.C.C. § 3–110.)

EXAMPLES　■　An instrument payable to the order of an estate may read as follows: "pay to the order of the estate of John J. Jones"; "pay to the order of Mary Jones, Executrix, John J. Jones Estate"; or "pay to the order of the executrix of the John J. Jones Estate." In each of these examples, the instrument is payable to the order of the representative of the estate.

■　An instrument payable to an office may read, "pay to the order of the treasurer of Long-Term Leasing, Inc.," while an instrument payable to a specific officer of the corporation may read, "pay to the order of W.G. Jones, Treasurer, Long-Term Leasing, Inc." In both examples, the instrument is payable to the corporation.

Payable to Bearer　　In contrast to an order instrument, a bearer instrument does not designate a specific payee and thus is payable to anyone who holds it. Further, an instrument is "payable to bearer" when it is payable to bearer or order of bearer, a specified person or bearer, or cash or the order of cash. In addition, an instrument is payable to bearer if there is any indication that it does not intend to designate a specific payee (U.C.C. § 3–111).

An instrument payable to bearer may read, "pay bills due," "pay holder," or any other notation that does not designate a specific payee.

RULES OF INTERPRETATION

The perfectly formed negotiable instrument is a written document that contains only the following four elements: (1) a maker's or drawer's signature; (2) an unconditional promise or order to pay a sum certain in money; (3) a statement that the instrument is payable on demand or at a definite time; and (4) a statement that the instrument is payable to order or bearer.

However, some instruments circulated in the world of banking and commerce are not always perfectly formed. An instrument may contain—in addition to the elements needed to make it negotiable—other terms, descriptive words, or ambiguous language. For example, a note may additionally state that property, such as a car or a home, has been given to secure payment of the note. This type of clause is called a **security provision.** An instrument also may be incomplete. For example, the amount of a check or the name of the payee may not be provided. In addition, a check may include descriptive words, such as "pay to the order of Jason G. Foley, President." Or the amount of a check may be ambiguous, because it is written in the sum of "one hundred and no/100 dollars" but also bears the figure "$1,000," as illustrated in figure 1.5.

Missing, contradictory, additional, or ambiguous language in an instrument cannot be ignored. The meaning of the language must be interpreted to assess its impact on either the negotiability of the instrument or on the rights and responsibilities of the parties to the instrument. Consider the foregoing examples. Does a security provision destroy the negotiability of an instrument? Is the payee of the check in figure 1.5 Jason G. Foley or the unidentified organization he presumably serves as president? Is this check properly payable for $100 or $1,000?

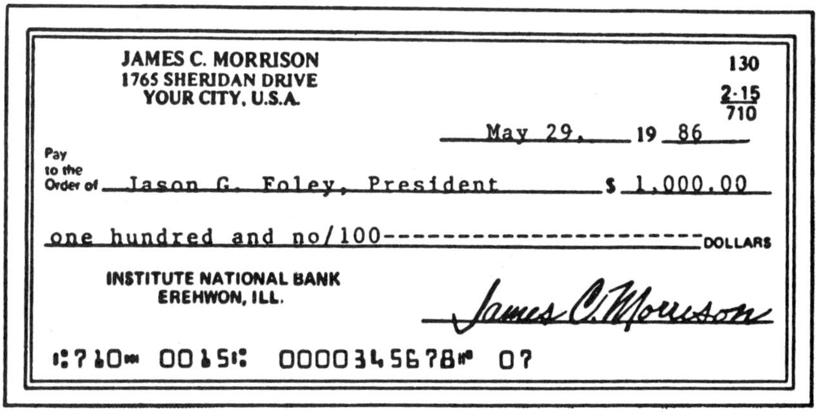

JAMES C. MORRISON
1765 SHERIDAN DRIVE
YOUR CITY, U.S.A.

130

2-15
710

May 29, 19 86

Pay to the Order of Jason G. Foley, President $ 1,000.00

one hundred and no/100-------------------- DOLLARS

INSTITUTE NATIONAL BANK
EREHWON, ILL.

James C. Morrison

⑆710⑈ 0015⑆ 0000345678⑈ 07

Figure 1.5 Check with Ambiguous Amount

To answer these questions, the UCC provides uniform rules of interpretation. For example, under these rules, an instrument's negotiability is not affected by the inclusion of a security provision. Thus, the transferee of a note can reasonably assume that he or she is receiving a negotiable note even if it contains a security provision in addition to the elements of negotiability. The UCC also provides that a check containing descriptive words, such as "Jason G. Foley, President," is payable to Jason G. Foley and not to the organization that he may serve as president. Guided by this rule, a teller may be confident that Foley is the proper payee and cash this check for him. The UCC also provides that words control figures; that is, the words used prevail over the figures used. Given this rule, a teller should pay the check in figure 1.5 for $100 and not $1,000.

The need for these uniform rules of interpretation becomes apparent when we consider what might happen if they did not exist. Without the rule that words control figures, one teller might cash the check in figure 1.5 for $100, while another might cash it for $1,000. Still a third teller might refuse to cash the check altogether.

The possibility of such a situation underscores the need for uniform rules of interpretation. Otherwise, uncertainty about the effects of missing, additional, ambiguous, or conflicting language on either the negotiability of an instrument or the rights and responsibilities of the parties to the instrument would make people reluctant to accept such instruments as meaningful substitutes for money.

To maintain negotiable instruments as meaningful substitutes for money, the UCC rules clearly define

- terms (in addition to the elements of negotiability) that do not affect the negotiability of an instrument

- omissions that do not affect the negotiability of an instrument

- the effect of certain terms and ambiguous language on the rights and responsibilities of the parties to an instrument

By clearly defining these matters, the rules ensure the ready acceptance and rapid circulation of negotiable instruments in the marketplace.

Terms Not Affecting Negotiability

Although to be negotiable an instrument must contain an unconditional promise or order to pay and no other promise, order, obligation, or power, the UCC provides several specific exceptions to this rule. For instance, the negotiability of an instrument is not destroyed even if it contains any of the following terms or provisions in addition to the unconditional promise or order to pay:

- a term stating that property securing the payment of a note may be sold if the maker fails to pay the note as agreed (default provision)

- a maker's promise to protect the property that secures payment of the note (protection-of-collateral provision)

- a statement of the place where an instrument is drawn or payable

- a statement of the date of an instrument

- a reference in the instrument to another writing

- a statement that the instrument is given in full satisfaction of a debt owed by the drawer to the payee

---

EXAMPLE ■ A promissory note states that it is "secured by a mortgage on real property located at 152 Idlewood Avenue and reference should be made thereto for additional agreements or provisions that may affect this note." Since this provision merely refers to a mortgage, it does not destroy the promissory note's negotiability.

However, if the note had stated that it was "subject to the terms of the mortgage securing it," then the note would be nonnegotiable.

Omissions Not Affecting Negotiability

Like an additional term, a missing term may affect an instrument's negotiability. For instance, an undated instrument may state that it is due 30 days after its date. Will the missing date prevent the instrument from ever being negotiable, since the time of its payment is uncertain? Similarly, what is the effect on the negotiability of an instrument if the payee's name or the amount of the instrument is not provided? Will these missing terms prevent the instrument from ever being negotiable? The UCC provides answers to these questions.

Incomplete Instruments

An instrument that is missing a term essential to its formation as a negotiable instrument will not always remain nonnegotiable. The UCC recognizes that the parties to an instrument may either inadvertently or intentionally leave an instrument incomplete. For instance, a person paying for groceries by check may be rushed and forget to fill in the amount, or a father may make out a blank check payable to his daughter and tell her to spend no more than $50 on school supplies.

The UCC (section 3–115) permits the holders to complete such checks according to the authority given them by the drawers. Thus, the grocer has the authority to complete the check up to the amount of the groceries purchased. Similarly, the daughter has the authority to complete the check she holds up to $50 for school supplies purchased.

Terms and Language Affecting Parties' Rights and Responsibilities

While the inclusion or omission of certain terms may affect the negotiability of an instrument, certain terms and ambiguous language can also affect the rights and responsibilities of the parties to an instrument. An example of a right that a party has to an instrument is a holder's right to receive payment when due (presuming that the instrument is not subject to a defense against its payment). For instance, if a note is payable 30 days from its date, the holder has the right to demand and receive payment from the maker on the maturity date. An example of a responsibility that a party has under an instrument is the obligation of the maker of a note to pay it at maturity.

Instruments containing the following terms and language can affect the rights and obligations of parties to them:

- instruments payable to two or more persons

- instruments with words describing the payee

- instruments with ambiguous or conflicting language

Instruments Payable to Two or More Payees

Frequently, a check will be drawn to the order of two or more payees. For example, insurance companies commonly issue claim checks to more than one payee. Typically, these instruments are payable to both the party whose property is insured, such as the owner of a car, and the institution that holds a security interest in the property, such as a bank.

Instruments payable to two or more payees create questions about who has the right to receive payment. The UCC (section 3–116) and case law determine whether the signatures of only one or all the payees are needed to properly cash a check in any of the following situations when the payees' names are

- joined by the word "and"

- separated by the word "or"

- joined and separated by the words "and/or"

- separated by a virgule (slash)

- not joined by the word "and," and not separated by a virgule or the word "or"

PAYEES' NAMES JOINED BY THE WORD "AND"

If the word "and" joins payees' names on an instrument, it is only payable to all of them (U.C.C. § 3–116(b)). Accordingly, before a teller can negotiate, cash, or accept such an instrument for deposit, all payees must endorse (sign) it. For instance, an instrument that is payable to the order of Sally Smyth and Julian Smyth designates joint payees and is only payable to both Sally and Julian. Thus, both Sally and Julian must endorse the check before a teller can cash or accept it for deposit.

PAYEES' NAMES SEPARATED BY THE WORD "OR"

If the word "or" separates payees' names on an instrument, it is payable to any one of them (U.C.C. § 3–116(a)). Accordingly, before a teller may properly cash or accept such an instrument for deposit, only one of the payees needs to endorse it. For instance, an instrument that is payable to the order of Robert Williams or Judy Williams is payable to either Robert or Judy. Thus, only one of their signatures is required for a teller to cash or accept it for deposit.

PAYEES' NAMES JOINED AND SEPARATED BY THE WORDS "AND/OR"

If the words "and/or" both join and separate payees' names on an instrument, it is payable to any one of the payees or to all of them (U.C.C. § 3–116(a)). For instance, an instrument that is payable to Ron Jones and/or Sam Jones is payable to one or both of the payees. In other words, all or any one of the payees may endorse such an instrument before a teller can properly cash or accept it for deposit.

PAYEES' NAMES SEPARATED BY A VIRGULE

A check payable to the order of Laura Deane/Stewart Deane separates the payees' names by a virgule (slash). Under case law in some states, such a check is payable to either payee. Courts in those states treat the virgule as if it were the word "or." Accordingly, the rules that apply to checks where the word "or" separates payees' names would also apply to checks where a virgule separates payees' names. However, since many states have not yet established laws on the effect of a virgule separating payees' names on checks, counsel's advice should be sought on such checks.

PAYEES' NAMES WITHOUT "AND," "OR," OR A VIRGULE

Sometimes two or more payees' names appear on a check without "and," "or," or a virgule separating them, as in "Andrew Baker Billy North." Cases considering this type of omission treat the instrument as though the word "and" separated the payees' names. Accordingly, such a check is only payable to all the payees.

Instruments with Words Describing the Payee

An instrument often describes a payee as holding an instrument for the benefit of another person, entity, or business. For instance, suppose a check is payable to "Frank Dwyer, Treasurer of Universe Steel, Inc." Since Dwyer is described by both the office he holds (treasurer) and the name of his company (Universe Steel, Inc.), the UCC (section 3–117) provides that the check is payable to his company. Frank Dwyer's name appears on the check only for convenience and permits him either to cash or deposit the check for his company's benefit.

Related to this rule is a common bank policy that forbids tellers to cash checks payable to corporations or other business entities such as partnerships. Instead, under such a policy, tellers may only accept these checks for deposit to corporations' accounts. This is because the case law in several states makes banks responsible for ensuring that corporate checks are either cashed or deposited only for the corporations' use. If a bank permits a dishonest corporate employee either to cash or deposit a corporate check into his or her own account for personal use, it is liable to the corporation for the amount of the check. Such a policy, then, protects banks from the dealings of dishonest corporate employees.

Case for Discussion

WORLDWIDE TRAVEL V. STAR STATE BANK

Facts

Marsha Mather, the treasurer of Worldwide Travel, Inc., wants to deposit into her personal account at Star State Bank a check in the amount of $15,000, payable to the order of "Marsha Mather, Treasurer, Worldwide Travel, Inc." Mather is a friendly person, well known to bank employees. She assures the teller, Greg Gregory, that the check represents commissions due to her from the drawer. Although Star State Bank's policy requires that corporate checks be deposited only to corporate accounts, Gregory allows Mather to make the deposit since he knows her and believes her story. A few days later, Mather returns to the bank, withdraws the money from a different teller, and departs for a two-month safari in Kenya. Worldwide Travel sues Star State Bank.

Decision

Unfortunately, Star State Bank is located in a state where the case law makes banks responsible for ensuring that corporate checks are cashed or deposited only for corporations' use. Consequently, the court rules that Star State Bank is liable to Worldwide Travel for the $15,000. According to the court, although Gregory knew Mather and believed her to be honest, he should not have permitted the deposit. The check clearly designated Worldwide Travel as the payee and bank policy prohibits the deposit of corporate checks into personal accounts. Gregory should thus have accepted this check only for deposit into an account in the name of Worldwide Travel, Inc.

Questions for Discussion

1. What steps should a teller take when a customer insists on depositing a corporate check into his or her personal account and bank policy prohibits such action?
2. What defenses could the bank have raised in this situation?
3. What procedures should banks use to prevent this kind of situation?

The UCC also provides that, if an instrument merely describes the payee as having a particular title or office but fails to designate on whose behalf he or she may be holding the instrument, it is payable to the individual. For instance, if an instrument is payable to "Frank Dwyer, Treasurer" or "Frank Dwyer, Trustee," a teller may treat the instrument as payable to Frank Dwyer individually.

Instruments with Ambiguous or Conflicting Language

Unfortunately, instruments are not always precisely written. Sometimes they contain conflicting or ambiguous language that calls into question the respective rights and responsibilities of the parties to the instruments. For instance, if a teller is confronted with a check bearing the figure "$1,000" but written in the amount of "one hundred and 00/100 dollars," how much cash should the teller give for it? Or if a check is typewritten in the amount of "$100" and machine printed in the amount of "$1,000," for how much is it payable? To answer these questions, the UCC (section 3–118) provides rules to resolve conflicts or ambiguities between (1) words and figures and (2) handwritten, typewritten, and printed terms.

WORDS AND FIGURES

The UCC rule governing conflicts between words and figures contained in an instrument is straightforward: words control figures. However, if the words are ambiguous, the figures control the words.

EXAMPLES ■ A teller is presented with a check to cash that bears the figure "$1,000" and is written in the amount of "one hundred and 00/100 dollars." In this situation, the teller may properly cash the check for $100 since words control figures.

■ A teller is presented with a check to cash that bears the figure "$365" and is written in the amount of "thirty six-five and 00/100 dollars." In this case, since the words "thirty six-five" are ambiguous, the teller may properly cash the check in the amount shown by the figure—$365.

Handwritten, Typewritten, and Printed Terms

The UCC rule governing differences between handwritten, typewritten, and printed terms in an instrument is also straightforward: handwritten terms (any writing done by hand) control both typewritten and printed terms, and typewritten terms control printed terms.

EXAMPLES ■ An instrument is either typewritten or printed in the amount of "$100" and handwritten in the amount of "one thousand dollars." Since handwritten terms control both typewritten and printed terms, the instrument is properly payable in the amount of $1,000.

■ An instrument is typewritten in the amount of "$1,000" and printed in the amount of "$100." Since typewritten terms control printed terms, the instrument is properly payable in the amount of $1,000.

CONCLUSION

Negotiable instruments are simply contracts to pay money which may take the form of a draft, check, note, or certificate of deposit. Drafts and checks are normally order instruments involving an agreement between three parties: the drawer, drawee, and payee. Notes and CDs are promissory instruments involving two parties: the maker and payee.

Whether a draft, check, note, or CD is negotiable is determined solely from the face of the instrument. To be negotiable, an instrument must be in writing and contain the maker's or drawer's signature, an unconditional promise or order to pay a sum certain in money, a statement that the instrument is payable on demand or at a definite time, and a statement that the instrument is payable to order or bearer.

Instruments circulated in the world of banking and commerce are not always perfectly formed. Besides the elements needed to make them negotiable, some instruments may also contain other terms, descriptive words, or ambiguous language. Consequently, the UCC has established rules of interpretation to enable the holder of an instrument to assess quickly and consistently the effect of a missing, additional, conflicting, or ambiguous term on an instrument's negotiability and the rights and responsibilities of the parties to the instrument. These rules promote the ready acceptance and rapid circulation of negotiable instruments and make them meaningful substitutes for money.

Questions for Review and Discussion

1. What are the four types of negotiable instruments?

2. What is the basic difference between an order and promissory instrument?

3. What two types of negotiable instruments are classified as order instruments? What two types are classified as promissory instruments?

4. How many parties to a draft are there? What is each party called?

5. How many parties are there to a promissory instrument? Name them.

6. Can a negotiable instrument be written on a napkin?

7. Can an illiterate person sign a negotiable instrument?

8. Is an instrument negotiable if its payment is conditioned on the occurrence of some event, such as graduation from college?

9. In what medium of exchange must a promise or order to pay be payable?

10. Is an instrument negotiable if the holder cannot determine from its face when payment is due?

11. To whom is a bearer instrument payable?

12. Can a check made out to John Fig and Carole Augenstein be endorsed and cashed by only one of them?

13. In whose account may a check made out to "Tom Wit, President, Allied Shoelace Co." be deposited?

14. One UCC rule holds that words control figures. What does this mean? Does this rule have an exception?

15. How should a teller interpret a check on which handwritten terms conflict with typewritten and printed terms?

Holder in Due Course

After studying this chapter, you will be able to

- identify actions necessary to transfer a negotiable instrument

- define assignment under ordinary contract law

- explain the difference between transfer by negotiation and transfer by assignment

- describe the concept of and list the requirements for becoming a holder in due course

- explain what is meant by taking an instrument for value, in good faith, and without notice of defect

- discuss the meaning and significance of the shelter doctrine

- describe the rights of a holder in due course, especially the right of protection from competing claims of ownership and personal defenses and a holder's susceptibility to certain real defenses

- explain the rights of one who is not a holder in due course

Negotiable instruments (checks, drafts, notes, and certificates of deposit) are readily accepted in banking and commerce as substitutes for the money they represent. One reason they are so widely used is that, under commercial law, they are easily transferred from one person or business to another by the simple process of negotiation.

Transfer by negotiation gives the person receiving the item (the **transferee**) the opportunity to obtain greater rights in the instrument than those of the person who transferred the item (the **transferor**). To obtain greater rights in the instrument, the transferee must achieve the status of a **holder in due course**. To comprehend holder-in-due-course status fully, you must first master the concept of negotiation.

NEGOTIABLE VERSUS NEGOTIATION

It is important to distinguish between the terms "negotiable" and "negotiation." **Negotiable** refers to an instrument that contains all the elements of negotiability (as discussed in chapter 1) and thus refers to the form of the instrument. **Negotiation** refers to the procedure by which one person or entity transfers a negotiable instrument to another.

Since negotiable instruments function as substitutes for money, they must be easily transferable from person to person and carry a reasonable expectation of payment. To ensure free circulation of negotiable instruments, the Uniform Commercial Code (UCC) provides certain safeguards to people accepting such instruments as payment, which are unavailable to those accepting nonnegotiable instruments as payment.

ASSIGNMENT VERSUS NEGOTIATION

Both assignment and negotiation are methods by which a person or entity transfers ownership rights (**title**) to an instrument to another. Ordinary written (nonnegotiable) contracts are normally transferred by assignment, while negotiable instruments are normally transferred by negotiation. The ease of transfer by negotiation over transfer by assignment sets negotiable instruments apart from ordinary contracts.

Assignment As discussed in chapter 1, an instrument containing a conditional promise to pay, while legally enforceable, is not a negotiable instrument.

EXAMPLE ■ In a promissory note, John Mercer agrees to pay Frank Smith $2,500 for a 1974 Dasher, "subject to the terms of a separate purchase and sale agreement." Such a note is nonnegotiable since its terms subject it to a separate agreement governing Mercer's purchase of the Dasher. Thus, ordinary contract law governs these kinds of nonnegotiable instruments.

Accordingly, if the owner of the instrument desires to sell (transfer) his or her interest in the instrument to another person, he or she will normally do so by assignment. Thus, **assignment** means that the owner of the instrument transfers all right, title, and interest in the instrument to the purchaser.

EXAMPLE ■ Because Frank Smith of the preceding example needs money, he sells the promissory note to his friend, Jim Morris, for $2,000. Smith uses these words to transfer the note to Morris: "For $2,000 and other valuable consideration, I hereby sell, assign, and grant to Jim Morris all my right, title, and interest in and to this promissory note, (signed) Frank Smith."

In this example, the **assignor** (Smith) has "assigned" to the **assignee** (Morris) whatever interest he has in the note. The effect of this action is to place the assignee (Morris) in the assignor's (Smith's) shoes and to grant Morris the same, but no greater, right to enforce payment of the instrument than Smith had. It should be noted that assignment is a valid legal process that creates rights and liabilities in the parties. Such rights and liabilities differ from those created by negotiation. If the maker of the note (Mercer) can claim a reason (defense) for not paying the assignor, then the maker can also claim that same defense against the assignee, even if Morris did not know about the defense when he purchased the instrument.

EXAMPLE ■ Frank Smith never delivers the car to Mercer. When the note matures, Morris (the assignee) demands payment from Mercer (the maker). Mercer refuses Morris's demand and claims the defense of nondelivery of the car. In this situation, Morris cannot enforce payment of the note (even if he did not have notice of the defense), because he possesses no greater rights in the instrument than Smith had. Thus, he is subject to Mercer's defense of nondelivery. However, the result in this example would have been dramatically different if Mercer had transferred the note to Smith by negotiation instead of assignment.

Negotiation

One party can transfer a negotiable instrument to another party either by endorsing the instrument and delivering it to the other party or by delivery alone. The party who transfers the note is the transferor, and the party who receives it is the transferee. How an instrument is negotiated depends on whether the instrument is in order or bearer form.

As was stated in chapter 1, an order instrument is payable to a specific person's or entity's order (U.C.C. § 3–110). For example, a check that states, "payable to the order of Joseph Walsh" or "payable to the order of Truckline, Inc.," is considered an order instrument. A **bearer instrument**, however, does not name a specific payee (U.C.C. § 3–111). For instance, a check that states, "pay bearer" or "pay cash," is considered a bearer instrument. The rules for the negotiation (transfer) of order and bearer instruments differ.

Order Instruments

The UCC defines negotiation as the transfer of an instrument in such a form that the transferee becomes a **holder**. Before a transferee can become a holder of an order instrument, however, two events must occur: (1) the instrument must be delivered to the transferee and (2) the transferor must endorse the instrument (U.C.C. § 3–202(1)).

EXAMPLES ■ Gerry Dixon wants to deposit a check payable to his order into his checking account. Dixon must both endorse his name on the back of the check and deliver the check to the teller before the bank becomes a holder.

■ Paul Fields has a check payable to his order that he delivers to Al Carter but fails to endorse. In this case, transfer by negotiation has not occurred and, upon receipt of the instrument, Carter is not a holder. As a result, he cannot become a holder in due course.

Bearer Instruments   A bearer instrument does not require an endorsement for negotiation (U.C.C. § 3–202(1)). Instead, a bearer instrument is negotiated by delivery alone. Upon delivery, the transferee becomes a holder.

EXAMPLE ■ Suppose the check Fields delivered to Carter in the preceding example was payable to cash instead of to Fields's order. In this case, Fields only has to deliver the check to Carter for Carter to become a holder. Thus Carter would be eligible to be treated as a holder in due course if he also meets the other legal requirements for becoming a holder in due course (if he received the instrument for value, in good faith, and without notice of a defense against it).

Negotiation is a method of transfer that supports the underlying goal of article 3 of the UCC to make negotiable instruments meaningful substitutes for money. A person who receives an instrument by negotiation becomes a holder and thus has the opportunity to obtain greater rights in the instrument than those of the transferor. To obtain greater rights in the instrument, however, a transferee must become a holder in due course. As such, a transferee receives the instrument free from certain defenses against payment. This reasonable expectation of payment makes a negotiable instrument a meaningful substitute for money.

HOLDER-IN-DUE-COURSE REQUIREMENTS

The concept of a holder in due course is the cornerstone of the law of negotiable instruments. This concept assures the holder in due course of a free market for his or her instrument. Therefore, the objective of UCC article 3, which is the free and rapid circulation of negotiable instruments, is achieved.

To qualify as a holder in due course, a transferee must first become a holder of the instrument. This simply means that the transferor must transfer the instrument to the transferee through the process of negotiation. Further, a holder in due course is a holder who takes the instrument

■ for value

■ in good faith

■ without notice of defect (that it is overdue, has been dishonored, or is subject to any defense against or claim to it by any other person) (See U.C.C. § 3–302.)

Defenses may be real or personal, as explained later in this chapter. Basically, a **defense** is a claim that one has a right to deny or avoid an obligation to pay an instrument.

Value   To become a holder in due course, a holder must first give something of value, such as money, in exchange for the instrument. For instance, a person who receives a negotiable instrument as a gift does not give value and, as such, does not qualify in his or her own right as a holder in due course. (The significance of the phrase "in his or her own right" will be explained later in the section on the shelter doctrine.)

The reason for this requirement is that, until a holder gives value, he or she does not need the protections given to a holder in due course. One such protection is the ability of a holder in due course to enforce the payment of an instrument, even though a defense against payment exists. Consequently, if a holder does not stand to lose something of value, he or she does not need to enforce the payment of an instrument. Instead, to protect him- or herself adequately, the holder can simply refuse to complete the transaction that caused receipt of the instrument in the first place.

EXAMPLE ■ Kathleen Seaver deposits a check into her account at Third

National Bank. Before she is allowed to draw against the deposit, Third National Bank learns that the drawee has dishonored payment of the check. Accordingly, to protect itself, Third National can simply refuse to allow her to draw against the deposit, and does not need the protection of a holder in due course in this situation.

On the other hand, once a holder gives value for an instrument, one of the holder's only protections against loss is the ability to enforce its payment, even if a defense against such payment exists. In other words, a holder for value needs the protection of a holder in due course.

EXAMPLE ■ Instead of depositing the check into her account, Kathleen Seaver of the preceding example cashes the check over the teller's counter. Before the check is returned unpaid because payment was stopped, Seaver closes her account and moves out of town. In this situation, since Third National has given value in exchange for the check (cash over the counter), it needs the protection of a holder in due course or it will suffer a loss. Accordingly, Third National may enforce payment against the drawer (the person or business against whose account the check was drawn), even though the drawer may claim a defense against paying other parties who are not holders in due course.

Thus, as long as a bank takes an instrument for value, in good faith, and without notice of a defect, it—like any other person or business—may become a holder in due course. Further, a bank generally takes an instrument for value when it permits "withdrawal of the credit" given for a deposited check or when it "cashes" the check over the counter (U.C.C. §§ 4–208 and 4–209).

The UCC (section 3–303) provides guidelines for assessing whether or not a holder has taken an instrument for value. A holder takes the instrument for value under one or more of the following situations:

- when the agreed consideration has been performed

- when the instrument is taken in payment of or as security for a prior claim against any person, whether or not the claim is due

- when a negotiable instrument is given for it

- when an irrevocable commitment to a third party is made

Performance of the Agreed Consideration

The giving of money or other property of value is a straightforward means of giving value for an instrument and thereby becoming a holder in due course. The crucial step here is the performance of the agreed consideration, not just the agreement or promise to perform.

Questions may arise when a negotiable instrument is transferred on the basis of a promise. Again, the performance of a promise, not simply the giving of it, is necessary for value to be sufficient to make a person a holder in due course.

EXAMPLE ■ Dwyer has a $10 check drawn by Ann Porter and made payable to him. He plans to transfer the check to Smith, who has promised to shovel his driveway. Smith's promise to shovel Dwyer's driveway for $10 is sufficient consideration to form a binding contract; it does not, however, constitute value. Smith must give value (shovel the driveway) to meet the first requirement of a holder in due course.

Receipt of an Instrument in Payment of Prior Claim

Value is also given when a person receives an instrument in payment of (or as security for) a previously existing (antecedent) debt unrelated to the instrument.

EXAMPLE ■ On April 15, Brian Wilson purchases a television set from Geraldine Browne. He agrees to pay $150 for it in 30 days, but on May 15, Wilson is short of funds and asks Browne for a 60-day extension. As security, Wilson transfers to Browne a $200 promissory note due on August 15. (He had received that note from Inez Calder in payment for a tape deck he had sold to her.) Browne has given value for the $200 note since it was transferred to her as security for a prior debt (arising from the sale of the television set) unrelated to the instrument issued as security (which arose from the sale of Wilson's tape deck). Thus, because she has given value, she meets the first requirement for becoming a holder in due course.

The Exchange of One Negotiable Instrument for Another

Value is also given when a holder takes one negotiable instrument in exchange for another.

EXAMPLE ■ Brady, the payee of a $1,000 note drawn by Alexander, sells it to Carter in exchange for Carter's personal check for $800. By taking the note in exchange for another negotiable instrument (in this case, a check), Carter has given value for the note, thereby meeting the first requirement of a holder in due course.

The Making of an Irrevocable Commitment to a Third Party

Recall that a person's promise to do something in exchange for an instrument does not constitute value. There is an exception to this rule however. A person might, in reliance upon receiving an instrument, make an irrevocable commitment (one that cannot be broken) to another person. Such a promise may constitute value. Thus, the person who makes an irrevocable commitment gives value and meets the first requirement for becoming a holder in due course.

EXAMPLES ■ Third National Bank, at its customer's request, exchanged its own cashier's check for a check drawn on another bank and payable to its customer's order. The check is subsequently returned unpaid to Third National marked "payment stopped."

Third National is a holder for value and thus a holder in due course (assuming the other requirements for becoming a holder in due course have been met) since, when it took the check in exchange for its own cashier's check, it irrevocably committed itself to pay its own cashier's check to any subsequent holder in due course. Once a bank issues a cashier's check, it is deemed to have agreed to pay it when presented. Accordingly, the bank may enforce the payment of the check against the drawer, even though the drawer might have a defense against paying some other party on the check.

■ Stein promises to plow Atchison's driveway during winter. In payment, Atchison transfers to Stein a $750 note he holds from Clark. Two days after receiving the note, Stein enters into a contract with Taylor (an unrelated third party) to buy a used car. Although Stein, after receiving the note in exchange for his mere promise (to plow Atchison's driveway), made an irrevocable commitment to purchase a car from Taylor, he has not given value. Under the UCC, in order for Stein's irrevocable commitment to have constituted value, it should have been made at the same time he received the note. Thus Stein is not a holder in due course. But if he pays for the used car by endorsing the note to Taylor, Taylor becomes a holder in due course.

Good Faith

In order to become a holder in due course, the holder must also take an instrument in good faith. Under the UCC, good faith means "honesty in fact in the conduct or transaction concerned." Under contract law, the two principal measures of good faith are the objective and subjective tests. The **objective** or **prudent-person test** uses the standard of a reasonably knowledgeable and careful person. If this hypothetical person would regard the instrument as valid, it may be assumed that the holder took it in good faith.

In contrast, the **subjective test** accepts the honesty of the holder in taking the instrument as the sole measure of good faith. In other words, the subjective test of good faith is met if the holder honestly believes he or she is taking a valid instrument, even though a prudent person would regard the instrument as invalid. The UCC relies on this subjective test of good faith. That reliance is tempered, however, by the final requirement for holder-in-due-course status—that a holder receive an instrument without notice of a defect.

EXAMPLES ■ In violation of his bank's regulations, a teller for First National took a check from a payee who was not a bank customer and exchanged it for a cashier's check. Before making the exchange, however, the teller called the bank on which the check was drawn to confirm that the account existed and had sufficient funds. Later, the check was returned to First National marked "payment stopped." The teller honestly believed he had taken a valid instrument. Thus, even though its teller had violated regulations, the bank acted in good faith according to the subjective test. As long as the bank also received the instrument for value and without notice of a defect, it could enforce its payment as a holder in due course against the drawer.

■ Stein draws two checks payable to Wilson's order in exchange for Wilson's promise to pay Stein in cash the next day. Wilson does not pay Stein, so Stein stops payment on his checks. Meanwhile, Wilson has gone to his bank and cashed the checks. Wilson's bank knew only that he had a history of bounced checks and a poor credit standing. Since the bank, when it cashed the checks, did not know that payment had been stopped, it acted in good faith according to the subjective test. Wilson's check-cashing history and his credit rating had nothing to do with the validity of the checks in question.

Without Notice of Defect

The final requirement for a holder in due course relates closely to the good faith requirement. The holder must take the instrument without notice that it is overdue, has been dishonored, or is subject to any defense against or claim to it by any other person.

Notice of an Overdue Instrument

To be a holder in due course, a person must take the instrument before its maturity.

EXAMPLE ■ Sherman made a note which was due on January 15, 1986, payable to the order of Jacobs. On January 16, Jacobs sold the paper to Rogers who bought it in good faith and for value. Nonetheless, Rogers was not a holder in due course, because the note was overdue when he purchased it.

The UCC (section 3–304(3)) provides that a holder has notice that an instrument is overdue if the holder has reason to know one or more of the following. That

■ any part of the principal amount is overdue

■ the maturity date has been accelerated

■ he or she is taking a demand instrument after demand has been made or more than a reasonable period has elapsed after its issue

The phrase "reason to know" simply means that, from all the facts and circumstances known to a person, he or she has reason to know that a particular situation exists (U.C.C. § 1–201).

PRINCIPAL AMOUNT OVERDUE

If a holder, upon taking an instrument, has reason to know that any part of the principal amount is overdue, he or she is ineligible to be a holder in due course.

EXAMPLE ■ Taylor gives Long a promissory note payable in installments. One installment falls due and remains unpaid and this fact is clearly shown on the face of the note. Long then sells the note to Hall. Since the note clearly shows that one installment of principal is past due, Hall has reason to know of this defect and cannot claim the status of a holder in due course.

ACCELERATED MATURITY DATE

Negotiable instruments that are payable in installments frequently include a provision that the entire principal amount shall immediately become due upon default in the payment of any installment. This type of provision is known as an acceleration clause. If a holder knows, upon taking an instrument, that the maturity date has been accelerated, he or she cannot be a holder in due course. However, a holder who accepts such an instrument without reason to know that it has been accelerated remains eligible for holder-in-due-course status.

EXAMPLE ■ Johnson fails to pay the first installment of a note when due to Taylor, the payee. Since the instrument contains an acceleration clause, the note is immediately payable in full. Taylor, at this point, sells the note to Bigman without telling him that the first installment on the note is outstanding. Since this fact is not apparent from the face of the note, Bigman still has holder-in-due-course status.

DEMAND INSTRUMENT OVERDUE

A demand instrument is payable when issued, but becomes overdue only after demand has been made or an unreasonable length of time has elapsed since its issue. Recall that a check is defined as a draft drawn on a bank and payable on demand. Reasonable time, in connection with a check drawn and payable within the United States, is presumed to be 30 days. Reasonable time, in connection with a demand note, is not defined by the UCC; a period of two days is not unreasonable, but one year probably is.

EXAMPLES ■ Ivan Strep draws a check payable to Chuck Altman. Altman transfers the check to Philip Lang two months after it was drawn. Presumably, Lang does not qualify as a holder in due course since he took a check more than 30 days after it was issued.

■ Jane Miller gives Bill Delton a promissory note payable on demand. On the next day Delton demands payment, but Miller refuses. Delton then sells the note to Paul Allen, who knows that Miller refused to pay it. Allen cannot be a holder in due course since he knowingly took the note after demand for payment was made.

■ John Beasley made a demand note payable to the order of Steve Bright. Bright demanded payment a few days after he acquired the note, but Beasley refused to pay. Bright then sold the note to Ramirez without telling him Beasley had refused to pay. Although the demand instrument came due at the time Bright demanded payment, Ramirez had no reason to know that this had occurred, and therefore can be a holder in due course.

Notice of Dishonor

A transferee who knows that an instrument has been dishonored cannot become a holder in due course. For instance, a person who takes a check marked "payment stopped" has notice that the instrument's payment previously has been dishonored and thus is ineligible to become a holder in due course for that instrument.

EXAMPLE ■ A bank accepts for deposit into its customer's account a check clearly noting that payment previously has been dishonored. The bank's customer closes the account and the check is once again returned dishonored with the notation "payment stopped." The bank then attempts to enforce payment against the drawer. Since the bank had reason to know that the check previously had been dishonored, it cannot now achieve the status of holder in due course and is consequently subject to any defenses that the drawer may assert against payment.

Notice of Any Defense or Claim

A holder having notice of any defense against or claim to an instrument by any person does not qualify has a holder in due course. A person (transferee) who takes an instrument knowing that another person claims title as owner to receive payment on the instrument, is ineligible to become a holder in due course. Similarly, previous knowledge of a defense against an instrument also bars a transferee from holder-in-due-course status. For example, a transferee cannot claim holder-in-due-course status if he or she accepts an instrument whose incompleteness or irregularity should arouse suspicion that something is wrong. An instrument on which the drawer's signature, payee's name, or the amount is missing or altered is incomplete or irregular enough to create suspicion of wrongdoing. On the other hand, an instrument that shows an obvious change in date from January 2, 1990, to January 2, 1991, need not necessarily arouse suspicion of wrongdoing. At the beginning of a new year, individuals will often mistakenly date an instrument with the previous year.

EXAMPLE ■ A bank teller is asked to cash a check with obvious erasures on it. The word "hundred" has been changed to "thousand" and the original payee's name has been erased and changed. The alterations are sufficiently obvious that the teller refuses to cash it. If the teller had ignored the obvious erasures, the bank would be ineligible for holder-in-due-course status.

SHELTER DOCTRINE

The transfer of an instrument gives the transferee the same rights as those of the transferor (U.C.C. § 3–201(1)). This means that a holder who would not otherwise qualify as a holder in due course automatically obtains the rights of this privileged position if the transferor was a holder in due course. This principle is called the **shelter doctrine.** Thus, a person who receives a negotiable instrument as a gift and does not give value for it becomes a holder in due course if the person making the gift is a holder in due course. By the same token, a person who knows that an instrument is overdue, has been dishonored, or is subject to a claim or defense may still enforce its payment as a holder in due course, but only if the transferor is a holder in due course.

In other words, the first person on an instrument to qualify as a holder in due course must qualify under all the rules discussed in the preceding sections of this chapter. The person who next obtains title to the instrument (either by purchase or gift) also acquires the status of holder in due course, even if that second person would not have normally qualified as a holder in due course.

EXAMPLE ■ Lake signs a promissory note for $2,500 in payment for a car he is buying from Cobb. Cobb fails to deliver the car but transfers the note to Hart by negotiation. Having purchased the note for value and in good faith and unaware of any claims to or defenses against the instrument, Hart becomes a holder in due course. Hart then transfers the note by negotiation to Adams. Adams knows Lake and also knows that Lake never received the car that Cobb promised him. Adams thus has notice of Lake's defense and would normally be ineligible for the status of holder in due course. However, since Adams's transferor (Hart) was a holder in due course, Adams succeeds to his rights and can enforce payment of the note against Lake.

The shelter doctrine again underscores the prevailing theme of article 3 of the UCC—to assure the holder in due course of a free market for his or her instrument and thereby make it a meaningful substitute for money. Nevertheless, the UCC makes two exceptions to the shelter doctrine:

■ A transferee who has been a party to any fraud or illegality affecting the instrument cannot succeed to the rights of a holder in due course.

■ A transferee who, as a prior holder of an instrument, had notice of a defense against payment of an instrument, cannot reacquire the instrument and improve his or her position by succeeding to the rights of a later holder in due course.

EXAMPLE ■ Suppose Cobb of the preceding example transfers the note directly to Adams, who knows that Cobb never delivered the car to Lake. Adams, having notice of Lake's defense against payment of the instrument, is not a holder in due course. If Adams then transfers the note to Morris by negotiation, Morris—by accepting the instrument for value, in good faith, and without notice of any claims or defenses—becomes a holder in due course. Adams cannot at this point reacquire the note from Morris and himself become a holder in due course, thereby improving his position with respect to collecting the note. The same exception holds true for any party involved in a fraud or illegality affecting an instrument; such a transferee cannot, under any circumstances, become a holder in due course.

RIGHTS OF A HOLDER IN DUE COURSE

Significant legal consequences flow from the privileged status of a holder in due course. As noted earlier, in claims of title to an instrument, the law favors a holder in due course, and most defenses against payment of an instrument do not affect the holder's ability to force that payment. Thus, a holder in due course takes an instrument free from all claims to it by any other person and most defenses of any party to the instrument with whom the holder has not dealt (U.C.C. § 3–305). A transferee who has notice of a claim to or defense against an instrument is disqualified from the status of holder in due course, except when, under the shelter doctrine, a transferee with such notice succeeds to the rights of a transferor who is a holder in due course.

Freedom from Claims and Personal Defenses

A claim of title is any person's assertion of his or her right as owner to receive payment on an instrument. A holder in due course is free from all such claims of ownership by other people.

For instance, a payee to whom an instrument is delivered is generally the owner of the instrument and, as such, is entitled to receive payment on it. However, an instrument endorsed in blank becomes a bearer instrument, payable to the person who possesses it, and may be negotiated by delivery alone. Thus, if the payee endorses an instrument in blank and then loses it, any person who takes it as a holder in due course from the finder or other transferor is immune from other claims of ownership. This is why a bank requires any customer who owns a lost cashier's check to indemnify it before the bank will issue a duplicate check. **Indemnification** simply means that, if the bank has to pay the original cashier's check because a holder in due course presents it for payment, the customer agrees to reimburse the bank for the amount of the check.

EXAMPLES ■ Sam Avery purchases a cashier's check, made payable to his order, from Third National Bank. After endorsing the check in blank, he loses it. Gerry Gray finds the check and promptly deposits it into his account with State Avenue Bank. Before the check is presented to Third National for payment, Avery requests the bank to issue another cashier's check, which the bank does in exchange for his indemnification against loss for any further claims on the original check.

When State Avenue receives the check back unpaid with the notation "payment stopped," it demands reimbursement from Third National. If State Avenue can demonstrate that it is a holder in due course, Third National must pay the original cashier's check. Third National can then recoup its loss from Avery under his indemnification agreement and thus avoid double payment.

■ David Jones draws and delivers a check payable to Pam Peters. Peters endorses the check in blank and then loses it. Jones stops payment on the check when Peters tells him that she lost it. The check is found by Fred Russell who then delivers it to Hobart Dunn. When the check is returned to Dunn unpaid, he demands payment from Jones, the drawer. Jones refuses, stating that Peters is the real owner of the check. If Dunn demonstrates that he received the check as a holder in due course, he would be able to enforce the check against Jones and take ownership free from Peters's competing claim of ownership.

Although a holder in due course is free from all claims of ownership, the UCC does not give a holder blanket protection from all defenses against payment. Defenses to actions on negotiable instruments are either real or personal defenses. A holder in due course takes an instrument free from personal, but not real, defenses (also called absolute defenses).

Real defenses deny the existence of a contract and, when successful, render a contract null and void from its creation. Forgery, for example, creates a real defense. If the maker's name on a note or the drawer's name on a check is forged, he or she is not liable on the note or check, even though it is transferred to a person who takes it in good faith, for value, and without notice of the forgery.

Personal defenses do not deny the existence of a contract but assert that, because some act or circumstance occurred either at or after a contract's creation, the contract has become unenforceable. For instance, payment of a note that occurs after the contract is created can give rise to a personal defense. Other common personal defenses are failure of consideration, fraud in the inducement, and failure to deliver an instrument.

Payment   If a maker pays a note, he or she possesses a personal defense against any subsequent holder who demands payment. However, since payment is not a defense that can be used against a holder in due course, it is extremely important that the maker of a paid note get it back or have it marked "paid" to avoid double payment.

EXAMPLE ■ Morris Simon signs a note as maker. Fifteen days before the note is due, he pays the holder, Ralph Barnes, but fails to get the note back or to have it marked "paid." Barnes then transfers the note to his friend, Max Lyons, who knows that Simon has already paid it. On the note's maturity date, Lyons demands payment from Simon, who asserts the defense of payment. In this situation, Simon can successfully use the personal defense of payment against Lyons. Because Lyons knew Simon had already paid the note when he took it, Lyons cannot claim the status of a holder in due course. However, if Lyons had received the note as a holder in due course, Simon would have had to pay the note twice.

Failure of Consideration

Failure of **consideration** occurs when the price of the goods purchased is not paid or when the goods purchased do not work. A maker, drawer, or other person liable on an instrument may assert this defense against the payee or other holder but not against a holder in due course.

Case for Discussion

WAYNE V. EISEN

Facts
Walter Ajax promises to deliver a new microwave oven to Rachel Eisen. She in turn gives him a promissory note for $450. However, when Eisen receives the microwave oven, she finds that it is not new and does not work. Meanwhile, instead of holding the note to maturity, Ajax sells the note to Jake Wayne before its due date. Wayne pays $400 for the note and, when the note is due, he demands payment from Eisen. Since the microwave does not work, she refuses to pay the note, so Wayne sues her.

Decision
The court rules in favor of Wayne. According to the court, even though Eisen has a legitimate personal defense, this does not affect Wayne's ability to collect from her. As a holder in due course, he is not subject to Eisen's personal defense of failure of consideration against Ajax.

Questions for Discussion
1. What should Eisen originally have done in this situation to protect her personal defense against Ajax?
2. What recourse does Eisen have to obtain satisfaction from Ajax for his failure of consideration?

Fraud in the Inducement

The UCC distinguishes between two tyes of fraud: fraud in the factum (fraud in the making or signing of an instrument) and fraud in the inducement. **Fraud in the factum** covers fraud when a party to an instrument does not know that he or she is signing a negotiable instrument. This kind of fraud is generally a real defense against payment. Most often, however, the party knows that he or she is signing a negotiable instrument but is led to sign it by false representation. This second type of fraud, called **fraud in the inducement**, is a personal defense. As such, this defense does not affect the rights of a holder in due course.

EXAMPLE ■ Mary Kelly fraudulently induced Carl Beasley to buy her car on the representation that she had never used it, when in fact, she had driven the car often. When Beasley found out that Kelly had swindled him, he refused to pay the note he had given to purchase the car. Meanwhile, Kelly had transferred the note to Joe Mason, who met the requirements for a holder in due course, and Mason sued Beasley. In this situation, Mason would win. Although Kelly fraudulently induced Beasley to purchase the car, he knew that he was signing a negotiable instrument.

Thus, unlike fraud in the factum, fraud in the inducement is only a personal defense and, as such, cannot be asserted against a holder in due course.

EXAMPLE ■ Suppose Beasley pays for the car with his personal check. When he learns that Kelly has misrepresented her use of the car, he stops payment on the check. In the meantime, Kelly cashes the check at Revere State Bank, which takes it as a holder in due course. The drawee bank then returns the unpaid check to Revere Bank, which demands payment from Beasley since it cannot recover from its customer, Kelly. Beasley refuses Revere Bank's demand so the bank sues him. In this case, Revere State Bank, a holder in due course, wins. Beasley's defense of fraud in the inducement is a personal defense and, as such, cannot be successfully asserted against a holder in due course.

Failure to Deliver an Instrument

Delivery of an instrument occurs when its possession is voluntarily transferred from one person to another (U.C.C. § 1–201(14)). But until delivery occurs, any person—except a holder in due course—takes an instrument subject to the personal defense of nondelivery (U.C.C. § 3–306(c)).

Case for Discussion

ESTATE OF JIM GRAY V. FOUR-STAR NATIONAL BANK

Facts

Jim Gray purchases a cashier's check and names his daughter Mary (who is 16 years old) as payee, intending to give it to her as a gift. However, before Gray can deliver the check to Mary, he dies. Later, Mary goes to the drawer bank, Four-Star National, to cash the check. The bank is unaware that Gray never delivered the check to his daughter and thus cashes it for her in good faith. Later, Jim Gray's estate, claiming that it is the rightful owner of the check since the deceased never delivered it to the payee, demands reimbursement from Four-Star National. The bank refuses and the estate sues.

Decision

In this case, the court rules in favor of the bank. According to the court, the bank's claim as a holder in due course prevails over the estate's claim of ownership. Furthermore, the court points out that a holder in due course not only takes an instrument free from personal defenses but also free from competing claims of ownership.

Questions for Discussion

1. Can Gray's estate raise any other claims besides nondelivery of the instrument against the bank?
2. Describe a situation in which a bank's claim to ownership would not prevail over a competing claim beause of an instrument's nondelivery.

Case for Discussion

JANSON V. JANSON

Facts

William Janson drew a check payable to his son Paul and gave it to Paul's wife with instructions not to deliver it to his son until he said to do so. Afterward, Janson decided not to give the check to Paul and stopped payment on it. Paul then found the check and took it to his father's bank to cash it. The bank refused because of the stop-payment order. Paul then sued his father for the amount of the check.

Decision

The court rules in favor of the father. According to the court, William Janson never instructed his son's wife to deliver the check to his son. Thus, the father's personal defense of nondelivery would prevail. Also, Janson's son cannot claim that he is a holder in due course since, when he took the instrument, he had notice of a defense against its payment: the check had never been delivered to him. (In addition, he had not given value.)

Questions for Discussion

1. Under what circumstances would the father have to pay the check?
2. Does the bank have any liability to the son for its failure to pay the check?

Susceptibility to Real Defenses

Although free from personal defenses, a holder in due course is not free from real (absolute) defenses. Real defenses may be asserted against any party to an instrument, even a holder in due course. If successful, such a defense renders a contract null and void from is creation.

In balancing the need for negotiability against protecting those with real defenses, the UCC gives greater weight to the latter. Because of the nature of real defenses, protecting parties with real defenses is more important than protecting innocent purchasers and preserving the concept of negotiability.

Section 3–305(2) of the UCC lists the following as real defenses:

- infancy, to the extent that it is a defense to a simple contract

- such other incapacity, duress, or illegality of the transaction, which negates a party's obligation on it

- misrepresentation (fraud) of the nature of a contract that a party signs without knowledge or reasonable opportunity to learn of its character or its essential terms

- discharge in insolvency proceedings (bankruptcy)

■ any other discharge of which the holder has notice when he or she takes the instrument

Infancy **Infancy** may be asserted as a real defense, even against a holder in due course, on behalf of a minor who is liable to pay an instrument. The UCC protects an **infant** (minor) against those who would take advantage of one, although the circumstances under which a minor may use the defense of infancy vary from state to state.

In some states, a minor who has misrepresented his or her age may not use the defense of infancy. For instance, a 16-year-old boy who uses false identification that states he is 21 to buy a car under an installment contract cannot avoid making payments through the defense of infancy.

Case for Discussion   **STELLAR MULTIMEDIA V. BROWN**

Facts

George Brown, a minor, buys a $600 color television from Stellar Multimedia under a contract in which he agrees to pay $600 in monthly installments of $25 over two years. After paying $250, Brown stops making further payments. By this time, the television has depreciated in value to $300. Stellar Multimedia then sues George on the contract and he asserts his infancy as a defense.

Decision

In this case, the court rules that, before Brown is relieved of his obligations under the contract, he must restore to Stellar Multimedia the original value of the television. To do this, the court states that Brown may pursue one of two options:

■ He may pay $350 to Stellar Multimedia, which is the difference between the original purchse price ($600) and the amount he has already paid under the contract ($250).

■ He may return the television to Stellar Multimedia and pay the store $50.

Questions for Discussion

1. In this situation, does George have any further recourse?

2. Describe a situation in which a bank customer might assert infancy as a real defense.

In some states where minors can claim infancy as a real defense, a minor is entitled to recover from the holder of the instrument whatever he or she has already paid. The holder of the contract in turn is entitled to recover the property purchased if it still exists. However, even if the property does not exist, the holder must still restore to the minor whatever he or she paid.

EXAMPLE ■ Markus, a minor, bought a car from Dewey under a contract in which he agreed to pay $3,600 in monthly installments of $100 over three years. After Markus signed the note, Dewey sold it to Third National Bank, which took it as a holder in due course. After paying $1,000 on the note, Markus stopped making further payments. Third National sued Markus, who claimed the defense of infancy and also demanded the return of the $1,000 he had already paid on the note. At this time, the car was worth only $800 because of wear and tear and damage from a minor accident. In this situation, since infancy is allowed in that state as a real defense, Third National was only entitled to a return of the car. The bank could not recover on the note, and it had to return the $1,000 to Markus.

Incapacity, Duress, or Illegality

State law determines whether incapacity, duress, or illegality of a transaction is sufficient to constitute a real defense. For these charges to be a real defense against a holder in due course, state law must render the obligation of the instrument in such circumstances entirely null and void. If under state law the effect of the incapacity, duress, or illegality is to render the obligation voidable at the obligor's election, these defenses are merely personal ones and have no effect if asserted against a holder in due course.

INCAPACITY

Incapacity covers individuals who are mentally incompetent, are under guardianships or conservatorships, are wards of the state, or are otherwise incapacitated as defined by state law.

EXAMPLE ■ Under formal guardianship proceedings, Saul is declared mentally incompetent, and Wilson is appointed to take care of Saul's affairs. However, Baden knows nothing of these proceedings. Saul then makes a note payable to Baden's order to buy a car. When Wilson, Saul's guardian, learns of the transaction, he refuses to pay the note. Baden sues as a holder in due course. In this case, under applicable state law, mental incapacity declared under guardianship proceedings is a real defense. Therefore, even though he is a holder in due course, Baden is subject to the defense and cannot recover on the note.

Suppose instead that Saul, although mentally incompetent, has not been declared incompetent under formal guardianship proceedings. State law provides that mental incapacity is a real defense only when a person is declared incompetent under a formal guardianship proceeding or when a person dealing with the incompetent person knew or should have known of the mental incapacity. Since Baden had no reason to believe that Saul was mentally incompetent when he signed the note, Saul's defense of incapacity is only a personal defense, which cannot affect Baden's status as a holder in due course. Thus, under these circumstances, Baden is entitled to recover the amount of the note.

DURESS

Duress is a question of degree. Duress occurs when one person exercises pressure to overcome another person's will and forces that person to do something that he or she would not normally do. Like fraud, duress may be a personal or real defense. For example, a person forced at gunpoint to sign an instrument could probably claim a real defense under most state laws. On the other hand, a person who signs a note under the threat that his or her son will be arrested probably would not have a real defense in most jurisdictions.

EXAMPLE ■ Mason, a drug addict, needs money to support his habit, and asks Dwight for cash. Dwight does not have any cash, so Mason asks him to write a check. Dwight refuses, and Mason draws a knife and threatens to kill Dwight unless he writes Mason a check. Dwight does as Mason requests. After Mason leaves, Dwight calls the police and then calls his bank and stops payment on his check. Meanwhile, Mason cashes the check at a local bar. When the check is returned to the bar owner unpaid, she demands reimbursement from Dwight. Dwight refuses and the bar owner sues. In this situation, since Dwight wrote the check under threat of death, it is void even in the hands of a holder in due course. Thus, the bar owner's claim is no good.

ILLEGALITY

The defense of illegality is generally used in situations involving gambling or **usury** (charging a higher interest rate than is legally permissible). Again, whether the gambling or usury that led to the signing of an instrument is a real defense depends on applicable state law. If state law renders a party's obligation in such a circumstance a nullity, illegality is a real defense that may be asserted even against a holder in due course. Otherwise, such a defense cannot be used against a holder in due course.

EXAMPLE ■ Patton, a customer of a hotel casino, wrote a check payable to the casino to purchase gambling chips. The casino then sold the check to a collection agency, which received it as a holder in due course. Later, the check was returned to the collection agency unpaid. In this situation, the agency was unable to collect on the check against Patton, because state law provides that gambling debts are void and unenforceable.

Therefore, the defense of illegality becomes a real defense that can be asserted even against holders in due course.

Misrepresentation   Misrepresentation or fraud is generally a personal defense but, under certain circumstances, it may become a real defense. Fraud as a real defense occurs when the signer of an instrument neither knows nor has the opportunity to learn that he or she is signing a negotiable instrument. This type of fraud is called fraud in the factum, meaning fraud in the making or signing of a document.

The classic illustration of fraud in the factum is when an individual is tricked into signing a promissory note in the belief that it is merely a receipt or some other document. Because the person never intended to sign a negotiable instrument, the signature is ineffective and he or she has a real defense. However, if an individual knows that he or she is signing a negotiable instrument but is induced to do so by misrepresentation, this is considered a personal defense. Depending on the circumstances of the fraud, a holder in due course may or may not be protected from the defense of misrepresentation.

EXAMPLE ■ Burns wants to join the YWCA. She is handed a paper and told that it is an application for membership, so she signs it. The paper turns out to be a promissory note, which is sold to Rogers, a holder in due course. Burns refuses to pay the note, and Rogers sues her. In this example, Burns may win. Although Rogers is a holder in due course, he may be subject to real defenses. Depending on some other circumstances, fraud may have occurred in the signing of the note in this situation. Thus, when a person is deceived about the nature of the paper he or she is signing, such fraud constitutes a real defense.

Whether misrepresentation is a real or personal defense depends on all relevant factors. Those factors include the party's age, intelligence, education, business experience, and ability to read English, as well as the representations made to the party and his or her reason to rely on them or to have confidence in the person making them. Those factors also include the presence or absence of any third person who might read or explain the instrument to the party; any other possibility of obtaining independent information; or the apparent necessity, or lack of it, for acting without delay.

Discharge in Bankruptcy

Bankruptcy laws give the bankrupt party a chance for a new financial start. For this reason, the discharge of obligations on negotiable instruments in bankruptcy or other insolvency proceedings is a real defense. Even a holder in due course cannot compel payment of a negotiable instrument discharged in bankruptcy.

EXAMPLE ■ Jackie Preston borrows $1,000 from Universal Finance Company to purchase a car from a friend. She also signs a promissory note providing for repayment of the loan in 24 equal installments. The finance company then sells her note to First Street Bank, which takes the note as a holder in due course. Preston later runs into financial difficulties and files a petition for bankruptcy. The petition requests that she be discharged from any further obligation to pay her outstanding debts, including the note held by First Street Bank. If the bankruptcy court grants the discharge, it will operate as a real defense against further payment on the note, even though First Street Bank is a holder in due course.

Other Discharges

If a holder taking an instrument has notice that a party's obligation to pay it has been discharged, this also constitutes a real defense. However, notice that one party to an instrument has been discharged does not prevent a holder from becoming a holder in due course in relation to any other parties who remain liable to pay the instrument. For example, if a note bears an endorsement that has been crossed out and thus canceled, a subsequent holder acting as a holder in due course may still pursue the maker of the instrument. But this holder in due course cannot compel the discharged endorser to pay the note, since notice of such discharge operates as a real defense against payment.

EXAMPLE ■ Moody makes a note payable to the order of Greene. Greene then endorses the note and delivers it to Wilson. Wilson crosses out and thus cancels Greene's endorsement before he transfers the note to Hull, a holder in due course. In this situation, Hull does not have a recourse against Greene since Greene's obligation has been discharged. If Hull sues Greene, Greene's real defense of discharge will thwart Hull's claim.

RIGHTS OF ONE WHO IS NOT A HOLDER IN DUE COURSE

A holder in due course takes an instrument free from all claims and personal defenses (but not real defenses) on the part of any person with whom the holder has not dealt. One who is not a holder in due course (a person who neither qualifies in his or her own right nor has acquired such rights by transfer) takes an instrument subject to all valid claims and defenses on the part of any other person that would be available in an action on a simple contract.

Case for Discussion   **WHO ARE HOLDERS IN DUE COURSE?**

David Banner, a 22-year-old college student who needed money, visited his aunt, Loretta James, and took three checks from her purse. The first check was for $200 drawn by Sam Collins and made payable to the order of Banner's aunt. The reverse side of the check was signed "Loretta James." The second check was a blank check from his aunt's checkbook. The third check was for $800 payable to Scissor's Palace Beauty Salon. The reverse side of the check was blank.

Banner took the $200 check to Easy Ray's General Store where, without signing anything, he presented the check and received $200. Later that day, Easy Ray's endorsed and cashed the check at Full-Service National Bank.

Banner forged his aunt's signature as the drawer of the second check and made it payable to himself for $300. He then told his friend, Jerry Jones, that he needed to cash a check his aunt had given him for a birthday present. Banner endorsed the check "payable to the order of Jerry Jones, David Banner." Jones gave him the $300, took the check, and deposited it into his account at Full-Service National Bank.

Banner deposited the third check into his checking account at Eighth National Bank after he had signed the back "Scissor's Palace." He then went to Video Emporium and wrote a check to the store from his account for $800 to buy a video recorder.

Question for Discussion

In this situation, which individuals, banks, stores, or other parties qualify as a holder in due course for each instrument?

CONCLUSION

As the vehicle for the free circulation of negotiable instruments, the concept of a holder in due course is the essence of article 3 of the UCC. Such a holder takes an instrument free from all claims of ownership and personal defenses. In doing so, the holder assures the rapid and free circulation of negotiable instruments and thus helps to make them meaningful substitutes for money.

Questions for Review and Discussion

1. What is the distinction between the terms "negotiable" and "negotiation"?

2. What type of law governs the transfer of nonnegotiable instruments? By what method are nonnegotiable instruments transferred?

3. What two actions transfer order instruments by negotiation? What action transfers bearer instruments?

4. What is the privileged legal standing of a holder in due course?

5. What constitutes giving value for an instrument?

6. Does the UCC rely on the objective or subjective test of good faith? Describe these two tests.

7. Is a person a holder in due course if he or she purchases a note after its maturity date?

8. May a person become a holder in due course even if he or she does not fulfill the ordinary requirements of such status? What is the name of the doctrine that permits this?

9. Can anyone successfully claim title to an instrument against a holder in due course?

10. What two kinds of defenses may a party assert against a holder in due course? To which kind of defense is a holder in due course susceptible? Give some examples.

3

Liability

After studying this chapter, you will be able to

■ name the two types of liability associated with authorized signatures

■ explain the difference between contractual and warranty liability

■ explain the contractual responsibilities of a maker, acceptor, drawer, and endorser

■ explain the technical differences between special, blank, and restrictive endorsements

■ explain the difference between presentment and transfer warranties

■ distinguish between the use of a discharge for a real defense and the use of a discharge for a personal defense

■ discuss events that can lead to the discharge of a party's liability on an instrument

A major principle under the Uniform Commercial Code (UCC) is that a person is not obligated (liable) to pay an instrument unless his or her authorized signature appears on it (U.C.C. §§ 3–401 and 3–404). As discussed in chapter 1, any word or mark intended as a signature may form a signature. Further, a person may place a signature on an instrument by either signing his or her own name or requesting (authorizing) another person to sign his or her name. A person who signs an instrument at another's request is commonly called an **agent,** and the person on whose behalf the agent acts is commonly called a **principal**.

Two types of liability associated with an authorized signature are contractual liability and warranty liability.

CONTRACTUAL LIABILITY

Each party to a negotiable instrument assumes the contractual responsibility to pay it to the holder. The extent of this contractual responsibility, however, depends upon whether a party has signed an instrument as a **maker**, an **acceptor** (a drawee who has signed his or her name on a draft and thereby agrees to pay it), a **drawer**, or an **endorser**.

Makers and acceptors are primarily responsible for the payment of an instrument. This means that they are the first parties to whom a holder must look for payment of an instrument. By contrast, drawers and endorsers are secondarily responsible for the payment of an instrument. Their expectations are either that the maker of a note or the drawee of a draft will pay the instrument. Accordingly, a drawer or endorser is contractually responsible to pay an instrument only after he or she has received timely notice that the primary party has refused to pay it (dishonored payment).

Primary Liability

The parties primarily liable on negotiable instruments are makers, in the case of notes, and acceptors, in the case of drafts. All other parties to an instrument are secondarily liable.

Contracts of Makers

A maker's obligation to pay a note after it matures is absolute (U.C.C. § 3–413(1)). In other words, a maker's obligation to pay does not depend on other conditions first being fulfilled. For example, generally a maker cannot claim that his or her obligation to pay a note does not arise until the holder has presented it for payment. This means that, if a note is payable one month from its date, neither demand nor presentment for payment after maturity is necessary before the holder can sue and recover the amount of the note from the maker. This is true even though the note is payable on demand. Paradoxical as it may seem, a maker is obligated to pay a demand note without the holder's first demanding payment for it. Therefore, the holder of a demand note may bring suit against its maker at any time, even on the day he or she receives the note (U.C.C. § 3–122).

EXAMPLES ■ Bates signs a promissory note, payable to the order of Beck on August 16. Beck does not ask Bates to pay the note until September 18. Bates then refuses to pay the note because his contractual obligation is limited to payment on August 16. Beck sues Bates. In this situation, Beck wins since Bates's promise to pay is unconditional. He must pay the instrument anytime after its maturity date.

■ Wallace signs a demand promissory note, payable to the order of Sheehan. Sheehan sues Wallace on the note. Wallace defends herself on the ground that Sheehan never made a demand for payment of the note. In this situation, Sheehan wins since Wallace's obligation on the note is not conditioned on a demand for payment.

Contracts of Acceptors

Just because a drawer writes a check or draft does not mean that the drawee (that is, a bank in the case of a check) is contractually bound to pay the holder. Under the law of negotiable instruments, a drawee is not contractually obligated to pay a holder unless he or she has accepted the draft. To accept a draft, the drawee normally writes on its face the word "accepted," followed by his or her signature and the date of acceptance. However, a drawee's signature alone can operate as an acceptance (U.C.C. § 3–410). The drawee's acceptance constitutes his or her promise to accept primary responsibility for the payment of the draft. After acceptance, the holder acquires the legal right to pursue the drawee for payment. Figure 3.1 illustrates the documentation required for acceptance of a draft.

When a bank is the drawee, its act of accepting a check in writing is called **certification** (U.C.C. § 3–411). Under the UCC, a bank does not have to certify a check. However, if a bank employee chooses to do

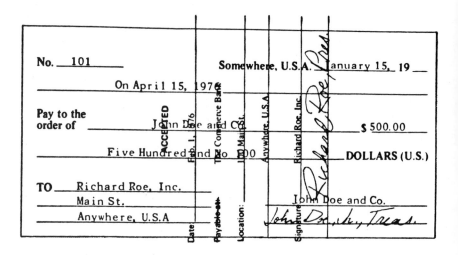

Figure 3.1   Documentation Required for Acceptance of a Draft

so, then he or she should ensure that the balance on deposit in the customer's account covers the amount of the check. Under federal law, an employee of a member bank of the Federal Reserve System commits a crime if he or she intentionally certifies a check for an amount over the balance on deposit in the customer's account (18 U.S.C. § 1004). The possible penalties imposed against an employee who intentionally violates this statute are severe: a fine up to $5,000, imprisonment up to five years, or both.

Banks frequently certify checks when a depositor purchases a car or home. The seller normally requests payment for such items by certified check, because he or she would rather rely on the bank's financial backing than that of the buyer-drawer. Figure 3.2 illustrates the documentation required for the certification of a check.

Case for Discussion   **HIGH-POINT STATE BANK v. T.V. SALES, INC.**

Facts

Jim Winegar draws a check payable to the order of T.V. Sales, Inc., for the purchase of a television. After receiving the check, T.V. Sales calls the drawee, High-Point State Bank, and asks whether sufficient funds are on deposit in Winegar's account to pay the check. The High-Point

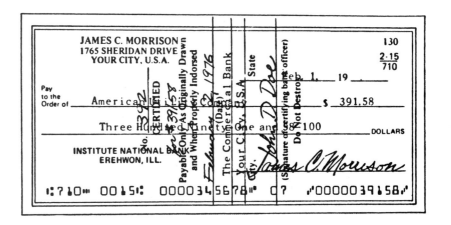

Figure 3.2   Documentation Required for Certification of a Check

employee who answers the inquiry responds that sufficient funds are currently available to pay the check.

Two weeks later, T.V. Sales presents the check for payment and it is dishonored. The company demands that High-Point pay the check and claims that the bank's previous statement that sufficient funds were available to pay the check constituted certification. High-Point refuses the company's demands, so T.V. Sales sues.

Decision

In this case, the court rules in favor of the bank. Under the UCC, certification of a check must be in writing. Furthermore, the bank's response referred only to the status of Winegar's account at the time it received the inquiry and was not a promise to pay the check when presented.

Questions for Discussion

1. What should T.V. Sales have done in this situation to protect itself from the dishonored payment?

2. Describe some procedures banks should establish so that employees do not improperly certify checks.

EXAMPLE ■ Oak Street Bank certified its customer's check payable to the order of Herbert. After the certification, the customer defaulted on a loan that Oak Street made to him. Consequently, the bank canceled the certification, used the proceeds of the check to pay the defaulted loan, and dishonored payment of the check when Herbert presented it. Herbert sued the bank. In this situation, Herbert won because, once the bank certified the check, it became primarily liable to pay it.

Generally, after certification, a bank's responsibility to pay a check is unconditional and cannot be reversed.

Secondary Liability

A drawer of a draft and an endorser of either a draft or note are secondarily liable to pay a negotiable instrument, unless they have expressly denied (disclaimed) this responsibility (U.C.C. § 3–414). For instance, if a drawer or an endorser writes the words "without recourse" after his or her signature, he or she has been effectively relieved from his or her secondary contractual obligation to pay the instrument. To be effective, however, the **disclaimer** must be written on the instrument.

EXAMPLE ■ Ann Smith drew a check payable to the order of Sam Rogers and signed her name as follows: "Ann W. Smith, without recourse." The drawee bank did not pay the check, so Rogers demanded payment from Smith. When Smith refused, Rogers sued her. In this situation, Smith won since, by writing the words "without recourse," she effectively disclaimed her contractual liability on the check.

Just because a drawer has disclaimed secondary contractual responsibility on a check, however, does not mean he or she is free from any liability to the payee. For example, although the payee cannot successfully sue the drawer on the instrument, the payee still may pursue the drawer on the underlying obligation. This obligation is simply the agreement between the parties that originally caused the negotiable instrument to be issued.

EXAMPLE ■ If Ann Smith had drawn the check in the preceding example to buy a radio from Sam Rogers, the agreement between Smith and Rogers for the purchase and sale of the radio would be the underlying obligation. Thus, although Rogers could not recover from Smith on the check (since she disclaimed her secondary contractual liability), he could still sue her on the underlying contract to recover the purchase price of the radio.

Thus, under the UCC (section 3–802), an instrument's underlying obligation is not discharged until the check is presented and paid.

Contracts of Drawers and Endorsers

Unless a drawer or an endorser has disclaimed secondary contractual liability on an instrument, he or she agrees to pay it if the following three conditions are met (U.C.C. § 3–414(1)):

■ The holder presents the instrument to the primary party for payment.

■ The primary party refuses (**dishonors**) payment.

■ The secondary party receives timely notice of the dishonor.

PRESENTMENT

Presentment is a demand for payment or acceptance of a negotiable instrument. A holder takes this action against the maker of a note or the drawee of a check or draft. As discussed in chapter 1, a negotiable instrument must be payable on demand or at a definite time. If an instrument is payable at a definite time, the presentment for payment is due on the instrument's stated maturity date (U.C.C. § 3–503). For example, a note dated April 1 states that it is due "30 days after date." In this situation, presentment for payment should be made on May 1, the note's stated maturity date.

If an instrument is payable on demand, then presentment is due within a "reasonable time." The nature of the instrument, banking custom, and the facts in each particular case determine the length of a "reasonable time" (U.C.C. § 3–503(2)). However, the UCC specifies that a reasonable time for presentment of a check is

- 30 days from its date or issue (first delivery to a holder), whichever is later, to charge a drawer with his or her secondary liability

- 7 days after an endorsement, to charge the endorser with his or her secondary liability

---

EXAMPLE ■ On January 1, Patterson drew a check on her account with Revere State Bank, payable to the order of Simon. Patterson delivered the check to Simon on January 2. On January 3, Simon endorsed the check over to Garner. Garner held the check until January 20, when he presented it to Revere State Bank for payment. The bank refused to pay the check, so Garner immediately notified Patterson and Simon of the dishonor. In this situation, Simon, an endorser, is not liable to Garner, since Garner failed to present the check within 7 days after Simon endorsed it over to him. However, Patterson, the drawer, is liable to Garner, since the check was presented for payment within 30 days after Patterson first issued it to Simon.

DISHONOR

Before a secondary party is held responsible to pay an instrument, it must also be dishonored. Dishonor simply means that the **payor** (maker or drawee) refuses to pay the instrument after proper presentment.

NOTICE OF DISHONOR

Finally, before being required to pay the instrument, a secondary party must receive timely notice of dishonor. Notice of dishonor may be given in any reasonable manner; that is, it may be oral or written

(U.C.C. § 3–508). Furthermore, the notice must identify the instrument and state that payment has been dishonored. A bank must give notice of dishonor before its **midnight deadline**, which is midnight of the banking day following the banking day on which the bank receives the item. For example, if a bank receives notice on May 1 that payment has been dishonored, it must give notice of such dishonor by midnight of May 2. Under the UCC (section 4–104(c)), a banking day is any day on which the bank is open to the public for carrying on substantially all its banking functions. Thus, if the bank receives notice of dishonor on a Friday and it is closed on Saturday and Sunday, then it has until midnight on Monday to give any necessary notice of dishonor. Parties other than banks must give notice of dishonor before midnight of the third business day after they receive ~~notice of the dishonor.~~ the instrument.

Once a party learns that an instrument has been dishonored, he or she may give any other party notice of the dishonor. Normally, however, a party will only give notice of dishonor to the party from whom he or she received the instrument.

EXAMPLE ■ Carter deposits a check drawn on Berg State Bank into her account at Third National Bank. Berg State dishonors payment of the check and returns it to Third National on May 1. In this case, Third National Bank must notify Carter of the dishonor by midnight on May 2 to charge her with secondary contractual liability.

The UCC (section 3–511) provides that presentment and notice of dishonor may either be waived or excused. Frequently, to waive these rights, parties will place certain language in an instrument, such as "presentment for payment and notice of dishonor are waived." The UCC further provides that, if this language appears on the face of the instrument, it binds all parties. However, if the language is written above an endorser's signature, it binds only the endorser.

EXAMPLE ■ Kandinsky makes a note payable to the order of Gunter. After endorsing the note, "presentment and notice of dishonor waived—(signed) Ray Gunter," Gunter delivers it to Meyer. Meyer then endorses the note over to Weems. However, Weems does not present the note at the proper time. When Kandinsky fails to pay the note, Weems sues the secondary parties—Gunter and Meyer. Meyer claims that Gunter's waiver does not bind him and thus he is not liable on the instrument because of the late presentment. In this case, Meyer wins because the waiver does not, in fact, bind him. However, if the waiver had appeared on the face of the instrument, it would have bound Meyer.

A waiver does not necessarily have to be expressly written on the instrument. A secondary party may waive his or her rights to presentment and notice of dishonor through his or her conduct. Whether such a **waiver by implication** has occurred must be determined on a case-by-case basis.

EXAMPLE ■ Margaret Allen, the president of a small corporation, personally endorses a corporate promissory note that she also signed on the corporation's behalf as maker. When she signed the note, Allen knew that the corporation was insolvent and would be unable to pay the note at its maturity. In this situation, she probably implicitly waived her right to receive notice of dishonor. The purpose of giving such a notice is to inform the secondary party that, because the primary party has defaulted, he or she will have to carry out his or her secondary contractual responsibility. Accordingly, a secondary party implicitly waives notice of dishonor if, when endorsing the instrument, he or she has no reason to believe that the primary party will pay it.

The UCC also provides that a holder may be excused from presenting an instrument for payment or giving notice of its dishonor. For example, under two circumstances, presentment for payment is entirely excused.

First, presentment is excused when the party primarily obligated to pay the instrument is dead or when insolvency proceedings begin after the instrument is issued. This **rule** recognizes that, if a maker or drawee is dead or insolvent, then the holder's expectation of immediate payment from the primary party is either impossible or so unlikely as to make presentment a wasted procedure. Instead, without first making presentment to the primary party, the holder is authorized to obtain payment from any secondary party. However, this rule does not excuse notice of dishonor, which still must be given to inform endorsers and drawers of their secondary liability on the instrument.

EXAMPLE ■ Prentiss makes a note, payable to the order of Ryan, that is due on May 1. Ryan endorses the note over to Grady. On April 30 Prentiss dies. In this situation, Grady does not have to **perform** the impossible act of presenting the note for payment to a deceased maker. However, although she is excused from presentment, she must still notify Ryan of the dishonor and his secondary liability to pay the instrument.

Second, presentment is entirely excused when the primary party refuses payment before presentment is required. The purpose of presentment is to determine whether the primary party will pay the instrument. Therefore, when the primary party clearly answers this question before formal presentment, the holder is excused from performing a useless act.

EXAMPLE ■ Dwyer makes a note payable to Watson's order, due on April 1. Watson then endorses it over to Meyer. On March 31, Meyer runs into Dwyer, who informs her that he will not pay the note on April 1 or at any other time. In this situation, Meyer is excused from presenting the note to Dwyer for payment.

Finally, both presentment and notice of dishonor are excused if circumstances beyond the holder's control prevent such actions. This rule would apply, for example, to a holder who is unable to present an instrument or give notice of dishonor because of interruptions in communication facilities, war, bad weather, or inability to find the primary party after a reasonable search. However, if the cause for the holder's inaction is removed, then the holder must make a reasonable effort to present the instrument or give notice of dishonor.

EXAMPLE ■ Kinney makes promissory note to Jones, due and payable on June 1. On June 1, a flood makes travel to Jones's place difficult and dangerous but not impossible. However, because of the flood, the holder does not present the note on that day. In this situation, the holder is probably excused from her failure to make presentment on June 1. However, she should make presentment as soon as it is safe to do so. If dishonor occurs upon presentment and she gives endorsers prompt notice of the dishonor, then she may hold them responsible for paying the note.

If a holder without an excuse fails to present an instrument on time or give notice of dishonor, then all endorsers are excused (discharged) from paying the instrument (U.C.C. § 3–502). However, the UCC is not as lenient toward the discharge of drawers.

A drawer is discharged from liability only when the drawee becomes insolvent (unable to pay its bills) during the delay in presentment and thus deprives the drawer of enough funds maintained with the drawee to pay the instrument. For example, if presentment is required on Monday but is not made until Friday and the drawee becomes insolvent on Wednesday, only then is the drawer discharged from liability on the instrument.

EXAMPLE ■ On January 1, Puryear draws a check on Third National Bank, payable to the order of Armstrong. Armstrong then endorses the check over to Baker, and Baker holds the check for five months.

Meanwhile, Puryear stops payment of the check. Baker finally presents the check to Third National for payment, but the bank refuses to pay it because of Puryear's stop-payment order. Baker then gives notice of the check's dishonor to both Armstrong and Puryear. In this situation, the endorser, Armstrong, is relieved from liability since presentment was late. However, the drawer, Puryear, is not released from liability since the bank was solvent when the check was presented for payment.

ENDORSEMENTS

An **endorsement** is a simple contract whereby the holder—by merely signing his or her name on an order instrument and delivering it to another party—transfers title to the instrument. An endorsement carries the promise that, subject to certain conditions, the endorser will pay the amount of the instrument if the maker of a note, or the drawee of a check or draft, dishonors payment. Furthermore, if payment of an instrument is dishonored, an endorser is contractually liable to pay any subsequent endorser. In other words, endorsers are liable to one another in the order in which they sign (U.C.C. §§ 3–414(1) and 3–414(2)).

EXAMPLE ■ A check is endorsed in the following order: "H. Muir, I. Lewis, M. Hollister." Hollister attempts to cash the check at the drawee bank but payment is dishonored. In this situation, Hollister has recourse against both Lewis and Muir on their endorsement contracts. If Lewis agrees to pay the check to Hollister, she may in turn pursue Muir for payment. However, if Muir pays the check, he may not pursue Lewis.

Forms of Endorsements

The three types of endorsement are special, blank, and restrictive.

Special Endorsements

A **special endorsement** specifies the person to whom or to whose order an instrument is payable (U.C.C. § 3–204(1)). Negotiable instruments so endorsed may be further negotiated only by the special endorsee's endorsement. This special endorsement provides some protection in case an instrument is lost, since it generally will be no good in another person's hands unless the special endorsee has endorsed it.

EXAMPLE ■ To make a special endorsement, Harold Taylor writes the words "pay to the order of James A. White, (signed) Harold Taylor," on the reverse side of an instrument (as illustrated in figure 3.3). In this situation, White is the special endorsee and the instrument may not be further negotiated without White's endorsement.

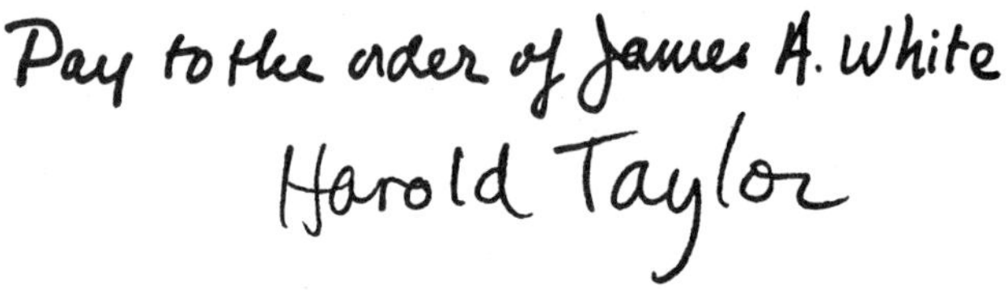

Pay to the order of James A. White

Harold Taylor

Figure 3.3   Special Endorsement

Blank Endorsements

A **blank endorsement** specifies no particular endorsee and may consist of only a signature (U.C.C. § 3–204(2)). A negotiable instrument endorsed in blank is payable to any bearer and, until specially endorsed, may be negotiated by delivery alone.

EXAMPLE ■ By merely signing her name on the reverse side of an instrument (as illustrated in figure 3.4), B. Brown makes a blank endorsement. In this situation, the note may be transferred to anyone without further endorsements. However, by writing a special endorsement over Brown's blank endorsement, any holder may make him- or herself, or a subsequent holder, into a special endorsee.

B. Brown

Figure 3.4   Blank Endorsement

EXAMPLE ■ Suppose White, upon receipt of the note in the preceding example, writes the words "pay to the order of Karen White" over Brown's blank endorsement (as illustrated in figure 3.5). In this situation, White makes herself a special endorsee.

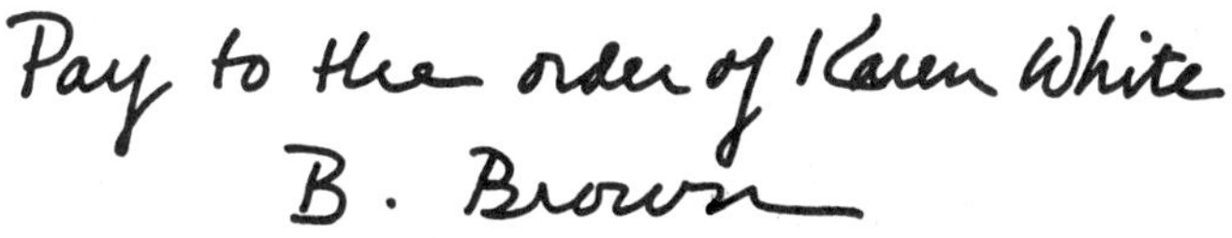

Pay to the order of Karen White
B. Brown

Figure 3.5   Special Endorsement Written over a Blank Endorsement

Restrictive Endorsements

Under the UCC (section 3–205), an endorsement is restrictive if it is one or more of the following:

■ It is conditional.

■ It attempts to prohibit further transfer of the instrument.

■ It includes the words "for collection," "for deposit," "pay any bank," or similar words signifying a purpose of deposit or collection.

■ It otherwise states that it is for the endorser's or another person's benefit or use.

Although **restrictive endorsements** are typically used in an attempt to prevent further transfers or negotiations of an instrument, they do not fulfill this purpose. Restrictive endorsements do not prevent further transfer or negotiation of an instrument (U.C.C. § 3–206(1)). However, they generally do require a transferee to give value or pay the item consistent with its endorsement.

A conditional endorsement might read, "pay to the order of Jimmie Jones when Jessie Jones becomes mayor, (signed) Jessie Jones." An endorsement purporting to prohibit further transfers might read, "pay to the order of Jimmie Jones only, (signed) Jessie Jones." An endorsement signifying the intent to make a deposit might say, "for deposit only, (signed) Jessie Jones." An endorsement for another's use might read, "pay to the order of Jessie Jones as trustee for Jamie Jones, (signed) Jessie Jones." Figure 3.6 illustrates these four types of endorsements.

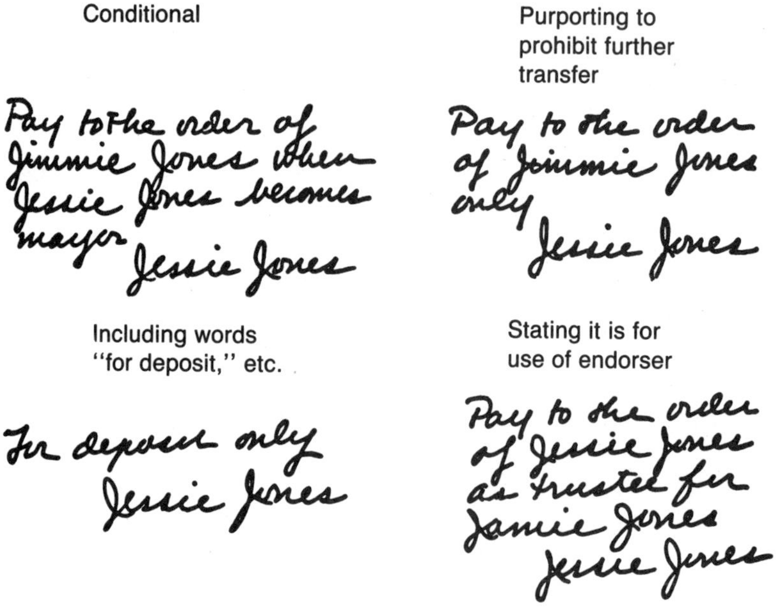

Conditional

Purporting to
prohibit further
transfer

Pay to the order of Jimmie Jones when Jessie Jones becomes mayor Jessie Jones

Pay to the order of Jimmie Jones only Jessie Jones

Including words
"for deposit," etc.

Stating it is for
use of endorser

For deposit only Jessie Jones

Pay to the order of Jessie Jones as Trustee for Jamie Jones Jessie Jones

Figure 3.6   Restrictive Endorsements

Places of Endorsements

As a general rule an endorsement may be placed anywhere on an instrument that is not governed by Regulation CC but is typically written on the reverse side (U.C.C. § 3–202(2)). If the instrument has insufficient space for an endorsement, it may be placed on an **allonge**, which is simply a piece of paper firmly affixed to the instrument.

Consequences of Endorsements

By the process of endorsement, order instruments may become bearer instruments and vice versa. A check payable to the order of cash is a bearer instrument, negotiable by delivery alone. Any transferee may, however, use a special endorsement to make the instrument payable to a specific party's order. This special endorsement transforms a bearer instrument into an order instrument, which can be further negotiated only by both delivery and a further endorsement by the special endorsee named in the endorsement. The special endorsee's blank endorsement could then transform the same order instrument back into a bearer instrument, payable to any holder and negotiated by delivery alone.

EXAMPLE ■ Figure 3.7 shows the reverse side of a negotiable instrument endorsed first with a special endorsement, then a blank endorsement, and finally a restrictive endorsement. Mary Martin makes a special endorsement with the words "pay to the order of William Williams, (signed) Mary Martin." Williams makes a blank endorsement simply with his signature, "William Williams," and transfers the instrument to Deborah Dix. Dix in turn makes a restrictive endorsement with the words "for deposit only, (signed) Deborah Dix." To become a holder, Dix's transferee must not only receive the instrument but must also comply with the terms of the restrictive endorsement.

Special endorsement

Blank endorsement

Restrictive endorsement

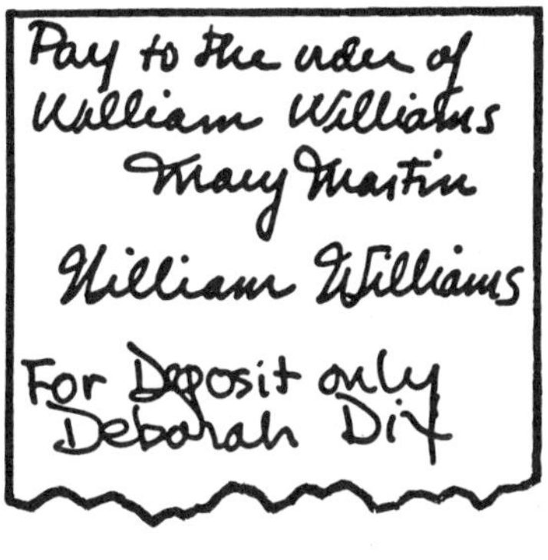

Figure 3.7   Special, Blank, and Restrictive Endorsements

| *Partial Endorsements* | An endorsement transfers title to the instrument from the endorser to the endorsee. For negotiation to occur, any necessary endorsement must convey title to the entire instrument (U.C.C. § 3–202(3)). Transfer of only part of the instrument destroys negotiation. Thus, a partial endorsement is in effect a partial assignment of an instrument. |

EXAMPLE ■ Sidney Barton holds a note payable to his order for $500. He endorses it "pay to the order of Frances Keyes in the amount of $250, (signed) Sidney Barton." Because the endorsement conveys only half of the instrument, it does not operate as negotiation. In accepting such a note, Keyes does not become a holder in due course, even if she receives the instrument for value, in good faith, and without notice that it is overdue or subject to any defense or claim. Instead, through such an endorsement Keyes only steps into Barton's shoes and is subject to any defenses against payment that can be asserted against him.

| *Wrong or Misspelled Names* | The UCC (section 3–203) provides that, when an instrument is made payable to a person under a misspelled or wrong name, the payee may endorse the instrument in the misspelled or wrong name, in his or her proper name, or in both the wrong and proper names. |

EXAMPLE ■ If Gerry Evans is properly the holder of an instrument payable to the order of Jerry Evans, he may endorse it as "Gerry Evans," "Jerry Evans," or both. The same would be true if Gerry Evans were properly the holder of an instrument payable in the wrong name, such as George Everett. However, the person paying the instrument in this situation, would usually require an endorsement in both names.

| *Rights to Endorsements* | Unless otherwise agreed, the transferee of an order instrument has the right to obtain the transferor's endorsement provided he or she has |

acquired the instrument for value (U.C.C. § 3–201(3)). Thus, a person who receives an instrument as a gift cannot demand an endorsement from the transferor.

EXAMPLE ■ J. White makes out a $1,000 check to "cash" and endorses it "pay to the order of J. White." White then presents the check to Gene Black as a gift but fails to sign the special endorsement. In this situation, Black cannot force White to endorse the check, since he received it as a gift.

WARRANTY LIABILITY

Makers, acceptors, drawers, and endorsers all have **contractual liability** on instruments, which relates to their obligation to pay the instruments when due. In contrast, only endorsers and other transferors have **warranty liability** on instruments. Further, a warranty is not a promise to pay the instrument when due. Rather, it is each transferor's promise to subsequent holders and to the payor that certain statements of fact about the instrument are true.

For instance, transferors state (warrant) that they have good title to the instrument they are transferring. **Good title** basically means legitimate ownership because the instrument does not contain any forged or unauthorized endorsements. If a transferor is discovered later not to have good title to the instrument, then he or she has "breached the warranty of good title." When a warranty is breached, the transferor is generally liable to the holder for the amount the transferor paid for the instrument.

Transferors' warranties are not normally written on the instrument. Instead, they are implied by the provisions of the UCC. In other words, the law of negotiable instruments in the UCC provides that transferors make certain warranties whether or not they are expressly stated in the instrument. Under the UCC, these warranties are divided into two categories: presentment warranties and transfer warranties.

Presentment Warranties

Each person or entity who transfers an instrument gives certain **presentment warranties**. These warranties run exclusively in favor of the payor (maker or drawee). Each transferor makes the following presentment warranties to the payor (U.C.C. §§ 3–417(1) and 4–207(1)):

■ that he or she has good title to the instrument

■ that he or she has no knowledge that the maker's or drawer's signature is unauthorized (a holder in due course does not give this warranty)

■ that the instrument has not been materially altered

Transfer Warranties

Each person or entity who transfers an instrument also gives **transfer warranties**. However, a transferor does not give these warranties to the payor but rather to the immediate transferee. Furthermore, if the transferor endorses the instrument, he or she gives these warranties to any other subsequent holder of the instrument. Thus, if the instrument is transferred by endorsement, a transferor makes the following transfer warranties to the immediate transferee and all subsequent holders (U.C.C. §§ 3–417(2) and 4–207(2)):

■ that he or she has good title to the instrument

■ that all signatures are genuine or authorized

■ that the instrument has not been materially altered

■ that no party's defense is good against the transferor

■ that he or she knows of no insolvency proceedings against the maker, acceptor, or drawer of the instrument

---

EXAMPLE ■ Genet issues a check payable to the order of Dwyer. Dwyer negotiates the check to Meyer, who deposits it into her account at State Bank. In turn, State Bank presents the check to Third National Bank for payment. In this situation, Dwyer, as a transferor, gives the transfer warranties to Meyer, his immediate transferee. In addition, since Dwyer transfers the instrument by endorsement, he also gives the transfer warranties to State Bank, a subsequent holder. In turn, when Meyer transfers the check, she becomes a transferor and gives the transfer warranties to State Bank, her immediate transferee. Last, Meyer, Dwyer, and State Bank are all transferors and thus give presentment warranties to Third National Bank, the payor.

DISCHARGES

Discharge simply means that a person no longer has a legal obligation to pay an instrument. Discharge is a defense against a claim that payment is due on an instrument. This defense may be either personal or real. As discussed in chapter 2, a real defense may be successfully asserted against a holder in due course, while a personal defense cannot. Under the UCC (section 3–602), discharge is a real defense only if a holder in due course, when taking an instrument, knows that a person's liability for it previously has been discharged.

If the person knew of the discharge they would not qualify for HDC status.

EXAMPLES ■ Kendall makes a note payable to the order of Boyd, who then endorses the note and delivers it to Wilson. Wilson crosses out Boyd's endorsement (cancels it) before he transfers the note to Hull, a holder in due course. In this case, Hull does not have recourse against Boyd since, when he took the note, he knew that Wilson had canceled Boyd's endorsement. Thus, if Hull sues Boyd, Boyd's real defense of discharge by cancellation will defeat Hull's claim.

■ Foster makes a note payable to the order of Jackson. Before the note's maturity, Foster pays Jackson but fails to obtain possession of the note or have it marked paid. Jackson immediately transfers the note to Abbott, who takes it as a holder in due course. In this case, Foster's payment of the note (an event of discharge) only operates as a personal defense, since Abbott was unaware of the payment when he took the note. Thus, if Abbott sues Foster, Foster's personal defense of discharge will not defeat Abbott's claim.

Scope of Discharges

The discharge of one party's liability on an instrument does not automatically lead to the discharge of liability for every other party. Since the primary party has the final responsibility to pay an instrument, once that party pays an instrument, he or she normally does not have the right to look to anyone else for reimbursement. By contrast, if a secondary party, such as an endorser, pays an instrument, he or she may normally obtain reimbursement from the primary party or any other party who endorsed the instrument before he or she did.

Accordingly, all parties to an instrument are generally discharged from liability when no party is left with the right to pursue any other party (**right of recourse**) for payment (U.C.C. § 3–601(3)). Since the primary party is normally without any such right of recourse, only his or her discharge results in the discharge of every other party to the instrument.

EXAMPLE ■ Gordon makes a note payable to the order of Finley and endorsed by Finley, Hughes, and Lynch. At maturity, Gordon pays the note. In this situation, Gordon's payment discharges him from further liability. In addition, since Gordon does not have the right to seek reimbursement from any other party on the instrument, his payment also discharges Finley, Hughes, and Lynch. If Lynch had paid the note instead of Gordon, Lynch's payment would have discharged only him from further liability. This is because Lynch would still have had a right of recourse against Hughes and Finley on their contracts as endorsers and against Gordon on his contract as a maker.

Events Leading to Discharges

The UCC (section 3–601) lists events that may lead to the discharge of a party's liability on an instrument. An earlier section in this chapter discussed one such event—the unexcused delay in presentment or notice of dishonor. Other events that may lead to the discharge of a party's liability on an instrument include the following:

■ when the holder is paid (payment)

■ when the holder refuses an offer of money to pay an instrument (tender of payment)

■ when a drawee certifies a check (certification)

Payment   The UCC provides a straightforward rule on when payment operates as a discharge: a party's liability on an instrument is discharged to the extent of his or her payment of the amount due (U.C.C. § 3–603).

EXAMPLE ■ Jewett makes a note, payable to the order of Adams, in the sum of $500. Jewett pays Adams $500 when the note matures. Thereafter, Jewett's liability on the note is completely discharged since he has fully paid it. However, if Jewett had paid Adams $300 instead of $500, Jewett's liability would only be partially discharged to the extent of $300. He would still remain liable to Adams for the $200 balance still due on the note.

PAYMENTS TO HOLDERS

Discharge from liability occurs only when a party makes payment to the holder of an instrument. However, not every person in possession of an instrument can be classified as a holder. As discussed in chapter 2, a person becomes a holder only when an instrument is transferred to him or her by negotiation. If a party does not pay a holder, then his or her liability on the instrument is not discharged and he or she may consequently be required to pay the instrument twice.

EXAMPLE ■ Huston makes a note payable to the order of Williams. The note is stolen and the thief forges Williams's endorsement. When the note is presented, Huston believes Williams's endorsement is genuine and pays the note to the thief. In this situation, since Williams did not endorse the note, it was not transferred by negotiation and thus the thief is not a holder. Consequently, Huston is still liable to Williams for the amount of the note.

WHO MAY MAKE PAYMENTS

Unless the holder objects, any person may pay an instrument, including a person who is not a party to the instrument (U.C.C. § 3–603(2)).

EXAMPLE ■ Bates makes a note payable to McLellan. At maturity, Bates cannot pay the note, so his father pays it for him. In this situation, as long as McLellan consents to the payment by the father, Bates's liability to McLellan is effectively discharged.

Tender of Payment

Tender of payment occurs when a party can pay an instrument and offers such payment to the holder. Under the UCC (section 3–604), a holder's refusal to accept a party's tender of full payment when or after an instrument is due discharges the various parties as follows:

■ The party tendering payment is discharged from subsequent liability for interest, collection costs, and attorney's fees.

■ Any party who has a right to require payment against the party whose tender was refused is completely discharged from liability on the instrument.

Case for Discussion

HOOKE V. ALBERT

Facts

Albert needed money to pay his bills, so he borrowed $5,000 from Hooke at the rate of 6 percent per year to maturity. Hooke was concerned about Albert's ability to repay him, so he required Albert's mother to endorse the note, making her secondarily liable for repayment. The note also called for an increase in the payment of interest to 12 percent and payment of attorney's fees if the note was not repaid when due. On the maturity date, Albert was unable to repay the note, so his mother offered $4,000 to settle Hooke's claims against them. However, Hooke refused the tender of payment and sued.

Decision

In this case, the court ruled that, since the tender was not for full payment of the note, Albert's mother is responsible for (1) the amount due on the note at maturity, including interest at 6 percent, (2) interest at 12 percent on the balance due from the maturity date to the date of final repayment, and (3) any attorney's fees associated with collecting the note.

Questions for Discussion

1. Does Albert's mother have any recourse in this situation? If so, what?
2. What steps might Albert's mother have taken to protect herself from this situation?

Facts

Suppose Albert's mother offers to pay the note in full. However, Hooke refuses her offer and says, "It's really Albert's responsibility, and I want him to pay the note."

Decision

The court rules that, since Albert's mother tendered full payment, she is discharged from paying any further interest on the note or any attorney's fees assessed in the collection of payment. She does, however, remain liable for the amount due at the time of tender.

Questions for Discussion

1. Is the court's decision in this case equitable? Why?
2. What defense might Albert raise in this situation?
3. Does Albert have any further recourse in this situation? If so, what?

Facts

Suppose that Albert tenders full payment of the note at maturity. However, because Hooke wants to collect more interest on the note, he refuses the tender and tells Albert to pay him in a few months. A month later, Albert goes bankrupt, so Hooke sues Albert's mother.

Decision

In this case, the court rules in favor of Albert's mother. The court states that Hooke's refusal of Albert's tender completely discharged Albert's mother from liability. This is because Albert's mother, as an endorser, had the right of recourse against Albert, who was primarily obligated to pay the instrument.

Question for Discussion
Why is the court's decision in this case equitable?

Certifications

To certify a check, the drawee bank places on its face the word "accepted" or "certified," usually with a stamp that bears a bank officer's signature. Such **certification** makes the drawee bank primarily liable for payment of the check. In addition, if a drawee certifies a check upon a holder's request, then this certification discharges the drawer and all other parties who endorsed the check before the certification (U.C.C. § 3–411).

EXAMPLE ■ Grove draws a check payable to the order of Johnson. After Johnson receives the check, she takes it to the drawee bank for certification. In this situation, if the drawee bank certifies the check, Grove's liability on the check is discharged. When the check is certified, the bank withdraws the money from Grove's account and places it into its own account.

CONCLUSION

Subject to certain exceptions, a person is not liable on an instrument unless his or her authorized signature appears on it. However, once a person willingly signs an instrument, depending on his or her interest in it, that person assumes contractual and/or warranty liability for the instrument until that liability is discharged.

A party's contract is generally discharged when it no longer has any force or effect as a legal obligation. The defense of discharge, however, cannot be asserted against a holder in due course unless he or she, when taking the instrument, knew of the party's discharge. Furthermore, a party's discharge does not necessarily lead to the discharge of every other party to the instrument. All parties to an instrument are discharged only when no party is left with the right to pursue any other party for its payment.

Questions for Review and Discussion

1. What obligates a person to pay an instrument?

2. Can a person sign an instrument on another's behalf? What is that person called?

3. Name two types of liabilities that may be incurred on an instrument.

4. What parties are primarily responsible to a holder for payment of an instrument? What parties are secondarily responsible to a holder for payment?

5. What phrase may drawers or endorsers write after their signatures on instruments to escape a contractual obligation to pay them? On what grounds can payees pursue drawers or endorsers who have thus disclaimed their secondary contractual responsibility to pay the instruments?

6. Name and describe three types of endorsements.

7. How may a payor endorse a check on which his or her name is badly misspelled?

8. What is a transferor's warranty on an instrument?

9. What three presentment warranties does a transferor make to a payor?

10. To whom are transfer warranties given?

11. What happens when no party is left with the right of recourse for payment of an instrument?

12. To whom must payment of an instrument be made for a discharge from liability to occur? Who may make such a payment?

13. What is the effect on liability of a drawer bank's written certification of a check?

Bank Collections

After studying this chapter, you will be able to

■ explain the purpose and substance of article 4 of the Uniform Commercial Code (UCC), the Expedited Funds Availability Act (EFAA), and Federal Reserve Regulation CC (Regulation CC) all of which govern bank deposits, collections, and returns

■ accurately describe the conditions under which a depositor has the legal right to withdraw cash and other items deposited into his or her account

■ describe the duties of banks in the forward collection of a check

■ describe the duties of collecting, paying, and returning banks during the return of a check

Article 3 of the UCC governs how a negotiable instrument is formed and the respective rights and responsibilities of the parties to an instrument. It codifies two principal common-law concepts that enable the free circulation of negotiable instruments: transfer by negotiation and holding in due course. In turn, article 4, EFAA, and Regulation CC govern the collection and return of a negotiable instrument during its journey through the payments mechanism. They codify and refine established rules that enable banks to deal comprehensively, consistently, and quickly with negotiable instruments. Thus, these laws combine to make negotiable instruments meaningful substitutes for money.

ARTICLE 4

The numerous checks handled by banks for collection nationwide (approximately 51 billion a year), coupled with inconsistent rules governing the rights and responsibilities of parties participating in the collection process, motivated the drafting of **article 4.**

One of the main purposes of article 4 is to create uniformity in the forward collection rules to assure a workable and predictable collection system that consistently resolves similar collection issues. This consistent treatment of similar issues maintains a confidence in the collection system, promotes an instrument's rapid circulation, and thus preserves a negotiable instrument's integrity as a meaningful substitute for money.

EXPEDITED FUNDS AVAILABILITY ACT AND REGULATION CC

On August 10, 1987, the Competitive Equality Banking Act (CEBA) was signed into law. CEBA is composed of 12 titles relating to the financial services industry. Title VI of CEBA is commonly referred to as the Expedited Funds Availability Act (EFAA). Under the provisions of CEBA, Congress charged the Federal Reserve Board with the responsibility of implementing the terms of EFAA, which the board accomplished with the adoption of Regulation CC in May 1988.

The purpose of EFAA is twofold: (1) to provide bank account customers with quicker access to deposits made into their accounts and (2) to expedite the return of unpaid items to the depositary institution.

COLLECTION PROCESS

Before beginning a discussion on the rights and responsibilities of depositary, collecting, paying, and returning banks when engaged in either the forward collection or return of checks, a description of the routes a check may take from issuance to payment may be beneficial.

A checking account customer expects the bank to pay the checks written on the account, to cash checks, and to credit the account with checks received. The key to fulfilling these expectations is the smooth flow of checks in the bank collection system. Figure 4.1 illustrates a common route that a check may follow in the collection system. As shown, both the drawer and payee are customers of the same bank. Thus, the collection route that this check follows is simple. It flows from the drawer to the payee and then to the bank. When the bank receives the check, it merely debits the drawer's account and credits the payee's account.

The bank in figure 4.1 has acted as both a depositary and payor bank. A **depositary bank** is the first bank to which an item is transferred for collection, even if it is also the payor bank (U.C.C. § 4–105(1)). A **payor bank** is one at which an item is payable as drawn (see U.C.C. § 4–105(b)).

Figure 4.2 illustrates a slightly more complex collection route, in which both the depositary bank and the drawee bank are located in the same metropolitan area and are members of the same local **clearing house**. The check flows from the drawer to the payee, ABC Store. ABC Store deposits the check at its bank, Local Bank, which then forwards the check for collection to the city clearing house, where it is presented to the drawee (payor) bank for payment. In this situation, Local Bank has acted both as a depositary and collecting bank. A **collecting bank** is any bank, except the payor bank, that handles an item for collection (U.C.C. § 4–105(d)).

Figure 4.3 illustrates an even more complex collection route, in which the depositary bank and drawee bank are located in different parts of the country. Suppose the drawer's check is drawn on a bank in Cleveland, Ohio, and is deposited into ABC's account at a bank in Hartford, Connecticut. The Hartford depositary bank then forwards the check to its local correspondent bank for collection. The Hartford correspondent bank then sends the check to the Federal Reserve Bank of Boston, which in turn sends it to the Federal Reserve Bank of Cleveland. The Cleveland Federal Reserve bank then forwards the check to the drawee's Cleveland correspondent bank, which then presents it to the drawee (payor) bank for payment. The correspondent banks can also be local clearing house associations.

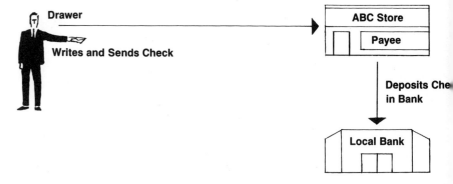

Figure 4.1   Bank Check Collection

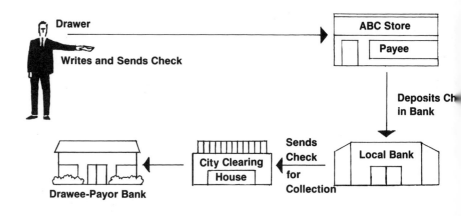

Figure 4.2   Bank Check Collection

The local Hartford bank in figure 4.3 has acted as both a depositary and collecting bank. In turn, the Hartford **correspondent bank** and the Federal Reserve Banks of Boston and Cleveland have acted as intermediary collecting banks. An **intermediary bank** is one to which an item is transferred during collection, except the depositary or payor bank (U.C.C. § 4–105(e)). The drawee's correspondent bank acted in this example as the **presenting bank,** which is any bank that forwards an item to another bank for payment (see U.C.C. § 4–105(e)).

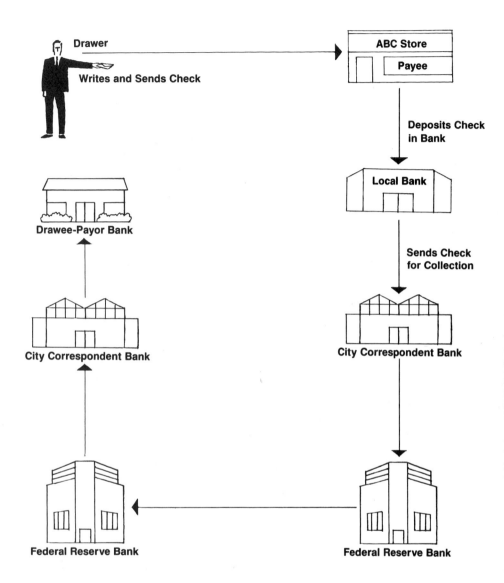

Figure 4.3   Bank Check Collection

WITHDRAWALS OF DEPOSITS

After making a deposit, which initiates the collection process, a customer often wants to know when the deposit may be withdrawn. Under Regulation CC the answer to this question depends on whether the deposit consists of

- cash; electronic transfers; or certain types of checks such as cashier's, certified, and teller's checks or checks drawn on or by certain government entities
- local checks
- nonlocal checks

Cash, Electronic Transfers, and Certain Types of Checks

The customer has the right to withdraw the deposit at any time during the next business day after the banking day the deposit was made, if a deposit consists of cash, electronic transfers or the following types of checks:

- checks drawn on the U.S. Treasury
- U.S. Postal Service money orders
- checks drawn on Federal Reserve banks or Federal Home Loan banks
- checks drawn by states or local government units
- cashier's, certified, or teller's checks
- checks drawn on the depositary bank

Under Regulation CC, a "business day" is defined as any day except Saturday, Sunday, and legal holidays. A "banking day" is defined as that part of a business day during which a bank is open to the public for carrying on substantially all its services.

EXAMPLE ■ Suppose Carpenter makes a deposit of cash on Friday. In this situation, Carpenter has the right to withdraw the deposit at the opening of business on Monday. This holds true even if Saturday qualifies as a banking day under the UCC (defined as any part of any day on which a bank is open to the public for carrying on substantially all of its banking functions) since, for the purposes of Regulation CC, Saturday is never a "business day." If a conflict arises between the provisions of the UCC and Regulation CC, the provisions of Regulation CC prevail.

Two preconditions exist for receiving next day availability on state and local government checks; cashier's, certified, and teller's checks; Federal Reserve bank and Federal Home Loan bank checks; and U.S. Postal Service money orders. First, the check must be deposited into an account held by the named payee. Second, the check must be deposited in person by the payee to an employee of the depositary bank. If any of these checks are deposited into the payee's account by means other than in person, then Regulation CC provides that the proceeds of such checks shall be available for withdrawal not later than the second business day after the banking day on which the funds are deposited.

The only condition attached to receiving next day availability on a U.S. Treasury check is that it must be deposited into an account maintained by the named payee. It does not have to be deposited in person by the payee to an employee of the depositary institution.

EXAMPLE ■ Suppose the payee of a certified check mails the check for deposit into his or her account and the check is received by the bank on Tuesday. In this situation, the check must be available for withdrawal at the opening of business on Thursday. If, however, the payee had presented the check for deposit in person to a bank employee on Tuesday, it would have been available for withdrawal at the opening of business on Wednesday.

Two other circumstances under which a depositor will receive next day availability exist. First, if a deposit consists of an **on-us item** (a check drawn on the depositary institution), then, as a general rule, the customer has the right to withdraw that deposit at any time during the next business day following the banking day of deposit. Second, if a deposit consists of items that are not subject to the next day availability rules, then the customer has the right to withdraw on the next business day the lesser of $100 or the aggregate amount of such checks deposited on any one banking day to all of the customer's accounts.

EXAMPLE ■ Suppose that on Monday a customer deposits five checks totaling $650, which are not subject to the next day availability rule. In this situation, the customer will be entitled to withdraw $100 of the deposit at the opening of business on Tuesday.

Local Checks   An item is considered a local check if it is deposited with a bank located in the same check-processing region as the paying bank. The routing and transit numbers, which generally appear as a fraction in the upper right hand corner of a check and in a nine-digit form in the magnetic ink strip at the bottom of a check (as shown in Figure 4.4), determine

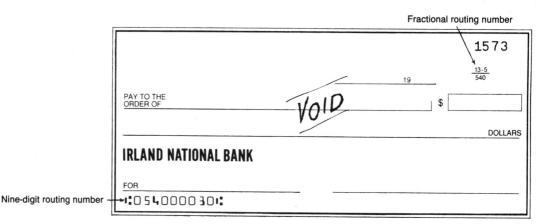

Figure 4.4   Check Routing and Transit Numbers

whether a check is a local or nonlocal item. The first four digits of the nine-digit routing number form the routing symbol. Appendix A to Regulation CC is a listing of routing symbols associated with each Federal Reserve office. This listing provides a ready reference to depositary institutions to determine whether checks deposited with it are drawn on paying banks located in the same check-processing region. If the routing symbols of both the depositary bank and the paying bank are listed in the same district, then the deposited item is considered a local item; otherwise, it is considered a nonlocal item.

If a deposit consists of local items, then under the temporary availability schedule contained in Regulation CC effective from September 1, 1988 through August 31, 1990, the customer has the right to withdraw the deposit at any time after the opening of the third business day following the banking day the deposit was made. For example, if a customer deposits a local item on Monday, he or she has the right to withdraw the deposit at the opening of business on Thursday.

In addition, U.S. Treasury checks; state and local government checks; cashier's, certified, and teller's checks; Federal Reserve bank and Federal Home Loan bank checks; and U.S. Postal Service money orders deposited and paid in the same check-processing region will be treated as local items if they fail to meet the next day or second day availability rules discussed earlier.

EXAMPLE ■ Suppose the payee of a cashier's check endorses it over to a third party who subsequently deposits it into his or her account on Tuesday at a bank located in the same check-processing region as the paying bank. In this situation, for the purposes of availability, the item will be treated as a local check and will be available for withdrawal on Friday. The next day availability rules do not apply in this case since the original payee did not personally deposit the check to an employee of the depositary bank.

On September 1, 1990, the temporary availability schedule governing the deposit of local items will be replaced by a permanent schedule, reducing the time period for availability of local and nonlocal checks. Under the permanent schedule, a local check must be available for withdrawal on the opening of the second business day following the banking day the deposit was made.

Nonlocal Checks
A nonlocal check is an item drawn on a paying bank that is not located in the same check-processing region as the depositary bank. If a deposit consists of a nonlocal check, then under the temporary availability schedule, the customer has the right to withdraw the deposit at any time after the opening of the seventh business day following the banking day the deposit was made. For example, if a customer deposits a nonlocal item on Monday, May 1, he or she has the right to withdraw the deposit at the opening of business on Wednesday, May 10. (Recall that under Regulation CC Saturday and Sunday are never "business days.")

In addition, state and local government checks; cashier's, certified, and teller's checks; and Federal Reserve bank and Federal Home Loan bank checks deposited with a bank located in a different processing region from the paying bank will be treated as nonlocal items if they fail to meet the next day or second day availability rules. U.S. Treasury checks and U.S. Postal Service money orders, however, are never treated as nonlocal checks. Instead, if these types of checks fail to meet the next day or second day availability rules, they are always treated as local items. This is because U.S. Treasury checks and U.S. Postal Service money orders are payable at any Federal Reserve office. Accordingly, the depositary bank will always be located in a Federal Reserve check-processing region where these items may be paid.

Under the permanent availability schedule, beginning September 1, 1990, a nonlocal check must be available for withdrawal on the opening of the fifth business day following the banking day the deposit was made.

Exceptions
Regulation CC sets forth certain exceptions that are applicable to the published schedules for local and nonlocal checks and, in limited situations, to the next day and second day availability rules. These exceptions recognize that depositary institutions frequently are placed at risk by having to release funds prior to the time a check could be returned unpaid. Therefore, to reduce this risk, the regulation permits depositary institutions to extend hold periods under the following circumstances:

■ when a new account is opened

■ when large deposits are made to an account

- when a check is redeposited to an account

- when a deposit account is repeatedly overdrawn

- when a bank has reasonable cause to doubt the collectibility of a check

- when certain emergency conditions arise

New Accounts

An account is considered new during the first 30 calendar days after it is opened. An account, however, is not considered new if a customer has previously established another open account relationship that is more than 30 calendar days old with the depositary bank.

Under the new account relationship, deposits of local and nonlocal checks are not subject to the availability requirements of Regulation CC. Furthermore, a depositary bank is not required to give next day availability on deposits of on-us items, nor is it required to give credit for the lesser of $100 or the aggregate amount on deposits of checks not subject to the next day availability rules. In addition, Regulation CC does not provide any maximum time frames within which holds may be placed on these types of items.

Cash deposits and electronic payments, however, are still subject to the next day availability requirements. A depositary bank is also required to give next day availability on deposits made in person by the payee to an employee of the bank, consisting of U.S. Treasury checks; U.S. Postal Service money orders; Federal Reserve bank and Federal Home Loan bank checks; state and local government checks; cashier's, certified, teller's, and traveler's checks, but only to the extent of the first $5,000 of funds deposited on any one banking day. Any amount of the deposit in excess of $5,000 shall be available for withdrawal any time after the opening of the ninth business day following the banking day the deposit was made.

EXAMPLE ■ Samuel Pike deposits a $10,000 cashier's check into a new account on Monday, May 1. In this situation, $5,000 must be made available for withdrawal on Tuesday, May 2, and the remaining $5,000 of the deposit must be made available for withdrawal on Friday, May 12.

Large Deposits   The availability rules governing local and nonlocal items are not applicable to deposits made on any one banking day that are in excess of $5,000. The rule applies in the aggregate to all deposits made into a customer's accounts at the depositary bank.

EXAMPLE ■ Suppose three separate deposits of $5,000 each are made into three separate accounts owned by one depositor on the same day. In this situation, only $5,000 must be made available in accordance with the availability schedules governing the deposit of local and nonlocal checks.

In this example, the excess amount of $10,000 should be made available for withdrawal within a reasonable period of time. Under Regulation CC, an extension of four business days after the day the funds would have been required to be available had the deposit been subject to the local and nonlocal check availability rules is presumed to be reasonable. A hold longer than four business days may be reasonable, but the depositary bank has the burden of so establishing. This extension rule is also applicable to redeposited items and repeated overdrafts (discussed later).

Redeposited Checks   The availability rules governing local and nonlocal items also do not apply to a check that has been returned unpaid and is subsequently redeposited for payment. This exception, however, does not apply to items that have been returned unpaid due to a missing endorsement.

Repeated Overdrafts   The availability rules governing local and nonlocal items do not apply to accounts that are repeatedly overdrawn. An account is considered repeatedly overdrawn if it has been overdrawn on six or more banking days during a six-month period or if it has been overdrawn in the amount of $5,000 or more on two or more banking days during a six-month period. The availability rules for local and nonlocal items under this exclusion are suspended for a period of six months following the last overdraft.

Reasonable Cause to Doubt Collectibility

If a depositary bank has reasonable cause to believe that a deposited item will not be paid by the paying bank, then the following availability rules are suspended:

- the next day and second day availability rules applicable to Federal Reserve bank and Federal Home Loan bank checks and cashier's, certified, and teller's checks
- the availability rules applicable to local and nonlocal checks

Funds that are subject to any delays under this exception must be made available for withdrawal within a reasonable period of time (four business days) after the day the funds would have been required to be available had the deposit been subject to the local and nonlocal availability rules.

A depositary bank may have reasonable cause to believe that a check will not be paid if the paying bank has indicated that a stop-payment order has been placed on the item or that there are insufficient funds on deposit in the account to cover the amount of the check. A stale-dated item may give a bank reasonable cause to believe that the item will not be paid, since under the UCC a bank need not pay a check, other than a certified check, that is presented for payment more than six months after its date. Also, if an item is postdated, a bank may have reasonable cause to invoke this exclusion, since under the UCC a postdated check is usually not properly payable until its date.

Under Regulation CC, reasonable cause to believe a check is uncollectible requires the existence of well-founded facts that would lead a reasonable person to conclude that the check will not be paid. Under no circumstances, however, should a depositary institution conclude that a check will not be paid based upon the fact that a check is of a particular class or is deposited by a person who is a member of a particular class or group.

Emergency Conditions

The availability rules, as they apply to local and nonlocal items, are suspended under one or more of the following conditions:

- an interruption of communications, computer, or other equipment facilities
- a suspension of payments by another bank

■ a war

■ an emergency condition beyond the control of the depositary bank

Funds that are subject to an extended hold, due to an emergency, must be made available for withdrawal within a reasonable period after the emergency has ended or within the period established for local and nonlocal checks, whichever is later.

As a general rule, if a depositary institution delays the availability of funds based upon any of the previously discussed exceptions, except the new account exception, then it must provide the depositor with a written notice of such delay. In addition, the notice shall be provided to the depositor at the time of deposit if made in person; otherwise, the notice shall be mailed or delivered to the customer on the first business day following the placement of the hold.

FORWARD COLLECTION OF CHECKS

Depositary, intermediary, and presenting banks all fall within the UCC definition of a collecting bank. Under the UCC (section 4–201), any bank handling a check for collection is the agent of the owner of the check until the payor finally pays it.

Duties of Collecting Banks

The collection of a check is normally initiated when it is deposited into a customer's account with a depositary bank. Under the UCC (section 4–202(1)(a)), when the depositary bank receives a check and any other collecting bank later handles it for collection, each must excercise "ordinary care" in promptly presenting the check to the payor for payment or sending the check to another collecting bank for its ultimate presentment to the payor.

Generally, a collecting bank exercises ordinary care when it properly performs these duties in a timely fashion. In addition, if the payor bank does not pay the check, then each collecting bank must exercise ordinary care in notifying the bank or person from whom it received the check that it was dishonored (U.C.C. § 4–202(1)(b)).

A collecting bank's responsibility in exercising ordinary care, however, is confined exclusively to its own actions. The bank need not assume responsibility for the actions of any other collecting or intermediary bank or agent to whom it sends the item for collection. For instance, a bank is not liable for another bank's or person's insolvency, neglect, misconduct, mistake, or default, or for the loss or destruction of an item while in the possession of others (U.C.C. § 4–202(3)). However, a bank must use ordinary care to select properly qualified banks and agents for the collection of an item. For example, a collecting bank that chooses an inexperienced private pilot to transport checks for collection may be held responsible for the pilot's actions, since it may not have used ordinary care to select a qualified agent.

Ordinary Care: The Midnight Deadline

Whether a bank collecting an item or giving notice of dishonor has exercised ordinary care is determined by whether it has acted "seasonably." A bank acts seasonably if it takes proper action within its midnight deadline (U.C.C. § 4–202(2)). The **midnight deadline** is defined as midnight of the banking day following the one on which an item or a notice is received. For instance, a bank that receives checks for collection on Tuesday exercises ordinary care if it forwards or presents them for payment by midnight on Wednesday.

EXAMPLE ■ A check drawn on Berg State Bank is deposited into Third National Bank on Friday morning. Third National Bank is not open on either Saturday or Sunday, and Monday is a legal holiday. In this situation, midnight on Tuesday is Third National Bank's deadline for presenting the check to Berg State or sending it to another collecting bank for presentment to Berg State.

Exceptions to the Midnight Deadline

The midnight deadline, however, is not an ironclad measure of whether a bank has exercised ordinary care in its collection activities. For instance, the UCC provides that the midnight deadline may be varied by (1) agreements, rules, or regulations; (2) a bank's establishing cutoff hours for handling of items for collection; or (3) excused delays.

TAYLOR V. THIRD NATIONAL BANK

Facts

On Wednesday, January 8, Third National Bank receives a check for collection drawn on Fifth State Bank. Because of a severe snowstorm on Wednesday night, Third National is unable to present the check to Fifth State Bank until Monday, January 13. Although sufficient funds are on deposit in the drawer's account on Thursday, January 9, they are not on deposit on Monday, January 13, so the check is dishonored. Taylor, the owner of the check, sues Third National Bank for failing to exercise ordinary care in collecting the check.

Decision

In this case, the court rules in favor of Third National Bank. According to the court, the bank's delay in taking action by its midnight deadline was excused because of a snowstorm, a circumstance beyond the bank's control.

Questions for Discussion

1. Does the owner of the check have any further recourse in this situation? If so, what?
2. How might a bank minimize problems caused by failure to act by its midnight deadline due to circumstances beyond its control?

DUTIES OF PAYOR-DRAWEE BANKS

The last bank in the collection chain to receive a check for payment is the **payor-drawee bank**. Under the UCC (section 4–105(b)), the payor is the bank at which a check is payable as drawn.

When checks are properly presented, a payor bank must decide which checks it will pay and which it will dishonor. This decision is based on whether the checks are "properly payable." The term "properly payable" includes the availability of sufficient collected funds on deposit in a customer's account at the time of the decision to pay or dishonor an item (U.C.C. § 4–104(i)). In other words, if a customer has sufficient funds on deposit in his or her account to pay a check, then the payor generally has a duty to pay it. If a payor breaches this duty and wrongfully dishonors a properly payable check, it is liable to its customer for the damages resulting from such wrongful dishonor.

On the other hand, if a check is not properly payable, a payor bank must return the check within a specific period as provided for under the provisions of Regulation CC. For example, a payor bank may legitimately refuse to pay a check under any of the following circumstances:

- The customer's account does not have sufficient funds to cover the amount of the check.

- The check is subject to a stop-payment order.

- The check is postdated.

- The check is presented more than six months after its date.

- The customer's account has been closed.

The concepts of properly payable checks and wrongful dishonor are discussed in chapter 5.

Time for Payment or Dishonor: The Midnight Deadline

Upon receipt of a check, a payor bank may take until its midnight deadline to decide whether to pay or dishonor the check (U.C.C. § 4–301). This practice is commonly called "deferred posting." Under deferred posting, all checks received by a payor bank on one business day are accumulated and posted to the drawer's demand deposit accounts on the next day. In other words, a bank can defer the decision to pay or dishonor a check for one business day after its receipt.

If the payor bank decides not to pay a check, then it must actually return the check within its midnight deadline. The payor bank's written notice of dishonor without the check is valid only when the check is no longer available. When a check is dishonored, it is ultimately returned to the depositor who initiated the collection process.

EXAMPLE ■ Marty Sheehan deposited a $15,000 check, drawn on Third National Bank, into his account at Berg National Bank. The check was presented for payment to Third National on Friday, January 24. Since Third National was not open on either Saturday or Sunday, it had until midnight on Monday,

January 27, either to pay the check or to send notice of its dishonor. During the evening of January 27, Third National returned the dishonored check to the presenting bank. However, Berg National's cancellation stamp on the check showed the date of receipt (return) to be January 28. In this situation, the notice of dishonor is valid because the check was returned to Berg National within Third National Bank's midnight deadline.

Suppose instead that on January 27, Third National sent written notice of the dishonor but did not return the check until January 28. In this situation, the notice of dishonor would be invalid unless the check was unavailable for return on January 27. Under the UCC, the payor bank's notice of dishonor is timely only if the unpaid check is returned within the payor's midnight deadline.

Exception to the Midnight Deadline

The deferred posting period for deciding whether to pay or dishonor a particular check does not apply to those checks presented to a teller over the counter for immediate cashing. Under the UCC (section 3–506), when a customer presents a check to a payor bank for payment over the counter, the bank must pay or dishonor the check before the close of business on the day of presentment.

EXAMPLE ■ On February 1, Schumacher presented a check to be cashed over the counter. The teller immediately dishonored payment because the drawer's account did not have sufficient funds on deposit to cover the amount of the check. In this situation, the dishonor of the check was timely because it occurred before the close of business on February 1.

RETURN OF CHECKS

Recall that under the UCC, upon receipt of a check, a paying bank may take until its midnight deadline to decide whether to pay or dishonor the check. In other words, a bank can defer the decision to pay or dishonor a check for one business day after its receipt.

Paying Banks' Responsibility for Return of Checks

If a paying bank decides not to pay a check, then it must actually return the check within its midnight deadline. Under the UCC, a check was considered returned when it was sent to the presenting bank. The UCC defines "send" to mean "deposit the check in the mail." However, Regulation CC imposes additional responsibilities on paying banks that decide to return items presented for payment. Not only must a paying bank that decides not to pay a check return it within its midnight deadline, but it must also return the item in an expeditious manner. A check is returned in an expeditious manner if it meets the requirements of either the two-day/four-day test **or** the forward collection test.

Two-Day/Four-Day Test

The two-day portion of this test applies to paying banks that are local with respect to the depositary bank. Under this test, a local paying bank returns a check in an expeditious manner if it sends the check so that the check would normally be received by the depositary bank not later than 4:00 P.M. (local time of the depositary institution) of the second business day following the banking day on which the check was presented to the paying bank.

For example, a check is presented for payment to a local paying bank on Monday. If the bank dishonors the check, it must return the check to the depositary bank by 4:00 P.M. on Wednesday.

The four-day portion of this test applies to paying banks that are nonlocal with respect to the depositary bank. Under this test, a nonlocal paying bank returns a check in an expeditious manner if it sends the check so that the check would normally be received by the depositary bank not later than 4:00 P.M. (local time of the depositary institution) of the fourth business day following the banking day on which the check was presented to the paying bank.

For example, a check is presented to a nonlocal paying bank on Monday. If the bank dishonors the check, it must return the check to the depositary bank by 4:00 P.M. on Friday.

Forward Collection Test

Under the forward collection test, a paying bank also returns a check in an expeditious manner if it forwards the returned item in the same way that a similarly situated bank would handle a check that is

- approximately the same amount as the returned check

- drawn on the depositary bank

- deposited for forward collection by noon on the banking day following the banking day on which the check was presented to the paying bank

In other words, if an unpaid check is returned to the depositary institution as quickly as a similarly situated bank would forward an item drawn on the depositary bank for payment, then the requirements under the forward collection test have been fulfilled.

EXAMPLE ■ Suppose a paying bank usually mails its forward collection checks to a Federal Reserve bank to avoid courier costs, but similarly situated banks use couriers to deliver forward collection checks to their Federal Reserve banks. In this situation, the paying bank must send its returned items by courier to meet the requirements of the forward collection test.

Notification of Return of Large Items

In addition to being charged with the duty to return unpaid checks in an expeditious manner, a paying bank is also charged with the duty to provide the depositary bank with notice of nonpayment of items in the amount of $2,500 or more. This notice must be received by the depositary bank by 4:00 P.M. on the second business day following the banking day on which the item was presented to the paying bank. Notice may be given by any reasonable means including, but not limited to, a writing (including a copy of the check), telephone, wire, fax, or telex. Once the depositary bank receives the notice of nonpayment, it must, in turn, notify its customer of the nonpayment by midnight of the banking day following the banking day it received notice.

Paying Banks' Liability

Upon receipt of a check, a paying bank may take until its midnight deadline to decide whether to pay or dishonor. However, if the paying bank fails to pay or return the check within its midnight deadline, then the UCC imposes strict liability on the bank for the full amount of any check. In other words, a paying bank is accountable for the amount of a check, whether or not it is properly payable, if the bank fails to either pay or return it within its midnight deadline.

This rule of accountability has not been changed by Regulation CC. A paying bank must still pay or return an item within its midnight deadline. What Regulation CC has done, however, is to impose an additional standard of care upon paying banks. Not only must paying banks act within their midnight deadlines, but they must also exercise ordinary care in returning unpaid checks in an expeditious manner by complying with either the two-day/four-day test or the forward collection test. The amount of damages that may be recovered against a paying bank that fails to exercise ordinary care in handling an item in an expeditious manner is the amount of the loss incurred, up to the amount of the check. This liability, however, may be reduced by the amount of loss that the claiming party would have incurred even if the paying bank had exercised ordinary care.

EXAMPLE ■ Suppose a paying bank returns a $2,000 check within its midnight deadline, but fails to exercise ordinary care in returning the item in an expeditious manner. By the time the returned check reaches the depositary bank, the depositor's account is closed, causing the depositary bank to sustain a $2,000 loss. Suppose further that the depositary bank could demonstrate that there was $750 on deposit in the closed account at the time the check should have been returned. Under these circumstances, the paying bank's liability is limited to $750, the amount that the depositary bank could have recovered had the paying bank exercised ordinary care in returning the item.

Returning Banks' Responsibility for Return of Checks

Under Regulation CC, a returning bank is defined to mean any bank handling a returned check except the paying bank and the depositary bank. Under the UCC, a returning bank is charged with the duty to exercise ordinary care in returning an item. Whether a returning bank has exercised ordinary care is determined by whether it has acted "seasonably." Recall that under the UCC, a bank acts seasonably if it takes proper action within its midnight deadline. For instance, under the UCC, a bank that receives an item for return on Tuesday exercises ordinary care if it forwards the item for return by midnight on Wednesday. Regulation CC imposes new responsibilities on returning banks. Not only must a returning bank act "seasonably" in returning an item by its midnight deadline, but it must also return the item in an expeditious manner.

The expeditious return requirement for a returning bank is more stringent in many cases than the duty of a collecting bank to act seasonably under the UCC. This is because a returning bank, as in the case of a paying bank, must meet either the two-day/four-day test or the forward collection test to be considered to have acted expeditiously.

Returning Banks' Liability

The two-day/four-day test for returning banks is the same test applied to paying banks. The forward collection test is similar to the forward collection test applied to paying banks. Under this test a returning bank must return an item as quickly as a similarly situated bank would forward for collection an item of similar size drawn on the depositary institution. Further, if a returning bank fails to return an item in an expeditious manner, then its liability for such failure is identical to that of a paying bank which fails to expeditiously return an item.

Endorsement Standards

Regulation CC has implemented certain endorsement standards for depositary, paying, and returning banks to facilitate the prompt return of checks. These standards specify where each endorsement should be placed on a check and the information each endorsement should contain. For instance, as illustrated in figure 4.5, the depositary bank's endorsement should be placed on the back of the check in an area which is 3 inches from the leading edge of the check to 1.5 inches from the trailing edge. The leading edge is defined as the right side of the check looking at it from the front; while the trailing edge is defined as the left side of the check looking at it from the front. In addition, the depositary bank's endorsement must be written in dark purple or dark black ink and must contain the following information:

■ the bank's nine-digit routing number, set off by arrows at each end pointing to the number

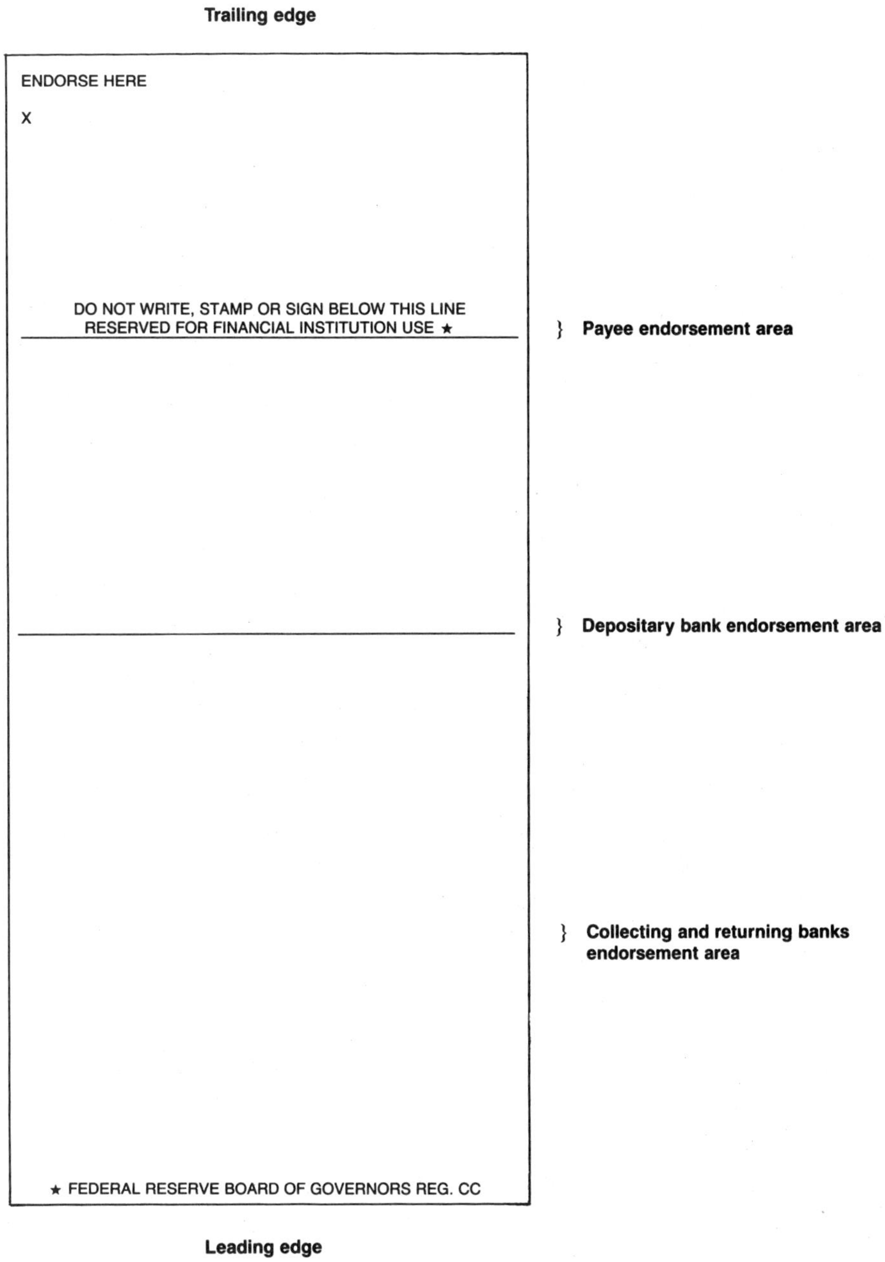
Trailing edge
ENDORSE HERE
X
DO NOT WRITE, STAMP OR SIGN BELOW THIS LINE
RESERVED FOR FINANCIAL INSTITUTION USE ★
} Payee endorsement area
} Depositary bank endorsement area
} Collecting and returning banks endorsement area
★ FEDERAL RESERVE BOARD OF GOVERNORS REG. CC
Leading edge

Figure 4.5 Endorsement Standards

- the bank's name and location

- the endorsement date

In turn, each subsequent collecting bank endorsement shall be in an area which is from 0 inches to 3 inches from the leading edge of the check. The endorsement must be written in an ink color other than purple and should include only its nine-digit routing number without the arrows, the endorsement date, and an optional trace/sequence number.

Each returning bank endorsement shall use an ink color other than purple and stay clear of the area on the back of the check from 3 inches from the leading edge to the trailing edge of the check. Also, the area from the trailing edge of the check to 1.5 inches from the trailing edge is where payees' endorsements are commonly placed.

Regulation CC places responsibility on the paying bank and the depositary bank to make certain that the back of the check is clear for the appropriate bank endorsements for both collection and return.

EXAMPLE ■ Suppose a paying bank permits its customer to place a carbon band on the back of the check that obstructs a bank endorsement and results in a delay in collecting or returning the item. Under these circumstances, the paying bank may be liable for any resultant damages. After the check is issued, the depositary bank then bears the burden of responsibility to make certain that its customer's endorsement or any prior endorsements do not inhibit the expeditious collection or return of the check; otherwise, the depositary bank may be held liable for any resultant damages.

CONCLUSION

If negotiable instruments are to serve as meaningful substitutes for money, they must be promptly paid. Article 4 of the UCC, therefore, imposes certain duties on both collecting and paying banks to ensure that negotiable instruments are rapidly circulated for their prompt payment in money. In turn, EFAA and Regulation CC impose certain duties on depositary, paying, and returning banks to ensure that deposited items are available for withdrawal within certain imposed deadlines and that dishonored items are returned in an expeditious manner.

Questions for Review and Discussion

1. Article 3 ensures the free circulation of negotiable instruments. What does article 4 ensure?

2. When is a cash deposit available for withdrawal from a customer's account?

3. When is an item considered a local check?

4. Under the permanent availability schedule, when is a local check available for withdrawal?

5. When is an item considered a nonlocal check?

6. Under the permanent availability schedule, when is a nonlocal check available for withdrawal?

7. There are six circumstances under which the published availability schedule may be extended. Name at least three.

8. What three kinds of banks are classified as collecting banks?

9. When is the midnight deadline for an item deposited on a Tuesday? If a bank is closed for the weekend, what is the midnight deadline for an item deposited on Friday?

10. Under what circumstances is a paying bank deemed to have returned an item in an expeditious manner?

5

Check Losses and Frauds

After studying this chapter, you will be able to

■ explain the liability of all parties to an instrument on which unauthorized signatures appear

■ describe customers' duty to inspect their statements and canceled checks and report any irregularities on them, such as forgeries or alterations, to the bank

■ discuss the circumstances under which a bank may either properly charge or refuse to charge its customers' accounts for the amount of their checks

■ explain a bank's liability for wrongfully refusing to pay its customers' checks

■ state the liabilities of collecting banks, including depositary, intermediary, and presenting banks

■ identify the liabilities of payor-drawee banks, which are responsible for paying checks drawn on their depositors' accounts

■ describe how the final payment of checks occurs

■ state the priorities of funds on deposit in a drawer's bank account

■ explain the practice of check kiting

So far, we have reviewed the basic aspects of negotiable instruments, including their types and forms; the concept of negotiability and its availability to holders in due course; the nature of contractual and warranty liability associated with authorized signatures; and the collection routes of checks from issuance to payment. However, our study of negotiable instruments has not yet confronted issues of error, forgery, or fraud.

For instance, who is liable on a negotiable instrument that bears a forged signature or unauthorized endorsement? What are the rights and responsibilities between the drawer and payor bank if an instrument is stale dated, postdated, incomplete, altered, drawn on insufficient funds, or subject to a stop-payment order? What happens if a payor bank dishonors a check it should have paid? What is the liability of collecting and payor banks if they fail to take proper action in handling an item within the time limits imposed by the Uniform Commercial Code (U.C.C.)? And what are some common schemes used to defraud a bank? This chapter will endeavor to answer these and other questions concerning final payment.

UNAUTHORIZED SIGNATURES

Under the UCC (section 3–404), an unauthorized signature does not operate as the signature of the person whose name is signed. However, a person who in good faith pays an instrument bearing an unauthorized signature is not without a remedy. This is because the person who made the unauthorized signature is personally liable, even if he or she used a name other than his or her own (U.C.C. § 3–404(1)).

An **unauthorized signature** is normally made under one of two circumstances: either it is forged or an agent, when placing the principal's signature on an instrument, has exceeded his or her authority.

EXAMPLE ■ Al Hays fraudulently identifies himself to May's Stereo Shop, Inc., as Donald O'Keefe. Since the stereo shop reasonably believes Hays to be O'Keefe, it permits him to purchase stereo equipment with a check that bears O'Keefe's forged signature as the drawer. When the check is returned to the stereo shop unpaid because payment was stopped, the shop owner immediately calls O'Keefe and demands payment. O'Keefe tells the shop that he did not purchase stereo equipment and that the man who posed as him was probably the thief who recently stole his checkbook and wallet. In this case, the stereo shop cannot recover from O'Keefe since the signature on his check was unauthorized. However, since the shop gave value for the check—the stereo equipment—it can recover the amount of the check from Al Hays, the unauthorized signer, if it can find him.

Under the UCC, the general rule that an unauthorized signature does not operate as that of the person whose name is signed has four basic exceptions. These exceptions arise under any of the following circumstances:

- when the person whose signature is forged or unauthorized decides to adopt it as his or her own (ratification)

- when a person tricks a drawer or maker into issuing an instrument in the name of a payee that he or she intends will have no interest in the instrument (as in the case of impostors, fictitious payees, and padded payrolls)

- when a person's own negligence substantially contributes to the making of his or her forged or unauthorized signature

- when a person fails to inspect his or her statement and canceled checks promptly to discover any forged signatures and to notify the bank of such a discovery

Ratification

An unauthorized signature does not operate as that of the person whose name is signed, unless he or she ratifies it (U.C.C. § 3–404(2)). **Ratification** means that a person agrees to adopt a signature that was unauthorized when originally placed on the instrument. Ratification may occur through a person's express statement or retention of benefits obtained from the issuance of the instrument.

Suppose that Al Hays of the preceding example is O'Keefe's good friend and roommate. Further, Hays signs O'Keefe's check without his authority but brings the stereo equipment back to the apartment for both of them to use. Later, O'Keefe discovers that Hays purchased the equipment with his check. In this situation, a strong argument can be made tht O'Keefe ratified Hays's unauthorized act of forgery and consequently is liable to the stereo shop. O'Keefe's retention and use of the stereo equipment after he learned how it was purchased shows ratification of Hays's unauthorized act.

Impostors, Fictitious Payees, and Padded Payrolls

As discussed in chapter 3, an endorsement is a simple contract whereby title to a order instrument is transferred merely by the holder's endorsing and delivering it to another party. Thus, a forged or unauthorized endorsement cannot generally pass good title to the instrument on which it is written. However, situations involving impostors, fictitious payees, and padded payrolls are exceptions to this rule (U.C.C. § 3–405). This does not mean that such actions are legal or proper. Instead, these UCC exceptions ensure that a holder in due course will not be forced to incur a loss because of an invalid instrument.

Impostors

An **impostor** is anyone who introduces him- or herself as some other person to a drawer or maker. An impostor attempts by fraud to induce a drawer or maker to deliver to him or her an instrument naming the person being impersonated as the payee. If the impostor succeeds in this fraud, then an endorsement by any person using the payee's name is effective to transfer good title to the instrument.

EXAMPLE ■ Green comes to White and introduces himself as Johnson, a respected art dealer. Green then induces White to draw a check, payable to Johnson, as an investment in a rare work of art. Once the check is drawn, by endorsing it in Johnson's name, Green or anyone else can transfer good title to the instrument.

Fictitious Payees When a person who signs an instrument on a maker's or drawer's behalf intends the payee to have no interest in the instrument, an endorsement by any person in the name of the named payee is effective. Although this rule is commonly called the **fictitious-payee rule,** its application does not depend on whether the named payee is fictitious but on whether the signer intends the payee to have an interest in the instrument.

EXAMPLES ■ Hart, treasurer of ABC Rental, Inc., draws a corporate check, payable to Judson Lewis, who does not exist. In this situation, an endorsement in the payee's name is effective to transfer title.

■ Bonnie Smith, as treasurer of Widget, Inc., draws a corporate check, payable to Rand, who Smith believes is a fictitious payee. In fact, Rand does exist. In this situation, an endorsement in the payee's name is also effective to transfer good title to the instrument. Whether Rand is a fictitious payee does not matter, since Smith never intended Rand to have an interest in the check.

Padded Payrolls A **padded payroll** is a common scheme among employees to defraud employers. This happens when an agent or employee of a maker or drawer includes a name on a payroll but intends to take the instrument him- or herself. In this situation, the agent's, employee's, or any other person's endorsement in the payee's name is effective. Again, whether the payee is real or fictitious does not matter.

EXAMPLE ■ Al Dix, a bookkeeper for Larry's Autos, Inc., prepares a payroll to submit to the company's treasurer and includes the name Pam

Minute. Dix knows but the treasurer does not know that Minute does not exist. The treasurer issues a payroll check payable to Pam Minute's order. In this situation, Dix's or any other person's endorsement in Pam Minute's name is effective to transfer good title to the instrument.

Suppose Pam Minute does exist and Dix knows it, but he does not intend her to have any interest in the check. Again, in this situation, the bookkeeper's or any other person's endorsement in Pam Minute's name is effective to transfer good title to the instrument.

Thus, in the cases of impostors, fictitious payees, and padded payrolls, the payee is not intended to have any interest in the instrument. If the payee had an interest, then any other party's signature would be a forgery and good title would not be passed to the holder.

Negligence

Negligence is also an exception to the general rule that an unauthorized or forged signature does not operate as that of the person whose name is signed (U.C.C. § 3–406). Reduced to its simplest definition, **negligence** means carelessness. The UCC provides that a person's unauthorized signature is considered genuine if his or her carelessness substantially contributed to the making of the unauthorized signature.

The UCC does not attempt to define all acts or omissions that constitute negligence. Instead, the code leaves the question of negligence to be resolved on a case-by-case basis. The UCC does, however, give some examples of negligent acts that substantially contribute to the making of an unauthorized signature. For instance, an obvious case of such negligence is when a drawer who uses a signature stamp (**facsimile signature**) fails to secure it and another person uses it to obtain funds fraudulently. Another example is when a check is carelessly mailed to the wrong person having the same name as the payee and such person negotiates the check.

EXAMPLE ■ The treasurer of Hal's New and Used Cars, Inc., signs all company checks with a rubber stamp that reads, "Hal's New and Used Cars, Inc., by James Good, Treasurer." At the end of each day, Good places the company checkbook and signature stamp in an unlocked filing cabinet. One evening, after Good leaves work, Jones, a bookkeeper for the company, retrieves the checkbook and stamp from the file cabinet and writes several checks payable to his own order. Jones then negotiates them for deposit into his account at Berg State Bank and, as the drawee, Berg State pays the checks. When Good discovers the fraud, Jones has already moved out of town. Good demands that Berg State recredit the account for Hal's New and Used Cars, since the company's signature on the checks was unauthorized. Berg State Bank refuses Good's demand, so Hal's New and Used Cars sues. In this case, the bank can make an excellent argument that Good's failure to safeguard the signature stamp was a major contributing factor to Jones's unauthorized acts. Under such circumstances, the court would consider the company's signature genuine and Berg State would win.

Customers' Duty to Review Statements and Canceled Checks

Under the common-law rule established in the eighteenth century English case of *Price v. Neale*, a drawee of a draft is presumed to know the signature of its customer, the drawer. Thus, generally, a drawee-payor bank is strictly liable to its customer for the amount of any check it pays over its customer's forged signature. However, section 4–406 of the UCC has modified this rule somewhat.

Case for Discussion

PRICE V. NEALE

Facts

Mr. Lee forged Benjamin Sutton's signature on a draft. The draft was payable to Mr. Roger Ruding for $250 at John Price's banking offices. (At this time in history, individuals ran banking houses because no uniform banking regulations existed.)

Upon receiving the draft, Roger Ruding endorsed the instrument to Edward Neale, who took it for value and did not know of the forged drawer's signature. Neale presented the draft for payment at Price's banking house, and Price paid Neale the value of the draft.

Mr. Lee was later proved to have forged Sutton's signature and was hanged for his crime, an extreme punishment even for the eighteenth century. When Price learned of the forgery, he demanded repayment plus damages from Neale. Neale claimed he acted innocently and in good faith, without the least knowledge of the forgery. Price claimed he paid Neale on the supposition that the instrument was a genuine draft. In addition, he could not collect against the drawer, Sutton, because the latter did not sign the draft. Further, he could not collect against Lee, because he was hanged for his crime. Price argued that Neale should have known the signature was a forgery, particularly since he had participated in the exchange of the instrument for value.

Decision

Although the court ruled that both parties acted in good faith and were innocent of any fraud, in this case, Price had to bear the loss. As a banker, Price had the responsibility to ensure that the draft did not contain a forged drawer's signature. Neale, on the other hand, had no responsibility to recognize Sutton's signature. Since Price was negligent in accepting these drafts instead of dishonoring them, the court ruled that he alone had to accept the loss. (See *Price v. Neale*, 3 Burrow's 1355 (1762).)

Questions for Discussion

1. What precautions should banks take to ensure that a drawer's signature is not forged on an instrument?
2. Today, what recourse does a bank have if it inadvertently accepts an instrument on which the drawer's signature is forged?

Under the UCC, a drawer has the responsibility to inspect his or her statements and any canceled checks promptly and report to the bank any forgeries discovered. If the drawer fails to comply with this statutory duty, then he or she—instead of the drawee—may be responsible for the amount of any check bearing a forged signature charged to his or her account. Accordingly, the drawer should treat his or her checkbook as a valuable possession. To prevent loss through forgery, the drawer should

- keep checkbooks, statements, and canceled checks in a safe place

- inform the bank of any loss or theft of blank checks

- compare statements with checkbook records and inform the bank immediately of any irregularities

- notify the bank if monthly statements and canceled checks are not received at the usual time

- destroy both blank checkbooks and loose checks that are no longer needed

- notify the bank promptly of any change in address

- write checks carefully and leave no blanks or spaces where any additional figures or words can be inserted

When the bank returns a customer's canceled checks, they are normally accompanied by a statement showing the amounts charged against the account and the resultant balance. Examination of this statement and a comparison of the canceled checks with the stubs in the customer's checkbook will show whether any forged checks have been charged to the account. If the customer discovers that a check has been forged, he or she is obligated to notify the bank of this fact. Prompt notification may enable the bank to recover the amount from the person who received the proceeds of the forged check and to prevent any further forgeries.

Fourteen-Day Rule Under the UCC, a customer must exercise reasonable care in inspecting his or her statement and report any forgery to the bank within a reasonable period, not to exceed 14 days after receipt of the statement. If the customer carries out this duty, then he or she is not liable for any forgeries discovered in the statement and the bank must recredit the customer's account. Under the UCC, a statement is made available to a depositor under any of the following circumstances:

- The statement is sent to the depositor.

- The bank holds the statement and canceled checks pursuant to the customer's request.

- The bank otherwise makes the statement and canceled checks available for inspection in a reasonable manner. (This situation most commonly arises when a customer moves and neglects to notify the bank of his or her new address.)

EXAMPLE ■ On March 15, the bank sends a monthly statement and canceled checks to Marshall for inspection. One check dated March 1, bears Marshall's forged signature. On March 25, Marshall notifies the drawee bank of the forgery. Because Marshall reported the forgery within 14 days after the drawee bank sent the statement and canceled checks to him, the bank must recredit his account for the amount of the forged check.

CUSTOMERS' FAILURE TO DISCOVER AND REPORT FORGERIES WITHIN 14 DAYS

If a customer fails to discover and report the first forgery contained in a statement within a reasonable period, not to exceed 14 days, then he or she may be prevented from recovering from the bank the amount of any forged check paid before the expiration of the 14-day period. Such a situation will occur if the bank can establish that (1) its customer failed to exercise reasonable care and promptness in examining the statement and canceled checks to discover such forgery and in notifying the bank of such discovery, and (2) the bank suffered a loss because of such failure.

Accordingly, even if the customer is negligent in discovering and notifying the bank of a forgery within the 14-day period, the bank cannot resist recrediting its customer's account if it cannot demonstrate that timely notification could have prevented the loss. Presumably, the bank must show that, with timely notification, it could have recovered the amount of the forgeries from the wrongdoer. In most cases, however, a bank may have difficulty demonstrating that its losses from a forged check paid within the 14-day period directly resulted from a customer's delay in discovering and reporting such forgery.

EXAMPLE ■ Suppose Marshall from the preceding example does not report the March 1 forgery to his bank until April 15, which is 30 days after the bank sent him the statement containing the forgery. Suppose also that the forger is Marshall's bookkeeper, who disappeared during February. In this situation, the drawee bank must recredit Marshall's account for the March 1 forgery, even though he did not report the forgery by March 29, the last day of the 14-day period. This is because the bank would still have suffered a loss, whether or not Marshall reported the forgery in a timely manner, since the forger left town in February and could not be located.

FORGED CHECKS PAID AFTER THE 14-DAY PERIOD

Under the UCC, for a bank to resist recrediting its customer's account for any forged checks paid after the 14-day period, it does not need to demonstrate that the customer's delay caused it to suffer a loss that it otherwise could have prevented. The UCC (section 4–406) provides that the bank is not responsible for any forgeries by the same wrongdoer that occur (1) 14 calendar days after the bank sends the statement and canceled checks containing the first forgery to the customer, and (2) before the customer notifies the bank of such forgeries.

EXAMPLE ■ Suppose that Marshall in the previous examples never inspects his March 15 statement containing the first forgery. On April 15, the bank again sends a monthly statement and canceled checks to Marshall. This statement contains two checks that bear his forged signature, one dated April 2 and the other dated April 5. Furthermore, the same wrongdoer committed all the forgeries. On April 18, Marshall inspects his statement and canceled checks, discovers the April 2 and 5 forgeries, immediately calls his bank, and demands that it recredit his account for the amount of the checks. The bank refuses Marshall's demand, so he sues. In this situation, as long as the bank exercised ordinary care in paying the forged checks, it does not have to recredit

Marshall's account for the April 2 and 5 forged checks. This is because Marshall failed to report the first forgery within 14 days after the bank sent the March 15 statement containing the first forgery to him.

Banks' Responsibility to Exercise Ordinary Care

By imposing a new duty on depositors to reconcile their monthly statements and accompanying canceled checks and then promptly notify banks of any forgeries among the canceled checks, the UCC rule on bank statements appears to favor banks. However, a question still exists about whether banks are negligent in paying such checks.

Under the UCC (section 4–406(3)), even if a customer is negligent in discovering and then reporting forgeries, he or she may still assert the forgeries against the bank if the customer can establish that the bank failed to exercise ordinary care when it paid the forged checks. For example, a bank paying a check with a customer's forged signature may not have exercised ordinary care if it does not have procedures to compare its customer's known signature (for instance, against a signature card) with the signature on the check. Even when the bank does have such procedures, if it does not reasonably follow them, then once again it may not have exercised ordinary care in paying a forged or altered check. The issue of whether a bank or customer has exercised ordinary care to prevent a successful forgery is therefore determined on a case-by-case basis.

EXAMPLE ■ In the previous examples, suppose that Marshall discovers that the bank did not compare his known signature on a signature card with the forged signature on his checks. In this situation, although he was negligent in failing to discover and report the first forgery, Marshall will probably win. Because the bank failed to exercise ordinary care in paying the forged checks, Marshall is entitled to have his account recredited.

Customers' Failure to Discover Forgeries within One Year

A customer is absolutely precluded from asserting a forged signature against a bank if he or she fails to discover and report the forgery within one year after the bank sends the statement containing the forgery to the customer (U.C.C. § 4–406(4)). This preclusion applies even if the bank, in paying the forged check, fails to exercise ordinary care.

EXAMPLE ■ Suppose that Marshall of the preceding examples reports the forgeries to his bank on April 20 of the following year and demands that his account be recredited. The bank refuses, so Marshall sues. In this situation, Marshall is absolutely precluded from asserting the forgeries against the bank, because he failed to notify the bank within one year from the dates (March 15 and April 15 of the preceding year) on which the bank sent the statements containing the forgeries to him.

FORGED ENDORSEMENTS

Generally, a drawee-payor bank is strictly liable for the amount of a check bearing a drawer's forged signature. Normally, when a drawer's signature is forged, only two parties are at odds with one another, the drawer and drawee. However, such is not the case when a check bears a payee's forged endorsement. These situations are extremely complex and involve almost every party to the forged instrument. For instance, the payee will have claims against both the drawer and drawee. The drawer in turn will have a claim against the drawee, while the drawee will have a claim against the presenting bank and all previous collecting banks, including the depositary bank. Each collecting bank will also have a claim against any previous collecting bank. Finally, the depositary bank is left with the forged check and the remaining claim against the least desirous defendant—the thief.

Payee Versus Drawer

As discussed in chapter 3, the underlying obligation on a check is not discharged until the check is presented and paid (U.C.C. § 3–802).

EXAMPLE ■ Marsha Bright owes Kim Kelly $100 for the purchase of a radio. She pays for the radio by a check drawn on her account at Third National Bank, but the check is stolen in the mail. In this situation, Bright still owes Kelly the $100.

The issuance of a check does not release (discharge) the drawer from liability on the underlying obligation. Discharge of the obligation does not occur until the check is presented and paid.

Payee Versus Drawee Bank

The UCC (section 3–419) provides that an instrument is **converted** when it is paid on a forged endorsement. Conversion is defined as wrongful control over the personal property of another. Thus, if a bank cashes a check for someone other than the owner, it has deprived the owner of control over his or her property.

EXAMPLE ■ Kelly of the preceding example is unable to recover the $100 from Bright. The thief who stole the check forges Kelly's endorsement and deposits the check into his own account at Berg State Bank. Further, Third National Bank pays the check upon its presentation by Berg State. In this situation, Kelly could look directly to Third National Bank for payment. Under the UCC, Third National Bank (the drawee bank) is liable to Kelly (the payee) for the face amount of the instrument ($100).

Drawer Versus Drawee Bank

A check is not "properly payable" if it bears an unauthorized or forged endorsement. This is because only a holder can properly present an instrument for payment (U.C.C. § 3–504).

EXAMPLE ■ Suppose Marsha Bright of the preceding examples acknowledges that she still owes Kelly $100, since her check was stolen in the mail, so she pays Kelly the $100 in cash. Because Third National

Bank has paid the stolen check, Bright is now out $100. Consequently, under the UCC, Bright can compel Third National Bank to recredit her account for $100, since the check was not properly endorsed.

Drawee Versus Depositary Bank

Good title generally means that an instrument does not contain any forged or unauthorized endorsements.

EXAMPLE ■ Once Third National Bank of the preceding example recredits $100 to Bright's account, it may turn to Berg State for refund of the $100 check, because Berg State breached its presentment warranty of good title. If the check had been deposited with a bank other than Berg State, Berg State could then turn to such depository institution for refund of the $100 check, because that institution breached its transfer warranty of good title.

Depositary Bank Versus Thief

The ultimate responsibility for forged endorsements is often placed on a depositary institution, because it is usually the first to deal with the forger and thus has the opportunity to verify the endorsement. The same reasoning applies to placing the ultimate responsibility for forged drawer's signatures on payor institutions, since a drawee bank can compare and verify the signature on a check with that on a signature card.

EXAMPLE ■ Unfortunately for Berg State in the preceding examples, it was both the presenting and depository institution. Accordingly, it can only recover the $100 from its customer, the thief, because he breached his transfer warranty of good title. However, in this situation, Berg State will probably have difficulty locating the thief because he has already left town.

The allocation of responsibilities for forgery is reflected in the distinction between transfer and presentment warranties governing signatures. As discussed in chapter 3, each person or entity who transfers an instrument gives the following **presentment warranties** to the payor (maker or drawee) (U.C.C. §§ 3–417(1) and 4–207(1)):

■ that the transferor has good title to the instrument

■ that the transferor has no knowledge that the maker's or drawer's signature is unauthorized

■ that the instrument has not been materially altered

In addition, a transferor makes the following **transfer warranties** to his or her immediate transferee and all subsequent holders if the instrument is transferred by endorsement (U.C.C. §§ 3–417(2) and 4–207(2)):

■ that the transferor has good title to the instrument

■ that all signatures are genuine or authorized

■ that the instrument has not been materially altered

■ that no party's defense is good against the transferor

■ that the transferor knows of no insolvency proceedings against the maker, acceptor, or drawer of the instrument

Thus, under transfer warranties, a transferee receives the warranty that all signatures on an instrument are genuine or authorized. The comparable presentment warranty, however, is much less generous. The warranty a payor receives on signatures is only that the transferor has no knowledge that the maker's or drawer's signature is unauthorized. Further, a holder in due course does not give this warranty to the payor.

The distinction between transfer and presentment warranties continues the common-law rule established in *Price v. Neale*. Under that decision, a drawee of a draft is presumed to know the signature of his or her customer, the drawer, and thus bears the burden of loss if he or she pays an instrument over the drawer's forged signature.

EXAMPLE ■ Suppose the thief in the preceding examples forged Bright's, instead of Kelly's, signature. Bright convinces Third National to recredit her account because the check was not properly drawn (that is, it has an unauthorized signature). In this situation, Third National cannot look to Berg State for refund because of breach of warranty. Berg State's presentment warranty given to Third National is not that the drawer's signature is genuine or authorized but only that it does not know that it is unauthorized. Furthermore, since Berg State is a holder in due course, it does not make any presentment warranty on the authenticity of the drawer's signature.

Case for Discussion

PACIFIC INSURANCE CO. V. COMMERCIAL BANK AND BAKERSFIELD NATIONAL BANK

Facts

Marie Porter was seriously injured in an automobile accident in August 1984. Following the accident, she hired an attorney, Marshall Lyons, to help her obtain a favorable settlement from Pacific Insurance Company. For his services, Lyons was to receive 30 percent of the settlement. The claim was eventually settled in June 1986, and Pacific sent a draft payment through Bakersfield National Bank for $5,860, payable to Marie Porter and Marshall Lyons.

When he received the draft, Lyons endorsed his name and forged Marie Porter's endorsement on the back. He then deposited the draft to his account on June 15, 1986, at the Commercial Bank of Bakersfield. Commercial Bank accepted the deposit and delivered the check to Bakersfield National Bank, which in turn presented the draft to Pacific Insurance Company for payment.

In May 1987, Porter contacted Pacific Insurance Company concerning the settlement of her claim. She reported that she was unable to locate her attorney and that he had apparently closed his account at the Commercial Bank of Bakersfield. Further, she reported that she had never received any money from the settlement of her claim.

When Pacific Insurance discovered the forged endorsement, it demanded payment of $5,860 from the Commercial Bank of

Bakersfield. In this situation, Pacific Insurance Company had authorized Bakersfield National to pay all drafts under $10,000.

Commercial Bank contended that its liability on warranty of endorsement did not extend to Pacific Insurance Company but only to Bakersfield National, the payor bank. Commercial Bank further contended that the insurance company should seek to recover the $5,860 from Bakersfield National.

Bakersfield National in turn argued that Pacific Insurance should be unable to recover that amount from it under the statutory warranty, because section 4–207 of the UCC makes the right of recovery conditional upon the payment of a draft in good faith.

Decision

In this case, the court ruled that Bakersfield National was not the payor bank. The draft had clearly stated that it was payable through Bakersfield National. Under sections 3–120, 4–105, and 4–207(1) of the UCC, Pacific Insurance was the payor. Therefore, the insurance company could make a claim against the Commercial Bank of Bakersfield for "endorsement warranties." In that respect, the court further ruled that Pacific Insurance could "rely on the prior endorsement as a guarantee of prior endorsements," because the Commercial Bank was in the best position to verify the validity of the payees' signatures.

However, Commercial Bank chose to rely on the integrity of its depositor, Marshall Lyons, and no one could accuse it of bad faith in doing so. Likewise, the Pacific Insurance Company also chose to rely on the integrity of the endorser, Commercial Bank, and could not be accused of bad faith in doing so.

Questions for Discussion

1. In this case, identify the depositary, collecting, and payor-drawee banks. Explain your reasons.
2. What final decision by the court would be equitable in this case? Should any of the parties to this suit be liable for the $5,860? Why?
3. What recourse does Marie Porter have in this situation?

If an endorser or drawer uses the words "without recourse" to qualify his or her responsibility to pay an instrument, this only means that he or she has disclaimed the contractual liability to pay. However, the endorser or drawer usually becomes liable in warranty upon the transfer of the instrument, and the qualified endorsement does not prevent that liability. Otherwise, drawers and endorsers could easily defraud other parties.

EXAMPLES ■ Mason makes a note payable to the order of Arthur Woodhouse. Before the note is due, insolvency proceedings are brought against Mason. Woodhouse knows that Mason will be unable to pay the note on presentment, so Woodhouse transfers the note to Preston and qualifies his endorsement as follows: "A. Woodhouse, without recourse." When the note is due, Preston presents it to Mason and discovers that he has been insolvent for some time and cannot pay it. Preston then sues Woodhouse. Although Woodhouse is not liable on his endorsement contract in this situation, he is liable for breach of his transfer warranty that he did not know of the drawer's insolvency proceeding. Thus, Woodhouse must pay the amount of the note to Preston.

■ Randall tricks Brown into making a note payable to Randall's order. Before the due date, Randall transfers the note to Miller. A month after the note is due, Miller presents it to Brown for payment. Brown refuses to pay the note because Randall had defrauded him. Miller then sues Randall. In this situation, Randall is not liable on his endorsement contract because Miller was late in presenting the note for payment. However, Randall is liable for breach of warranty and must pay Miller. When Randall transferred the note to Miller, he warranted that he did not know of any good defense against him. Since he defrauded Brown, Randall obviously knew that Brown had a good defense against him.

Case for Discussion   **WESTBURY TRUST V. FRANKLIN NATIONAL BANK**

Facts

Mary Winter receives a check for $13.50 from the Nassau County Social Services Department. Because she has debts that far exceed the value of the check, Winter carefully types a "3" in front of the $13.50. This alteration makes the check appear to be payable for $313.50. Winter then goes to Westbury Trust to cash the check. The teller is familiar with the Nassau County checks, verifies that Winter is the proper payee, and pays her $313.50.

The Nassau County checking account is with Franklin National Bank. Through the collection process, Westbury Trust delivers the check for payment to Franklin National, which pays the check and sends the canceled check to Nassau County. A clerk at the Social Services Department detects the alteration and promptly notifies Franklin National, which credits the county's account for $300 and returns the check to Westbury Trust for payment.

Westbury Trust contends that Franklin National must suffer the loss of $300, since it was the payor bank. Westbury Trust claims that it was a holder in due course, acted in good faith, and made no warranty that the item had not been materially altered. Franklin National argues that Westbury Trust may have been a holder in due course, but it was also the collecting bank. Under the UCC (section 4–207(1)), the collecting bank makes presentment warranties, one of which is that the instrument has not been materially altered.

Decision

The court states that, under the circumstances, neither bank was negligent in accepting the check. Clearly, Winter is guilty of fraud but cannot be located. In this case, however, the court rules in favor of Franklin National Bank. According to the court, presentment warranties override the status of a holder in due course for Westbury Trust. The only exception would have been Franklin National's acceptance of the check before Westbury Trust cashed it, which would have happened if Franklin National had certified the check.

Questions for Discussion

1. Why does Westbury Trust's presentment warranty that the instrument has not been materially altered override its status as a holder in due course?
2. What is the extent of Westbury Trust's liability in this case? What is the extent of Nassau County's liability?

WHEN ARE CHECKS PROPERLY PAYABLE?

A bank does not have to open an account and receive deposits from a person or entity with whom it chooses not to do business. Similarly, a bank may close an undesirable account if it gives reasonable notice of such action to its customer. However, when a bank does choose to do business with a depositor, it has a fundamental responsibility to pay its depositor's checks that are properly payable (U.C.C. § 4–401). The proper performance of this duty cannot be overemphasized, since a bank may otherwise face significant liabilities. For instance, if a bank pays a check that is not properly payable, then it must recredit its customer's account for the amount of the check. Further, if a bank fails to pay a check that is properly payable, then it is liable to its customer for the damages that result from its wrongful dishonor. The provisions of the UCC (section 4–104(i)) defining what constitutes a properly payable check are somewhat vague. According to those provisions, properly payable checks require the availability of funds for payment at the time the decision is made to pay or dishonor the check. In other words, a bank may properly pay a check if sufficient funds are on deposit in the customer's account to cover the amount of the check. However, this provision by itself provides little guidance to a bank confronted with the issue of whether a particular check is properly payable.

For instance, even though a customer has sufficient funds on deposit to pay a particuar check, is it still properly payable if it is postdated, stale dated (over six months old), or subject to a stop-payment order? Fortunately, section 4–104(i) of the UCC is not the sole source of answers to these and other questions relating to whether a particular check is properly payable. Common law and certain provisions of articles 3 and 4 also help to determine whether checks are properly payable under any of the following circumstances:

- when a check is stale dated, that is, presented for payment more than six months after its date

- when the payment of a check results in a creation of an overdraft in the customer's account

- when a bank pays a check after its customer has died or become incompetent

- when a signature is missing, forged, or unauthorized

- when a check has been altered or is incomplete

- when a check is postdated

- when a check is subject to a stop-payment order

Stale-Dated Checks

A stale-dated check is one that is presented for payment more than six months after its date. Under the UCC (section 4–404), a bank need not pay a check, other than a certified check, that is presented for payment more than six months after its date. However, the UCC gives a bank the option to pay a stale-dated check if it does so in good faith.

As discussed in chapter 2, good faith is measured by the subjective test defined as actual honesty in the conduct of a transaction. Thus, if a bank knows that a check is stale dated, under what circumstances does it pay it in good faith? The UCC provides that a bank pays a stale check in good faith if it knows that the drawer wants payment to be made. Accordingly, if any question arises about whether payment should be made, the bank should consult the drawer or else dishonor the check.

What happens if a bank does not know that a check is stale, such as when it is paid in a normal computer run or when a teller inadvertently fails to notice the stale date? Under the UCC subjective test, as long as the bank has acted honestly—that is, without knowing the check is stale—then it has acted in good faith and is not liable to the customer for the payment of the stale check. However, some courts have disagreed with this view. These courts state that a bank's failure to discover that a check is stale dated constitutes a breach of its duty to exercise ordinary care in payment of a check. Consequently, these courts would require the bank to recredit the drawer's account if he or she did not want the check paid. Because of these conflicting viewpoints, a bank's counsel should always be consulted to determine whether the payment of a stale check was proper.

EXAMPLE ■ Newman presented a check, payable to her order, to a teller to be cashed. The teller noticed that the check was seven months old and refused to pay it. Since the check was stale dated, the dishonor in this situation was not wrongful.

However, suppose the teller noticed the stale date, had no idea whether the drawer wanted the check paid, but still cashed the check. When the drawer learned that the bank paid the check, he demanded that it recredit his account, because two months earlier he had issued a replacement check to Newman (the payee) after she had told him that the first check was lost. The bank refused to recredit the account, so the drawer sued. In this case, the drawer would probably win. Under the comments to section 4–404 of the UCC, a bank pays a stale check in good faith when it knows the drawer wants the payment made. Since the teller knew that the check was stale dated but still cashed it without finding out whether the drawer wanted it paid, he did not act in good faith.

Overdrafts

The provisions and comments in section 4–401 of the UCC expressly provide that a check is properly payable, even though its payment will create an **overdraft** in a customer's account. By creating the overdraft, the bank in effect loans money to its customer and, under the UCC, the check carries with it the customer's implied promise to reimburse the bank for this loan.

EXAMPLE ■ Third National Bank paid a check that created a $500 overdraft in its customer's account. When the bank asked the customer to cover the overdraft, she refused and said that the bank did not have her permission to overdraw on her account. The bank sued and, in this case, won.

Thus, under the UCC, a bank does not need its customer's permission to overdraw on his or her account. If it chooses to do so, then the customer must reimburse it for the amount of the overdraft.

Customer's Death or Incompetence

Among a bank's many concerns in dealing with customers is what to do when a depositor dies. Suppose, for example, the bank honors a depositor's checks, only to learn later that the depositor died before their payment. Under the circumstances, are these checks properly payable?

A bank's authority to pay its depositor's checks generally ends when the depositor dies or becomes mentally incompetent. The UCC (section 4–405) refines this rule to state that bank employees need not read the obituary columns nor feel compelled to distinguish between eccentricity and lunacy at their own peril. Specifically, under the UCC, a bank's authority to pay checks is not revoked until it actually knows that either its depositor is dead or has been declared incompetent by a court of law. In fact, even after it is aware of its customer's death, a bank may continue to pay his or her checks for 10 days following the death (U.C.C. § 4–405(2)).

An interesting aspect of this section of the UCC is that any person claiming interest in a deceased or incompetent customer's account, whether such a claim is founded on merit, may order the bank to stop payment on any outstanding checks. Such an interested party is usually a creditor, relative, or personal representative of the estate of a deceased depositor.

EXAMPLE ■ On March 5, Tim Brown issued a check for $1,500, payable to the order of Cecil de Caxton. Unknown to the bank, Brown died in an accident on the following day. On March 25, the bank paid Brown's check. When Brown's estate learned of the payment, it demanded reimbursement from the bank. The estate argued that the check was not properly payable, because it was paid more than 10 days after Brown's death. The bank refused the demand and the estate sued. In this situation, the bank would win. The check was properly payable because the bank did not know of its depositor's death when it paid the check. The 10-day rule only applies when the bank actually knows that its depositor has died. However, if the bank had known of Brown's death when it paid the check, the estate would win because the bank's authority to pay the check ended on March 17, 10 days after its customer died.

Missing, Forged, or Unauthorized Signatures

Unless a drawer is negligent, a check that bears a forged or unauthorized signature or is missing a signature is not properly payable. A person is not obligated to pay an instrument unless his or her signature appears on it. In other words, a check is not properly payable until the drawer orders with his or her authorized signature the drawee to pay it to the holder. This rule also applies to checks that bear a forged endorsement.

As discussed in chapter 2, negotiation is a special form of transfer that makes the transferee a holder. A bearer instrument is negotiated by delivery alone, while an order instrument is negotiated by delivery to the transferee accompanied by the transferor's endorsement. If that endorsement is unauthorized (forged), then any subsequent transferee taking the instrument cannot be classified as a holder. Consequently, an instrument bearing an unauthorized endorsement is not properly payable, because only a holder can properly present an instrument for payment in money (U.C.C. § 3–504).

EXAMPLE ■ Morris owes Hoffman $3,000 for the purchase of a used car. She pays for the car by a check drawn on her account at Avenue State Bank. The check is stolen in the mail and the thief forges Hoffman's endorsement. Avenue State Bank subsequently pays the check. Since Hoffman never received payment, Morris still owes him $3,000, which she pays in cash. Morris then demands that Avenue State recredit her account. The bank refuses Morris's demand, so she sues. In this case, Morris wins. The check was not properly payable because it bore the payee's forged endorsement.

Incomplete or Altered Checks

In most instances, a check is **altered** when enough space is left on the amount line to permit such alteration. On the other hand, an **incomplete check** is most often completed contrary to the drawer's authority when the amount line is left completely blank. In either case, whether such checks are properly payable depends on whether the bank acted in good faith and according to reasonable commercial standards and the customer acted with **reasonable care**.

Incomplete Checks

A drawer who habitually signs blank checks can scarcely claim that he or she has acted with reasonable care. Consequently, a blank check that leaves such a drawer's possession is properly payable in the amount subsequently completed, unless the bank has not acted in good faith or has received notice that the completion was improper (U.C.C. § 4–401(2)(b)).

EXAMPLE ■ Martin gives Jacobs an incomplete check and instructs him to complete it for $3,000. Contrary to Martin's instructions, Jacobs completes the check for $5,000, which the drawee bank pays in good faith and without notice of the unauthorized completion. Once Martin receives her statement, she immediately informs the bank that the completion was improper and her account should have been debited for only $3,000, instead of $5,000. She then demands a credit of $2,000. The bank refuses and Martin sues. In this case, the bank wins. Under the UCC, a bank may charge its customer's account in the amount of a completed item, unless it receives notice that the completion was improper.

Case for Discussion

BULLITT COUNTY BANK V. PUBLISHERS PRINTING CO.

Facts

Publishers Printing was a small company consisting of three officers who also served as directors. William Young, an employee of Publishers, was considered the chief clerk, officer manager, and a trusted employee. Young's primary duties were to deposit checks to Publishers' accounts, to cash small checks that he was required to endorse, and to ensure that the company's balances were maintained.

From October 22, 1975, through January 18, 1980, Young began presenting checks at the bank drawn on Publishers' accounts, payable to the Bullitt County Bank. Young requested that checks presented in this manner be exchanged by the bank for cashier's checks payable to another bank, in which Young kept a private account. During this period, the president of Publishers often left presigned, blank checks in Young's possession, which another officer would later cosign. Also, during this time, a CPA firm audited Publishers' bank statements, as well as its corporate accounting books, and reported no discrepancies.

Publishers sued Bullitt for $147,481 for failure to exercise ordinary care in payment of checks drawn to the bank's order, with the proceeds of the checks paid to another party. The bank contended that the drawer, Publishers, was negligent in its business practices and should be barred from recovery. The bank further contended that William Young had apparent authority to cash checks on behalf of his principal, Publishers; that is, as office manager, Young had authority to handle certain banking transactions. According to the bank, the officers of Publishers had given the bank the impression that Young had the authority to handle the transactions in this case.

Decision

The court ruled that, in handling Publishers' accounts, the bank did not exercise good faith and ordinary care (U.C.C. §§ 1–103, 3–406, 3–419(3), 4–103(1), and 4–406(2)). The court also stated that the bank had an obligation to notify Publishers of Young's departure from his regular banking duties. Thus, according to the court, the bank's exchanging unendorsed checks drawn to the bank's order without question was unreasonable. (See *Bullitt County Bank v. Publishers Printing Co., Inc.*, Kentucky Court of Appeals, No. 83–CA–2201–MR (September 7, 1984).)

Questions for Discussion

1. What procedures should the bank have followed in this situation?
2. The UCC requires a customer, in examining his or her statements and canceled items, to exercise reasonable care and promptness and to notify the bank promptly of any discrepancies. Why did the court not apply that rule in this situation?

Altered Checks Generally, altered checks are only properly payable in the amount in which they were originally drawn, as long as the drawee bank paid the check in good faith.

EXAMPLE ■ Suppose a $100 check is altered to $1,000. If the bank paid it in good faith, then the check is properly payable in the original amount of $100. Under these circumstances, the bank would have to recredit $900 (the difference between the altered amount and the original amount) to its customer's account. However, if the customer's own negligence substantially contributed to the alteration, then the customer would not be entitled to a recredit of $900 (U.C.C. § 3–406). Under these circumstances, the check would be properly payable in the altered amount of $1,000.

An obvious case of negligence that substantially contributes to an alteration is when the drawer leaves spaces on a check where words or figures may be placed.

Postdated Checks

A **postdated check** bears a date later than the one on which it is issued. The making of a postdated check implies a promise to have money in the bank account at a future date. Consequently, a postdated check is usually not properly payable until the day of its date (U.C.C. § 3–114).

EXAMPLE ■ On March 1, Crane presented a check, payable to her order, to a teller to be cashed. The teller refused to cash it because the check was dated April 1. In this situation, the dishonor was not wrongful, since the check would not be properly payable until April 1.

Stop-Payment Orders

Because a check is simply the drawer's order to the drawee bank to make a payment, the drawer has the right to revoke that order and stop payment of the check. Once a bank receives a **stop-payment order,** its sole duty is to obey it. Consequently, a check on which a customer has placed a valid stop-payment order is not properly payable (U.C.C. § 4–403).

Time of Orders

To be effective, however, a bank must receive a stop-payment order at a time and in a manner (the check must be accurately described) that gives the bank a reasonable opportunity to act on the order before it finally pays the check.

EXAMPLE ■ Lewis stops payment on one of his checks on Monday at 9:05 A.M. At 9:10 A.M. on the same day, the bank cashes it over the counter. When Lewis finds out that the bank paid the check over his stop-payment order, he demands that it recredit his account. The bank refuses, so Lewis sues. In this case, the bank probably wins. Although the bank received the stop-payment order before it made the final payment, five minutes is probably not a reasonable period for the bank to act on such an order and thus it is not effective.

Method of Stopping Payments

In most states, a customer may give a stop-payment order either orally or in writing (U.C.C. § 4–403(2)). However, in those states that allow such a procedure, an oral order only binds the bank for 14 calendar days, unless the order is confirmed in writing within that period. By contrast, a written order is effective for six months. To extend that period, the customer must then renew the written order in writing within the six-month period.

EXAMPLE ■ On April 15, Andrews called her bank and orally stopped payment on one of her checks. However, she failed to confirm the order in writing, so the check was paid on May 15. In this situation, the payment was proper because an oral stop-payment order that is not confirmed in writing only binds the bank for 14 calendar days from the day it is received.

Who May Stop Payments

Under the UCC, only the drawer has the right to stop payments on his or her checks. The sole exception to this rule involves the bank's payment of a check after a customer dies. As previously discussed, in that situation, any person claiming an interest in the decedent's account can stop the payment of a check.

EXAMPLE ■ Simon drew a check payable to the order of Wise. Wise endorsed the check over to Beck for the purchase of a rolltop desk. Beck never delivered the desk to Wise, so Wise called the drawee bank and demanded that it stop payment on the check. The bank refused to stop payment and subsequently paid the check. In this situation, the bank's actions were proper because only the drawer can stop payment on a check.

Stopping Payments after Certification

As discussed in chapter 3, a drawee bank is not liable on an instrument until it certifies it. Once a check is certified, the drawer no longer has the right to stop payment. This is because certification is the drawee's own commitment to pay the instrument and the drawee is not required to harm its own credit and reputation through refusal to pay a certified check for the drawer's convenience.

Drawee's Liability for Failure to Stop Payments

If a bank pays a check over a valid stop-payment order, the customer must demonstrate that he or she suffered a loss before he or she can recover damages from the bank (U.C.C. § 4–403(3)).

EXAMPLE ■ Birch draws a check on her account at First State Bank, payable to Wilson's order, for the purchase of an antique lamp. As soon as Birch receives the lamp, she stops payment on the check. First State inadvertently pays the check and Birch demands that it immediately recredit her account for the amount of the check. The bank learns that Birch received the lamp and thus refuses to recredit her account. Birch sues and, in this case, First State wins. Since Birch received the lamp, she did not suffer a loss from the bank's payment over her stop-payment order (U.C.C. § 4–407(b)).

What if Birch could demonstrate that the antique lamp she bought was a fake? Surely, under those circumstances, the drawee bank would be required to recredit her account, since its failure to stop payment would cause her to suffer a loss. Interestingly enough, the answer to this question is not always yes. This is because the drawee bank is entitled to step into the shoes of any holder in due course on the check (U.C.C. § 4–407(a)). If the holder in due course can enforce payment of the check against the drawer, then the drawer cannot make the drawee recredit his or her account. The reason is that, even if payment is stopped, the drawer is still obligated to pay the holder in due course. Therefore, if the drawer were entitled to have his or her account recredited, he or she would be unjustly enriched; that is, he or she would receive credit for an amount legitimately owed to the holder in due course, which the bank would then have to pay.

EXAMPLE ■ Suppose that Birch can demonstrate that the lamp is a fake. Further, the check is deposited with Third National Bank, which receives it in good faith, for value, and without notice of Birch's personal defense (failure of consideration) that the lamp is a fake. When Birch learns that her check has been paid over her stop-payment order, she demands that First State recredit her account, because she did not receive the lamp for which she had bargained and thus suffered a loss from the payment over her stop-payment order.

First State argues that, even if it had stopped payment, Birch would still lose the amount of the check, since she would be obligated to pay Third National Bank, which received the check as a holder in due course. Therefore, First State argues that Birch's loss did not result from its failure to stop payment but instead from the check's being received by a holder in due course. Thus, the bank refuses to recredit Birch's account. In this case, First State wins. Under the UCC, the bank is entitled to step into the shoes of any holder in due course on the instrument. Because Third National was a holder in due course that could have enforced payment of the check against Birch if the check had been dishonored, Birch cannot make First State recredit her account.

What is the bank's liability when a drawer demonstrates that a loss was suffered because the bank paid a check over a valid stop-payment order and the check did not pass through the hands of a holder in due course? Under these circumstances, the drawee bank must recredit the customer's account but does have a remedy to recover its loss. Once the drawee has recredited its customer's account, it steps into its customer's shoes and has the right to sue the payee on the underlying obligation that originally caused the issuance of the check (U.C.C. § 4–407(c)).

EXAMPLE ■ Instead of the check's being deposited with Third National Bank, suppose that the payee cashes the check in the previous example over the counter at First State. In this situation, Birch wins and First State must recredit her account. However, First State may then sue the payee on its customer's claim of failure of consideration (the fake lamp).

WRONGFUL DISHONOR OF CHECKS

A drawee bank has a duty to pay its customer's checks that are drawn against sufficient funds. If the bank fails to pay a properly payable check, then it becomes liable to its customer for the damages caused by its wrongful dishonor.

Under the UCC, when a wrongful dishonor of a check occurs through a mistake, then the payor bank is liable to its customer only for those damages actually sustained and clearly resulting from the wrongful dishonor (U.C.C. § 4–402). Generally, claims for speculative damages, such as embarrassment and humiliation, cannot be recovered. In other words, claims that cannot be measured in actual dollars lost cannot be recovered. However, the UCC provides that, if a customer is jailed on the charge of giving a bad check because of such a wrongful dishonor, damages may include those caused by the arrest and prosecution. A judge or jury will determine any damages caused by the wrongful dishonor of a check on a case-by-case basis.

EXAMPLES ■ Fisher owed Third National Bank $500 on a past-due note. The bank offset the balance of $450 in his checking account against the balance due on his note. After the offset occurred, Third National dishonored payment of a check drawn against Fisher's account because of insufficient funds. Fisher sued Third National for damages and claimed that the dishonor was wrongful. In this situation, the bank won because the offset was proper and thus the dishonor was not wrongful.

■ Citizen's Bank wrongfully dishonored payment of a check that was issued to make an installment payment on a car loan. Because the check was dishonored, the lender repossessed the drawer's car. The drawer then demanded the bank pay him $4,000 (the fair market value of the repossessed car) because of the wrongful dishonor. The bank refused the demand, so the drawer sued. In this situation, the drawer won since he could prove that the wrongful dishonor actually caused him $4,000 damage.

■ Union Bank by mistake wrongfully dishonored the payment of two checks. Because of the mistaken dishonor, the drawer claimed she suffered damages as follows: (1) $1.50 for a telephone call to the bank to get it to correct its mistake; (2) $130 for two weeks' lost wages; and (3) $500 for embarrassment. The drawer testified at the trial that she had respiratory trouble and, because of it and a case of nerves from the embarrassment she suffered from having her check dishonored, her doctor advised her to take two weeks off from work, which she did. In this situation, the drawer was not entitled to recover all the damages that she claimed. The only actual dollar amount of damages that she could prove resulted from the wrongful dishonor was the $1.50 for the telephone call. Her claim that she incurred a $500 damage because of embarrassment could not be measured in actual dollars of loss. Furthermore, her claim for $130 in lost wages because of illness did not directly result from the wrongful dishonor but from a respiratory problem that existed before the wrongful dishonor occurred.

PAYOR BANKS' LIABILITY FOR THE LATE RETURN OF CHECKS

As discussed in chapter 4, upon receipt of a check, a payor bank may take until its midnight deadline to decide whether to pay or dishonor it. However, if the payor bank fails to pay or return the check within its midnight deadline, then the UCC (section 4–302) imposes strict liability on the bank for the full amount of any check. In other words, a payor bank is accountable for the amount of a check, whether or not it is properly payable, if the bank does not either pay or return it within its midnight deadline.

EXAMPLES ■ Dunn, the payee of a check draw on Avenue State Bank, deposits it into his account at Fifth National Bank. On Monday, August 21, the check is presented to Avenue State Bank for payment. On Wednesday, August 23, Avenue State Bank returns the check, because the drawer's account is overdrawn. When Dunn receives the unpaid check, he demands payment from Avenue State Bank because of the late return. Avenue State refuses Dunn's demand and states that the check was not properly payable. Dunn sues Avenue State Bank and, in this case, wins. The payor bank failed to return the check within its midnight deadline and thus is accountable for the amount of the check, even though it was not properly payable.

■ On February 1, Wilson presents a check that he wants cashed to a teller of the drawee bank. Since Wilson does not maintain an account with the bank, the manager must approve the check before it is cashed. The manager tells Wilson to leave the check with her and return in a few hours. When Wilson returns, the manager has already left for the day. On the next day, Wilson again goes to see the manager and demands that the bank immediately pay the check. The manager refuses because the drawer's account is closed. Consequently, Wilson sues the bank for the amount of the check. In this situation, Wilson wins. Under the UCC, when a check is presented over the counter for immediate payment, the bank must pay or dishonor it before the close of business on the day of presentment. Otherwise, the payor bank is accountable for the amount of the check, even though it is not properly payable.

COLLECTING BANKS' LIABILITY

Under the UCC (section 4–103(5)), the amount of damages that may be recovered against a collecting bank that fails to exercise ordinary care in handling an item is the actual amount of the item in question. This liability, however, may be reduced by any amount that the collecting bank can demonstrate would not have been collected even if it had exercised ordinary care.

For example, suppose a bank handles two checks for collection that belong to the same owner. The amount of one check is $1,000 and the amount of the other is $700. Without a legitimate excuse, the bank fails to meet its midnight deadline. By the time the checks are presented for payment, the drawer has gone into bankruptcy. Under these circumstances, the collecting bank is ordinarily liable to the owner for the total amount of both checks, $1,700. However, suppose that the collecting bank can show that at no time between its receipt of the checks and the filing of the bankruptcy petition was more than $700 on deposit in the drawer's account. Thus, even if the collecting bank had exercised ordinary care, it would still have dishonored the $1,000 check for insufficient funds. In this situation, the collecting bank's liability is then limited to $700, the amount that could have been realized had it exercised ordinary care.

EXAMPLE ■ On Monday morning, Berg State Bank receives three checks for collection in the amounts of $500, $250, and $1,500. Without a legitimate excuse, Berg State does not present the checks to the payor bank until Friday. Upon receipt, the payor bank dishonors payment because the account is closed. The drawer had $150 on deposit in his account from Monday until Friday when he closed it. The owner of the checks sues Berg State Bank for the aggregate amount of the checks, based on its failure to exercise ordinary care in handling them for collection. In this situation, Berg State wins. Even if Berg State had acted by midnight on Tuesday, all the checks still would have been dishonored, since the drawer had only $150 on deposit, which was less than any one of the checks in question.

FINAL PAYMENT OF CHECKS

The final payment of checks is a significant collection event. It marks the end of the collection process and the time when the payor bank assumes liability for the payment of the check.

Final payment can occur when the payor bank fails either to pay or dishonor a check within its midnight deadline. The payor bank's failure to act makes it accountable for the amount of the check, whether or not it is properly payable. In addition, the UCC (section 4–213) provides that final payment also occurs when the payor bank has done one of the following:

■ paid the check in cash

■ finally settled for the check

■ completed posting the check to the drawer's account

Payments in Cash   Traditionally, when a holder presents a check over the counter for payment and receives cash in return, the payor bank has made a final payment. The UCC concurs with this common-law rule.

Final Settlements   Prior to the enactment of the Expedited Funds Availability Act (EFAA) and the adoption of Regulation CC by the Federal Reserve Board, when a check was presented to the payor bank, the presenting bank normally received what was called a provisional credit to its account maintained with the payor. Under the deferred posting section of the UCC, the payor then had until its midnight deadline to revoke this provisional credit. If the payor bank dishonored payment within the deadline, then each provisional settlement given by collecting banks could be revoked and the provisional credit given by the depositary bank to the depositor could also be cancelled. However, if the payor did not revoke its provisional settlement within its midnight deadline, then payment was final. All the provisional settlements thus became final, the proceeds of the check flowed back to the original depositor, and the credit in the account became usable money.

Under EFAA and Regulation CC, the concept of provisional settlements has been abolished. Settlements between banks made during the forward collection of a check are now considered final when made. This is because under Regulation CC a payor bank may bypass the presenting bank and return a dishonored check directly to the depositary bank. Thus, by following this more efficient return path, the payor bank does not recover the settlement made to the presenting bank. Instead, Regulation CC requires the payor bank to settle for a returned check in the same way it would settle for a similar check for forward collection. For example, under Regulation CC, a depositary bank is obligated to pay a payor bank that is returning a dishonored check to it the amount of the check before the close of business on the banking day on which it received the check.

Regulation CC, however, makes it clear that final settlement by a payor bank is not considered to be final payment for the purposes of the deferred posting section of the UCC. In other words, as long as a payor bank has neither paid an item in cash nor completed the process of posting, it may still dishonor payment of the item within its midnight deadline and recover settlement from the depositary bank. Conversely, if a payor bank neither pays an item in cash, nor completes the process of posting, nor dishonors payment within its midnight deadline, then payment becomes final.

Posting Checks

Even if a payor bank has not paid a check in cash or finally settled for it, certain internal procedures can still result in its final payment. Specifically, if the payor has completed posting the check, then its final payment has occurred (U.C.C. § 4–213(c)). **Posting** is the usual procedure that a payor bank uses to determine whether to pay a check and then record the payment. Posting may include one or more of the following steps taken by the payor bank (U.C.C. § 4–109):

- verifying any signature on the check

- ascertaining that sufficient funds are available to cover the amount of the check

- affixing a paid or other stamp to the check

- entering a charge or entry to a customer's account

- correcting or reversing an entry or erroneous action taken on the check

After its receipt by the payor, a check usually moves first to the sorting and proving departments, where it may also be photocopied. It then moves to the bookkeeping department, which begins posting. The bookkeeping department first examines the check for form and signature, then ensures that sufficient funds are on deposit to cover the amount of the check, and finally posts the check to the drawer's account. This final mechanical step normally evidences that posting has been completed and the decision to pay the check has been made.

EXAMPLES ■ A payor bank receives a check on Monday morning. It is sorted under the customer's name on Monday and, under the deferred posting routines (U.C.C. § 4–301), reaches the bookkeeper for that customer on Tuesday morning. The bookkeeper examines the signature, verifies that sufficient funds are available, and decides at 11:00 A.M. on Tuesday to pay the check. The bookkeeper then enters a debit for the amount of the check in the customer's account at 12:00 noon on Tuesday. In this situation, posting is completed at 12:00 noon on Tuesday.

■ A payor bank receives a check in the mail on Monday. The check is sorted and otherwise processed during the day on Monday. On Monday night, an electronic computer provisionally records the check as a charge to the customer's account. On Tuesday, a clerk examines the signature on the check to determine whether it should be finally paid. If the clerk determines the signature is valid and decides to pay the check, and all other processing of it is complete at 12:00 noon on Tuesday, posting is completed at that time. However, if the clerk determines that the signature on the check is invalid or that the bank should not pay the check for some other reason, the check is returned to the presenting bank. Then, in the regular Tuesday-night computer run, the debit to the customer's account for the check is reversed. In this situation, the bank has made no determination to pay the check and has not completed posting. Thus, final payment of the check has not occurred.

Therefore, posting is not completed until the payor has decided to pay the check and has recorded the payment. Once the payor completes posting, however, final payment of the check has been made.

PRIORITY OF FUNDS ON DEPOSIT IN DRAWERS' ACCOUNTS

Between the time a check is issued and paid, several events may intervene to upset the normal collection process. For instance, during this period, the payor bank may do any of the following:

■ acquire knowledge or receive notice that the drawer has filed a petition for bankruptcy

■ receive an order from the drawer stopping payment on the check

- receive a court order or IRS levy attaching the account for the benefit of the drawer's creditors

- exercise its own right to use funds on deposit in the account to repay a debt the customer owes to the payor

These four events are commonly called the **four legals**. Each legal may create a dispute between the owner of a check and the person asserting a legal over who has priority to the funds on deposit in the drawer's account. To resolve this issue, the UCC (section 4–303) states that notice or knowledge of the legal is too late if the payor does not have a reasonable period to act on it and has also taken any one of the following steps:

- certified the check

- paid the check in cash

- finally settled for the check

- completed posting

- become accountable for the amount of the check (that is, missed a midnight deadline)

- otherwise taken action that indicates its decision to make final payment of the check

As can be seen, certain tests used to determine the priority status of a check are also used to determine whether final payment of a check has been made. These tests include payment of the check in cash, final settlement of the check, completion of posting, and expiration of deadlines resulting in the payor's accountability for the amount of the check.

In addition, the UCC provides two tests to establish a check owner's priority over that of a legal: (1) the payor bank's certification of the check and (2) any other acts by the payor that demonstrate its final decision to pay the check. The final-decision-to-pay test provides for situations where the bookkeeping department has examined the check and the account to be charged and has decided to pay the check, but postpones the actual physical posting of the check to the account. This activity is called **sight posting**.

Generally, the test to determine whether the owner of a check or the person asserting a legal is entitled to the proceeds on deposit in the drawer's account is "first come, first served." Accordingly, if a check is finally paid or certified before the payor bank knows or receives any notice of a legal upon which it has a reasonable time to act, then the owner of the check is first in time and thus entitled to the proceeds on deposit in the account.

EXAMPLE ■ On Monday morning, Third National Bank provisionally settles for a check drawn on its customer's account. On Wednesday morning, Third National receives a restraining order that prohibits it from disbursing any funds on deposit in the same account. Upon receipt of the restraining order, Third National revokes the provisional settlement given for the check and returns it unpaid. The owner of the check (not the party who served the restraining order) is entitled to the funds in the account, because Third National failed to revoke the provisional settlement within its midnight deadline (on Tuesday at midnight) and thus became accountable for the amount of the check. Third National's accountability for the amount of the check constitutes final payment.

Suppose that instead of provisionally settling for the check, Third National pays the check in cash over the counter on Monday morning at 9:15. The bank received the restraining order that morning at 9:10. Although the bank received the restraining order before it paid the check in cash, the owner of the check would probably be entitled to the funds on deposit in the drawer's account. Under the UCC (section 4–303), the payor bank must have a reasonable time to act on a legal before the legal takes priority over payment of the check. Third National cannot reasonably be expected to act on a restraining order within five minutes after its receipt in order to prevent payment of the check in cash.

Suppose instead that on Monday morning Third National Bank sorts, proves, photographs, and posts the check to its customer's account. On Monday afternoon, Third National receives a stop-payment order on the check. Upon receipt of the order, Third National reverses the posting entries and returns the check unpaid to the presenter on Tuesday. The owner of the check sues Third National and states that final payment of the check occurred before the bank's receipt of the stop-payment order, because posting was completed on Monday morning before the stop-payment order was received. Thus, the owner claims the check's payment takes priority over honoring the stop-payment order. The courts are divided on the question of when posting is complete. A discussion of the different interpretations follows.

Under the facts of this latter situation, some courts have ruled that the posting process was incomplete and thus the bank did not make final payment of the check before receiving the stop-payment order. This is because, under the UCC (section 4–109(e)), posting also includes correcting or reversing an entry for erroneous action taken on a check. The effect of this ruling, however, is that posting remains incomplete until the expiration of the midnight deadline. Other courts, however, have ruled that posting was complete and thus payment of the check was final. These courts adhere to the view that banks should reverse entries only when they are erroneous from their inception and not because of subsequent, independent information received by the banks. This view is probably preferable to the former view. Otherwise, no matter when posting is completed, it will never constitute final payment until the midnight deadline has passed. The effect of the former view is to eliminate the completion of posting as an indication of final payment and clearly the UCC did not intend this result.

Order for the Payment of Checks

Under the UCC (section 4–303), a payor bank may pay checks presented to it in any order it desires. Thus, for accounts having insufficient funds to cover the payment of all the checks, payor banks have unlimited discretion to determine which checks should be paid and which should be returned unpaid. Payor banks are not, however, excused from their duty to pay or return checks within their midnight deadlines, although they might under the UCC (section 4–303) pay checks received on Tuesday before they pay other checks received on Monday.

EXAMPLE ■ On Tuesday, Third National Bank receives three checks for payment in the amounts of $100, $500, and $600. The checks are drawn on an account that has a balance of $1,100 in collected funds. The payor bank decides to pay the $500 and $600 checks, even though it received them after the $100 check was presented for payment. In this situation, the payor bank's action is proper, since (under the UCC) the bank may charge checks drawn on its customer's accounts in any order that it wishes.

CHECK KITING

Besides forgery, check kiting is another common method used to defraud banks. **Check kiting** is a scheme whereby a depositor with checking accounts in two or more banks, or two people living or banking in different localities, exchange checks on the respective banks. By using such schemes to take advantage of the time required for banks to process, clear, present, and pay checks, a depositor can acquire fictitious bank balances. Thus, the depositor obtains unauthorized use of bank credit and funds before the funds represented by the checks have been taken from their respective checking accounts and transferred to the appropriate depositary-collecting bank.

EXAMPLE ■ Mr. Sly has a business checking account at Bank C in Pittsburgh, Pennsylvania and personal checking accounts at Bank A in Scranton, Pennsylvania, and Bank B in Boston, Massachusetts. The following steps trace the check-kiting process:

1. Mr. Sly draws a check on Bank C payable to a creditor.
2. He deposits a check in Bank C drawn on Bank A before the check

given to the creditor arrives at Bank C.

3. He deposits a check in Bank A drawn on Bank B before the check drawn on Bank A (in step 2) arrives.
4. He deposits a check in Bank B, drawn on Bank C before the check drawn on Bank B (in step 3) arrives.
5. He draws a check on Bank C payable to creditors, increases the amount of the "tail on the kite" (increases the amount of money involved), and repeats the cycle.

This cycle continues until some bank stops paying against uncollected funds.

Check kiting results from a relaxation of banking practices whereby a bank grants special favors to a depositor who has presumably established a good credit position at the bank for payment of his or her checks against uncollected funds. Such fraud may also result from inadequate controls for determining when funds on deposited items are actually available or from too short a deferment period for availability of funds to depositors of transit items. In addition, the use of average deferments for computerized demand deposit accounting can also increase the dangers of kiting.

Because of banks' loose practices in the payment of checks against uncollected funds, and the abnormal delays in check processing and collection beyond the predetermined period, a depositor can repeat the process of kiting undetected indefinitely. In recent years, computerized accounting has also removed the visual awareness of the repetitive drawing of checks, which used to occur in manual bookkeeping.

To work the kiting operation successfully, the depositor must calculate exactly the amount of time required for checks to clear through the check-collection channels between the various banks involved. Generally, the amounts of these interest-free extensions of unsecured credit continue to increase during the kiting operation. In some instances, the resulting bank losses have been monumental and have directly caused bank closings. However, failure to meet checks as presented can result in an overdraft and expose the fraud.

A depositor's use of uncollected funds is not necessarily a kite. Most banks analyze and monitor active accounts, including the timing of transit items, to discover use of uncollected funds. To uncover a kiting scheme, however, the amount of the checks drawn on the account, and the amount of the deposits made to the account must be almost identical. Furthermore, infrequent check kiting is almost impossible to discover. An unusual number of checks made payable to the drawer and deposited in another bank, frequent checks made out to the same payee, and frequent requests for information about a depositor's account are all warning signs of a possible kiting scheme.

The only way a bank can collapse a kite is to stop paying against uncollected funds in such accounts. Today, software systems that can detect attempts to draw against uncollected funds as well as other unusual account activity are available.

As payment devices for the transfer of funds, checks serve an invaluable function for the economy. Thus, bank employees need to understand the legal implications inherent in the format and negotiation of checks. Careless practices and procedures in the endorsement of checks, handling of deposits, and availability of funds carry a high risk of loss. Banks will expose themselves to fraud and deceptive schemes unless their policies and employees are kept up to date on the proper practices and procedures for checks.

CONCLUSION

This chapter explained the fundamental principle, subject to certain exceptions, that a person is not liable on an instrument unless his or her authorized signature appears on it. If a drawer's signature is forged, then the ultimate responsibility for the forgery usually falls upon the drawee bank according to the common-law principle established in *Price v. Neale.*

However, if the payee's endorsement is forged, then the liability rules are different. The basic principle is that the person or entity that first deals with the forger loses. That entity may be a retail store or provider of services, such as a bank. Thus, in cases of forged endorsements, the ultimate liability is normally imposed upon the depositary institution if it is the first institution to deal with the forger and thus has the opportunity to detect the forgery. Of course, if possible, the depositary institution can always collect from the thief.

Both collecting and payor banks must take action on the collection and payment of negotiable instruments within their midnight deadlines. If a payor bank fails to act within its midnight deadline, the UCC imposes strict liability on the bank for the full amount of the check. If a collecting bank fails to act within its midnight deadline, it too may be liable for the full amount of the check. However, the collecting bank may reduce this liability by any amount that it can demonstrate would not have been collected even if it had acted within its midnight deadline.

A payor bank has the fundamental duty to pay its customers' checks that are properly payable. Under the UCC, a check is considered properly payable if sufficient funds are on deposit in the customer's account to cover the amount of the check. However, even if sufficient funds are on deposit to pay a check, it may not be properly payable. Common law and certain provisions of articles 3 and 4 determine whether a check is properly payable. If the bank wrongfully dishonors a properly payable check, then it is liable to its customer for damages that he or she actually sustains and that clearly result from the wrongful dishonor.

Questions for Review and Discussion

1. How does the UCC generally treat an unauthorized or forged signature? Describe a situation in which an unauthorized signature would be considered genuine and thus make the drawer liable on the instrument.

2. Who bears the loss if a bank pays a check that bears a forged signature?

3. What is the ordinary period in which a customer must discover and report a forged check paid from his or her account? What if a year has elapsed before a customer discovers a forged check among his or her canceled checks?

4. If a customer has sufficient funds in his or her account to cover a check, is the drawee bank compelled to pay it? Give an example of a circumstance in which a bank might still dishonor the check.

5. If a person finds his or her paycheck that was missing for nearly a year, would the bank act wrongfully if it decided to pay it?

6. For an altered check to be properly payable in the amount originally drawn, how must the drawee bank have acted? When is a customer liable for the altered amount?

7. What is the bank's duty when it receives a stop-payment order from its customer?

8. What is the extent of damages a person can recover from a bank that mistakenly dishonors a check?

9. What is the next step after a payor bank decides to dishonor a check?

10. Does a limit exist on a collecting bank's liability if the bank does not exercise ordinary care in handling a check?

11. What actions by the payor bank constitute final payment of a check?

12. What are the four legals? Does a person who asserts one of the legals automatically get paid first from the funds on deposit in the drawer's account? What determines the order of payment?

6

Letters of Credit

After studying this chapter, you will be able to

■ give a legally correct definition of a letter of credit

■ identify the parties to a letter of credit

■ explain the requirements for establishing a letter of credit

■ explain the difference between commercial and standby letters of credit

■ state issuers' obligations to beneficiaries of a letter of credit

■ describe issuers' liabilities for wrongfully refusing to pay drafts presented under a letter of credit

■ explain the conditions under which a letter of credit may be enjoined

WHAT IS A LETTER OF CREDIT?

As a payment device, a letter of credit is similar to a check, note, draft, or certificate of deposit. **Letters of credit** are instruments under which a bank agrees to substitute its credit for that of its customer.

Letters of credit are commonly used in such commercial transactions as when a local company imports goods from overseas and needs a letter of credit to finance the transaction. The foreign exporter may insist that the local company's bank establish a commercial letter of credit, so drafts may be drawn against that credit for immediate payment.

In addition, letters of credit are used both domestically and internationally as performance bonds or to support bids on projects. Unlike commercial letters of credit, these instruments—called standby letters of credit—are not expected to be funded in the normal course of business.

Sources of Law

The rules governing letter-of-credit transactions are derived from article 5 of the Uniform Commercial Code (UCC), entitled "Letters of Credit," and the *Uniform Customs and Practices for Commercial Documentary Credits* (UCP). The UCP is a compendium of customs and practices developed over the years for letter-of-credit transactions. The International Chamber of Commerce, which has existed since 1933, prepares and publishes the UCP. In contrast to UCC article 5, the UCP is not a statute and therefore does not in and of itself carry the force of law. However, courts will often look to the UCP in determining what standards apply to letters of credit. Also, the terms of the UCP often are incorporated by reference into the terms of letter-of-credit transactions.

The Parties

As with a draft, a letter of credit involves primarily three parties. First, the customer or **account party** requests the bank to establish a letter of credit. The bank that issues it in turn is called the **issuer**, while the person entitled to draw or demand payment under the terms of the credit is called the **beneficiary**. In addition to the account party, issuer, and beneficiary, a letter of credit may also involve advising and confirming banks.

An **advising bank** is one that notifies the beneficiary that another bank has issued a letter of credit in his or her favor (U.C.C. § 5–103(e)). Since frequently no relationship exists between the issuer and beneficiary, the terms and conditions of a letter of credit are often transmitted to the beneficiary through his or her own bank or a bank known to the beneficiary. Under the UCC, an advising bank does not assume any obligation to honor drafts drawn under a letter of credit. But the bank is responsible for any errors contained in its advice to the beneficiary.

The terms of a letter of credit may require that a bank with which the beneficiary is familiar agree to confirm the letter of credit. Under the UCC, a **confirming bank** is one that agrees to become liable under the terms of the letter of credit to the same extent as the issuer. A confirming bank provides a hesitant seller with additional comfort that he or she will be paid for the goods sold, since the seller may look to both the issuer and the confirming bank for payment.

Thus, a letter of credit is a commitment by a bank (the issuer), made at its customer's (the account party's) request, to honor drafts presented by a third party (the beneficiary) according to the terms of the credit.

Formal Requirements

In contrast to a negotiable instrument, no particular form is required to create a letter of credit. However, as with a negotiable instrument, a letter of credit must be in writing and signed by the issuer (U.C.C. § 5–104). Also, any modification of the letter of credit must be in writing and signed by the issuer or confirming bank.

Although it is not a formal requirement under the UCC, a letter of credit should also contain an expiration date. Since the account party's property often secures a letter of credit, neither the issuer nor the account party will know when the property can be released unless the letter contains an expiration date. In fact, the Comptroller of the Currency (the primary regulator of national banks) requires national banks to include an expiration date in all letters of credit that they issue.

When Is a Letter of Credit Established?

A letter of credit may be revocable or irrevocable. It is important for the parties to an **irrevocable letter of credit** to know when it is established. For instance, a seller who ships goods to a buyer before the establishment of an irrevocable letter of credit runs the risk that the issuer may cancel the credit or modify its terms and render the credit unacceptable to the seller. Under those circumstances, the seller may have either to rely solely on the buyer's credit for payment or locate a new buyer who can provide an acceptable credit arrangement. Thus, knowing when an irrevocable letter of credit is established is important, because it marks the point when the issuer is precluded from either unilaterally canceling or modifying the credit. The issuer of a

revocable letter of credit may unilaterally modify or cancel it even after it is established.

Under the UCC (section 5–106), a letter of credit is established for an account party when it is sent to the account party or when a written advice of its issuance is sent to the beneficiary.

EXAMPLE ■ On May 1, World Exporters, Inc., requests Second National Bank to issue a letter of credit for Universal Importers, Ltd. Second National agrees to issue the letter of credit, which it sends to World Exporters on May 5. Subsequently, Second National becomes concerned about World Exporters' ability to fund the letter of credit and notifies World Exporters on May 10, that the credit is canceled. In this situation, the cancellation is not effective, because Second National "established" the letter of credit on May 5 when it sent the letter to World Exporters.

Under the UCC (section 1–201(38)), a writing is "sent" when it is deposited in the mail or otherwise delivered for transmission by some other usual means of communication, such as a telex.

A letter of credit is established for a beneficiary under the UCC when he or she receives the letter of credit or a written advice of its issuance.

EXAMPLE ■ Suppose that Universal Importers, Ltd. in the previous example receives an advice from its bank on May 9 that the letter of credit has been issued. Based upon this advice, it ships the goods ordered by World Exporters, Inc., and sends its draft for payment to Second National Bank on May 11. Second National refuses to pay the draft, because it canceled the credit on May 10, before the draft was presented for payment. Universal sues Second National. In this situation, Universal wins. This is because the credit was "established" for Universal on May 9, the day on which it was advised of the letter's issuance, which was also the day before Second National attempted to cancel the letter of credit.

As we have seen, once a letter of credit is established, the circumstances under which it can be modified or canceled depend on whether the credit is revocable or irrevocable. A revocable credit provides little comfort to a beneficiary and is rarely used, since even after it is established the issuer may modify or cancel it without the beneficiary's or customer's consent (U.C.C. § 5–106(3)). However, such is not the case with an irrevocable credit. Once an irrevocable credit is established, the issuer can only revoke or modify it with the customer's or beneficiary's consent (U.C.C. § 5–106(2)). But an issuer is not required to amend or modify a letter of credit at the account party's and beneficiary's request.

Case for Discussion

HANSON V. COLUMBUS CADETS AND MID-CITY NATIONAL BANK

Facts

Peter Hanson, a highly skilled football player, agreed to sign a contract with the Columbus Cadets football team. The team played in the World Football League, which had just come into existence. Hanson was worried that the team and the league would be unable to compete successfully with the existing National Football League. Therefore, he demanded and received from the owners of the Columbus Cadets a contract backed by a letter of credit. Mid-City National Bank issued the letter of credit on August 15. The letter read in part

This letter of credit guarantees payment of $70,000 to Peter Hanson for services rendered to the Columbus Cadets Football Club. An affidavit stating that Mr. Hanson has not been paid under his contract must accompany drafts presented under this credit.

Later, the club did in fact fail and Hanson was not paid his $70,000 salary. Accordingly, he presented a draft and affidavit to Mid-City National for payment. A bank officer told him that the letter of credit had been revoked several weeks ago. Hanson, of course, was shocked. He had not been notified of the revocation, nor did he know that the letter of credit could be revoked. Hanson sued the owners of the football team and the bank. His attorney contended that, although the letter did not state that it was irrevocable, the term "guarantee" demonstrated the letter was irrevocable, since only an irrevocable letter would constitute any sort of guarantee to Hanson.

Decision

In this case, the court ruled in favor of the club. According to the court, the UCC (section 5–106(2)) provides that, once agreed upon, an irrevocable credit can only be modified with the beneficiary's consent. However, the UCC does not state what constitutes an irrevocable as opposed to a revocable letter of credit. The court then looked to the *Uniform Customs and Practices for Commercial Documentary Credits*, which clearly states that, if a credit is not designated as irrevocable, then it is revocable.

Questions for Discussion

1. What is the difference between a revocable and irrevocable letter of credit?
2. Did the court treat Hanson fairly in this case? State your reasons.
3. What are the general requirements to revoke a letter of credit? Can an irrevocable letter have a time limit on it? Should Hanson have been informed of the intent to revoke the letter of credit?

Commercial Letters of Credit

A commercial letter of credit supports the sale of goods and, in its simplest form, involves the payment of a draft in exchange for a document of title. This payment is made through a third party—the issuer. For instance, suppose an electronics dealer located in New York wants to import a certain line of personal computers manufactured overseas. Since the overseas manufacturer is unfamiliar with the New York dealer, it refuses to permit the purchase under either an open account or documentary sale.

If the purchase were made under an **open account**, then the seller would be shipping the goods based on unsecured credit. This is risky if the manufacturer is unfamiliar with the dealer's financial responsibility. If the purchase were made under a **documentary sale**, the manufacturer would mail to its agent in New York a bill of lading accompanied by a draft drawn on the buyer. A bill of lading is a document of title that normally permits the holder to obtain possession of the goods shipped. The manufacturer's agent would not release the bill of lading to the buyer until he or she paid the draft.

Although the manufacturer would maintain control over the goods under a bill of lading, it would still run the risk that the buyer might become insolvent or refuse to pay for the goods in order to obtain a better price. Under these circumstances, the manufacturer would then have to find a new buyer, which might result in additional storage costs until one was found. In addition, it might be forced to sell the goods for a lower price than the one for which it had bargained with the original buyer. So, instead, the manufacturer insists that the purchase be financed through a commercial letter of credit.

Under the terms of a commercial letter of credit, the buyer is the account party, the buyer's bank is the issuer, and the manufacturer is the beneficiary. Such credit also provides that the beneficiary may draw a draft on the issuing bank upon presentment of the draft accompanied by the following documents:

- an invoice

- a bill of lading

- an inspection certificate

- an insurance policy covering the value of the goods

Upon receipt of the documents, the issuer inspects them to ensure that they conform to the terms of the letter of credit. If they do, the issuer will pay the draft, and the bill of lading will be delivered to the buyer. Upon payment of the draft, the issuer has the right to seek reimbursement from the account party. Normally, to pay the issuer, the account party either funds his or her checking account for the amount of the draft, which the bank then debits, or draws on a line of credit extended to the buyer by the bank.

In addition, if the manufacturer is unfamiliar or uncomfortable with the issuer, it may request under the terms of the credit that a bank with which the beneficiary is familiar confirm the credit. Again, a confirming bank's obligation to pay the credit is the same as that of the issuer (U.C.C. § 5–107).

The use of a commercial letter of credit significantly reduces the seller's risk of nonpayment, since the bank's credit is substituted for that of the buyer. In addition, the use of commercial letters of credit reduces the buyer's risk of not receiving the goods bargained for, since the issuer will not pay the seller until the buyer receives the documents of title.

Standby Letters of Credit

Unlike commercial letters of credit, **standby letters of credit** do not deal with financing the purchase and sale of goods. Instead, they are like performance or surety bonds. As such, they normally guarantee the account party's performance of a monetary obligation owed to the beneficiary.

Standby letters of credit are used in various financial settings. For instance, they are used in real-estate development transactions whereby a contractor is required to obtain a standby letter of credit for the owner's benefit to ensure the completion of the construction project. A standby letter of credit may also be used as security for the nonpayment of a loan. Standby letters of credit also have served in place of supersedeas bonds to ensure the payment of a judgment recovered against the account party if his or her appeal fails. And they have been used in place of taking physical possession of property that has been attached pursuant to a writ of execution.

Although the issuer of a commercial letter of credit expects to pay the seller's drafts, the issuer of a standby letter of credit does not. Instead, the issuer of the latter fully expects its customer to complete the performance of the obligation owed to the beneficiary. However, when an account party does default on the obligation, the beneficiary usually needs the following documentation to draw on the credit:

■ a draft up to the amount of the credit

■ the beneficiary's statement certifying that the account party has defaulted on performance of the obligation

As with a commercial letter of credit, the issuer of a standby letter of credit has the right to seek reimbursement from the account party upon payment of the draft.

EXAMPLE ■ William Jenkins, a developer, required Galaxy Construction Company, Inc., to obtain a $100,000 standby letter of credit guaranteeing completion of a construction project. Under the terms of the letter, the issuer agreed to pay $100,000 to Jenkins (the beneficiary) upon presentation of a sight draft. Later, Galaxy defaulted in the completion of the construction project, and Jenkins presented the $100,000 draft to the issuer for payment. The issuer refused to pay because certification that the contractor had defaulted in its obligation did not accompany the draft. Jenkins sued the issuer for wrongful dishonor. In this case, Jenkins won. Under the terms of the credit, the beneficiary was required to present only the draft for payment.

If a letter of credit is conspicuously labeled as such and requires only the presentment of a draft for payment, then it is considered a **clean letter of credit** and is legally enforceable (U.C.C. § 5–102(c)).

ISSUERS' OBLIGATIONS TO CUSTOMERS AND THEIR BENEFICIARIES

What is an issuer's obligation to its customer once a letter of credit has been established? Once an issuer receives a draft and accompanying documents, it must carefully examine the documents to determine whether on their face they comply with the terms of the credit (U.C.C. § 5–109(2)). The issuer is not liable or responsible for determining whether the terms of the underlying contract have been met. This responsibility lies exclusively with the account party and beneficiary.

In addition, the issuer does not assume liability or responsibility for any documents presented under the credit that may be false, fraudulent, or without legal effect, as long as the documents appear to be acceptable on their face (U.C.C. § 5–109(2)). Consequently, if the documents conform to the terms of the credit, then the issuer must honor payment of the draft, even though the goods or documents may not conform to the terms of the underlying contract (U.C.C. § 5–114).

When Do Documents Conform?

Before payment can be made, must documents presented to the issuer strictly, or just substantially, comply with the terms of the credit? The issuer's duty to examine the documents is ministerial, not discretionary. If the documents do not comply with the terms of the credit, then the issuer must not make the payment. Under those circumstances, the issuer is not obligated to investigate the facts further to determine whether payment should be made. The issuer's sole duty is to examine the face of the documents.

The reason the beneficiary is required to present specific documents before a letter of credit is paid is to assure the buyer that he or she will receive the goods bargained for. If the issuer is given the discretion to make a payment as long as the documents substantially comply with the terms of the credit, this assurance may be thwarted. Accordingly, the courts in most jurisdictions adhere to the rule that the documents must strictly conform with the terms of the credit before the issuer can honor payment. However, courts in a few jurisdictions have instead adopted the rule of substantial compliance. Under this rule, courts refuse to permit nonpayment based on technicalities that do not interfere with the substantive terms of credit.

Because of the divergence in views concerning what constitutes compliance, bankers need to consult with counsel when confronted with documents that do not strictly, but appear substantially to, conform to the terms of the credit. For instance, if a particular jurisdiction adheres to the **substantial-compliance doctrine**, then the bank should make the payment. Otherwise, the beneficiary will succeed in an action against the issuer for wrongful dishonor. On the other hand, if the jurisdiction adheres to the **strict-compliance doctrine**, the bank should not make the payment. Otherwise, the bank may be precluded from pursuing the account party for reimbursement on the grounds that the payment was improper, since the documents did not strictly comply with the credit.

EXAMPLES ■ First National Bank issued a letter of credit naming Boyson as beneficiary. Boyson sells acrylic yarn, and the account party manufactures textiles. Under the terms of the letter, the invoices were to state that they covered "100 percent acrylic yarn." When the invoices were presented to the issuer, they instead bore the notation "imported acrylic yarn." Consequently, the issuer dishonored payment, even though the packing list did bear the notation "100 percent acrylic yarn." Boyson sued First National for wrongful dishonor. In this case, since the court adhered to the strict-compliance rule, First National won because the invoices did not conform to the terms of the credit.

■ Berg State Bank issued a standby letter of credit supporting the account party's purchase of real estate. To draw under the terms of the letter, the beneficiary was required to present a signed statement that the account party was in default and a sight draft. The beneficiary was also required to note the letter-of-credit number (3939) on both the statement and the sight draft. When the account party defaulted, the beneficiary presented the required documents but failed to note the letter-of-credit number on the signed statement. Consequently, the bank dishonored the draft and the beneficiary sued. In this case, since the court adhered to the substantial-compliance test, the beneficiary won. The court reasoned that the failure to note the letter-of-credit number on the statement did not prejudice either the account party's or issuer's rights under the terms of the letter of credit.

Cases for Discussion

JUNE'S SPORTSWEAR V. STATE BANK OF COMMERCE

Facts

The State Bank of Commerce agreed to issue a letter of credit for its customer, Wilson's Sporting Goods Store. The beneficiary of the letter of credit was June's Sportswear Company. When State Bank issued the letter of credit, its officers had not properly checked the current financial status of Wilson's Sporting Goods. After issuing the credit, the bank officers had reason to believe that Wilson's was unable to repay the bank for the amount of funds to be paid June's.

When June's presented its documentation to the bank for payment against the letter of credit, the bank officers were greatly relieved because June's had shipped the sporting goods to Cleveland, Ohio, instead of Baltimore, Maryland, as required by the terms of the credit. Consequently, the bank dishonored the payment of the draft that accompanied the documentation. June's immediately contacted officials at Wilson's to inform them of State Bank's dishonor. Although officials at Wilson's were able to convince the bank that the company was financially sound, they were unable to convince the bank to amend the letter of credit to provide for a different shipping point. Consequently, June's sued State Bank for wrongful dishonor.

Questions for Discussion

1. Is the issuer of a letter of credit required to amend or modify it at the account party's or beneficiary's request?
2. If the court abides by the strict-compliance standard, who wins? Why?
3. If the court abides by the substantial-compliance standard, who wins? Why?

WELTI SWIM CLUB V. SOVAY NATIONAL BANK

Facts

Sovay National Bank agreed to issue a letter of credit for Huszar Contractors, Inc., to secure payment of $45,000 to Welti Swim Club should Huszar fail to construct a swimming pool for Welti on or before April 1. The terms of the credit specified that in order to draw a draft for $45,000, Welti was to present a signed statement on or before April 1 that Huszar had failed to perform. The letter of credit did not specify an expiration date. On April 2, Welti presented the draft and signed statement to Sovay National Bank. The bank dishonored the draft on the basis that the documents failed to conform with the terms of the credit. Consequently, Welti sued Sovay National Bank for wrongful dishonor.

Questions for Discussion

1. Since the letter of credit did not specify an expiration date, did Welti have a reasonable time to comply with the terms of the credit?
2. Who wins under the strict-compliance standard? Why?
3. Who wins under the substantial-compliance standard? Why?

The Midnight Deadline

Upon presentment of documents for payment, an issuer must carefully examine the documents to ensure that on their face they conform with the terms of the credit. Since this examination takes time, the UCC provides the issuer with a longer period to make a payment decision for a letter of credit than for an ordinary draft.

As chapter 5 explains, a payor bank must either pay or return an item presented for payment within its midnight deadline, defined as midnight of the next banking day after receipt of the item. In the case of documentary drafts, however, the issuer may defer payment without dishonor until the close of the third banking day after receipt of the documents (U.C.C. § 5–112(1)).

EXAMPLE ■ On Monday, First National Bank is presented with documents for payment under a letter of credit. Before the close of business on Thursday, the bank honors payment. Since First National made its payment decision before the close of the third banking day after receipt of the documents, it has acted in a timely manner. If the party presenting the documents expressly consents to the deferment, an issuer may defer its payment decision beyond the close of the third banking day (U.C.C. § 5–112(1)(b)).

As discussed in chapter 5, once a payor bank decides to dishonor an item, it must return the item to the presenting bank within its midnight deadline. However, such is not the case with documents presented for payment under a letter of credit. To meet its duty to return the draft and documents, an issuer can simply advise the presenter that it is holding the documents at his or her disposal unless otherwise instructed (U.C.C. § 5–112(2)). This procedure keeps the documents of title at the same location where the goods are to arrive and thereby facilitates their resale.

Wrongful Dishonor

What is the liability of an issuer if it wrongfully dishonors the payment of a draft upon presentation of documents that comply with the terms of the credit? The UCC limits the issuer's liability to the beneficiary for wrongful dishonor to the face amount of the draft, together with any incidental damages and interest. However, this amount must be reduced by any amount realized on the resale of the goods. Incidental damages are also limited to any commercially reasonable charges incurred in connection with the return or resale of the goods, such as transportation and custody costs. In addition, if the goods are not resold, then they must be turned over to the account party upon payment of the judgment (U.C.C. § 5–115).

<table>
<tr><td>*Case for Discussion*</td><td>

ORIENT EXPORTS V. THIRD NATIONAL BANK

</td></tr>
</table>

Facts

Third National Bank agreed to establish a letter of credit at the request of its customer, Empire Imports, Inc., to pay for 1,000 wicker chairs manufactured by Orient Exports, Ltd. Under the terms of the credit, Third National agreed to pay a sight draft in the amount of $10,000 upon presentation of the draft, an invoice, a bill of lading, and an insurance policy. Third National sent the letter of credit to Empire on April 1 and advised Orient of its issuance on April 3. On April 10, Orient shipped the chairs and, on April 20, Third National received the documents required under the terms of the credit.

Meanwhile Empire learned that the chairs were constructed with a lower-quality wicker than that specified in the underlying sales contract and instructed Third National to dishonor the draft. Otherwise, Empire would withdraw its substantial account balances from the bank and hold it responsible for any damages caused by payment of the draft. Third National acquiesced and dishonored the draft.

Orient sued Third National claiming the following damages: (1) $10,000 representing the amount of the draft, (2) interest on the $10,000 from its due date until paid, (3) $2,000 in attorney's fees, and (4) the cost of transporting the chairs back to its factory.

Questions for Discussion

1. Name the account party, issuer, and beneficiary in this case.
2. When was the letter of credit established for the account party? Why?
3. When was the letter of credit established for the beneficiary? Why?
4. Was Third National justified in dishonoring the draft? Why?
5. If the dishonor was wrongful, what damages would Orient Exports be entitled to recover?

ENJOINING PAYMENTS

An issuing bank must carefully inspect documents to ensure that on their face they conform to the terms of the credit. If the documents conform, then the issuer must pay the accompanying drafts, even though the documents may not conform to the underlying sales contract between the account party and beneficiary.

Accordingly, even if an account party can demonstrate that the quality of the goods does not conform to the terms of the underlying contract, payment of the draft under the letter of credit still cannot be enjoined. The same holds true if the account party learns that the beneficiary does not intend to perform according to the terms of the underlying contract. Under those circumstances, the account party still cannot obtain an **injunction** against payment of the draft under the letter of credit.

These results buttress the proposition that a letter of credit is completely independent of the underlying sales agreement. The issuer's duty is to deal exclusively with the letter-of-credit documents. If the documents conform to the terms of the credit, then the issuer must pay the draft notwithstanding any disputes that may exist between the account party and beneficiary over the underlying contract.

In limited circumstances, however, a court can enjoin the payment of a draft, even though the documents on their face appear to conform with the letter of credit. Provided the documents have not fallen into the hands of a holder in due course, a court may generally enjoin payment based on a fraud or forgery in the documents or fraud in the letter-of-credit transaction (U.C.C. § 5–114). Thus, if a beneficiary submits a false or forged document that appears acceptable on its face or if the original letter-of-credit transaction is a sham, then and only then may a court enjoin payment.

EXAMPLE ■ At its customer's request, First National Bank issued a letter of credit for the benefit of Star Exporters. The terms of the letter required payment of the draft upon presentation of the draft, an invoice, and a bill of lading. After presentation of those documents, which appeared acceptable on their face, the customer informed First National that it believed the bill of lading to be fraudulent. First National informed its customer that it would have to pay the draft, unless it was enjoined from doing so, since the documents appeared to be in order. Before the bank paid the draft, however, the buyer was able to convince a court that the bill of lading was fraudulent. Consequently, the court enjoined payment on the draft. In this situation, the court's injunction was proper since it was based on fraud in the letter-of-credit transaction.

Suppose instead that the buyer convinced the court to issue an injunction because the quality of the goods was inferior to that to which the seller agreed in the underlying sales contract. In this situation, the issuance of an injunction would probably be incorrect since it would not be based on any fraud concerning the letter of credit.

Thus, any dispute concerning the underlying transaction is between the buyer and seller and should not serve as a basis for enjoining payment of the letter of credit.

CONCLUSION

A letter of credit is a widely used financing device to support the purchase and sale of goods (a commercial letter of credit) or the performance of an obligation owed by the account party to the beneficiary (a standby letter of credit).

A letter of credit permits transactions between buyers and sellers who are unfamiliar with one another. It assures the buyer the receipt of goods purchased, and the seller the receipt of payment for goods sold. As such, a letter of credit helps to stimulate the continuous flow of commerce.

Questions for Review and Discussion

1. Define the following terms: account party, issuer, beneficiary, advising bank, and confirming bank.

2. When is a letter of credit considered "established" for an account party? When is it considered "established" for a beneficiary?

3. What is the importance of knowing when an irrevocable letter of credit has been established?

4. Distinguish between a commercial and standby letter of credit and describe the main purpose of each.

5. Once a letter of credit has been established, what obligation does an issuer have to its customer?

6. What is a clean letter of credit?

7. What is the doctrine of strict compliance? How does it differ from the doctrine of substantial compliance? To which doctrine do most courts adhere? Discuss which doctrine you feel is most beneficial to bankers and why.

8. Once an issuer has been presented with documents under a letter of credit, how long does it have to decide whether to pay or dishonor the draft? How does that period differ from the period in which a payor bank has to decide whether to pay or dishonor any ordinary draft? Explain the difference.

9. If a draft presented under a letter of credit is wrongfully dishonored, what damages is the beneficiary entitled to recover?

10. State the circumstances under which the payment of a draft may be enjoined, even though the documents appear on their face to conform with the terms of the credit.

7

Secured Transactions: Attachment and Perfection

After studying this chapter, you will be able to

■ define security terminology

■ explain the concepts of attachment and perfection

■ describe the general types of property included in and excluded from the scope of article 9 of the Uniform Commercial Code (UCC)

■ describe the purpose and contents of a security agreement

■ describe the purpose and contents of a financing statement

■ give legally accurate definitions of possessory and nonpossessory security interests

All bankers know that granting loans brings the risk of nonpayment. Frequently, persuaded by a good credit report on a borrower, a lender will lend money on an unsecured basis and rely on the borrower's honesty and solvency for repayment. Often, however, the lender will require security as an added protection against nonpayment.

This chapter describes how a security interest in property pledged as collateral for a loan is created under article 9 of the UCC. The effective study of secured transactions begins with an understanding of certain concepts and terms in article 9.

179

SECURITY TERMINOLOGY

A lender or seller who possesses a security interest is called a **secured party**. The person who owes payment or other performance under a security agreement is the **debtor**. (The debtor is not necessarily the owner of the property involved in a security agreement.) **Security interest** means that the secured party has an interest in some property that it can take and sell if the debtor fails to pay the loan (**defaults**). The property taken as security is called **collateral**. The procedure by which the secured party sells the collateral upon the debtor's default is called **foreclosure**. By paying the debt, the debtor can avoid the secured party's right of foreclosure. This right to pay the debt and discharge the security interest is known as the **right of redemption**.

Attachment is a concept designed to grant a security interest in the debtor's property. Usually, attachment occurs when the debtor signs a security agreement or surrenders possession of the property to the lender, as long as the debtor has rights in the collateral and value has been given. **Perfection**, on the other hand, is a concept designed to protect the secured party with respect to the collateral against other parties who can also claim an interest in it. Usually, to perfect a security interest, the secured party files a financing statement with a specific public official. However, under some circumstances, the secured party can merely take possession of the collateral to perfect a security interest.

ARTICLE 9 COLLATERAL

Article 9 of the UCC applies to loans secured only by personal property and does not deal with transactions that use land as security (that is, **mortgages** and **deeds of trust**). Article 9 also excludes the following transactions:

- security interests governed by any U.S. statute, such as security interests in ships that come under the federal Ship Mortgage Act of 1920

- artisans liens
- landlords' liens
- liens for delivery of material or labor (**mechanics' liens**) governed by separate statutes
- transfers of claims for wages, salaries, or other employees' compensation
- equipment trusts covering railway rolling stock
- sales of accounts or chattel paper as part of the sales of businesses
- transfers of interest in any insurance policies
- rights acquired by consent judgments
- offsets
- fixtures (except as discussed in chapter 8)
- transfers of any claims arising from torts
- transfers of interests in any deposit accounts

However, when determining whether a particular item of collateral will be available on default, a lender cannot ignore these exclusions. A lender that has perfected its security interest in the collateral may find itself competing with another creditor whose interest in the collateral arises outside article 9. An example of such a creditor is a judgment creditor who has obtained a writ of execution that orders a sheriff to place a levy on the debtor's property.

Thus, when perfecting a security interest, a lender must determine whether the collateral comes under article 9. Article 9 defines collateral by type of personal property. The type of article 9 collateral involved will then determine whether a lender must file a financing statement or take possession of the collateral to perfect its security interest.

The UCC classifies article 9 collateral as either goods that are categorized as equipment, farm products, and inventory or intangibles that are categorized as instruments, documents, chattel paper, accounts, and general intangibles (including contract rights).

Goods   Goods are things that can be readily moved from one location to another when a security interest is created in them. **Consumer goods**

are those used or bought primarily for personal, family, or household purposes (U.C.C. § 9–109(1)).

Goods are **equipment** if they are used or bought primarily for a business (U.C.C. § 9–109(2)). Machinery is a good example of equipment. Machinery used on a farm is called "farm equipment." On the other hand, **inventory** is defined as goods held for sale and includes raw materials, work in process, and materials used or consumed in a business (U.C.C. § 9–109(4)). **Farm products** include crops, livestock, and other farm produce, such as eggs, that farmers hold for sale (U.C.C. § 9–109(3)). Farm products are similar to inventory but are held by a farmer rather than a business.

Intangible Personal Property

Unlike goods, the remaining types of article 9 collateral are intangible, that is, property that has no value in itself but instead has value because of what it represents.

EXAMPLE ■ Smith gives Jones her promissory note on a piece of paper worth less than $0.01. In the note, Smith promises to pay $500 to Jones or her order. Although the tangible value of the promissory note is less than $0.01, its intangible value is $500.

Again, **intangible property** includes instruments, documents, chattel paper, accounts (including contract rights), and general intangibles. **Instruments** are any negotiable instruments, certificated securities (such as stocks traded on a public exchange), or any other writings, whether negotiable or nonnegotiable, that evidence a right to payment of money (U.C.C. § 9–105(1)(i)).

Documents refer to documents of title that are the subject of an entire article of the UCC, article 7. Among the more common types of documents are warehouse receipts and bills of lading (U.C.C. § 9–105(1)(f)). **Chattel paper** includes writings that evidence both a monetary obligation and a security interest in or a lease of specific goods. For example, a loan form in which a bank's customer both promises to pay a debt and evidences collateral for that debt is chattel paper (U.C.C. § 9–105(1)(b)).

Accounts are any rights to payment for goods sold or leased or for services rendered that are not evidenced by instruments or chattel paper. Accounts include both **accounts receivable** (rights to payment for goods already sold or leased or services already performed) and **contract rights** (rights to payments). In addition, all rights to payment under charters or other contracts involving the use or hire of a vessel are accounts (U.C.C. § 9–106).

General intangibles (a catchall category) include any personal property other than goods, accounts, chattel paper, documents, instruments, and money. For instance, goodwill, literary rights, copyrights, trademarks, and patents are all general intangibles.

The classification of personal property may change with a change in either ownership or the purpose for which it is used. For example, a refrigerator for sale by an appliance dealer is inventory. If the refrigerator is sold to a restaurant, it becomes equipment. However, if the restaurant owner goes out of business and takes the refrigerator home for his family's use, it may become a consumer good.

CREATION OF SECURITY INTERESTS: ATTACHMENT

Article 9 of the UCC uses the term "attachment" to indicate when a security interest is created. Since a security interest is a property interest in a debtor's asset conveyed to the creditor, the security interest is created the moment the creditor obtains an interest in the assets, that is, the moment when the creditor's rights "attach" to the debtor's property. Attachment occurs when

- value has been given

- the debtor has rights in the collateral

- the secured party possesses the collateral pursuant to an oral or written agreement or the debtor signs a security agreement that describes the collateral

Value   The first element of attachment is giving value. Under the UCC (section 1–201(44)), a lender gives value to the debtor when it acquires a security interest in the debtor's property in return for a binding commitment to extend credit, as security for a preexisting claim, or in return for any consideration to support a simple contract. A loan of money is the most common type of value given by a lender to a debtor.

Rights in the Collateral

The second element of attachment is the debtor's rights in the collateral. The debtor acquires such rights of ownership before, at the time of, or after signing the security agreement. However, a debtor who acquires collateral by theft does not have ownership rights and thus attachment cannot occur.

EXAMPLE ■ Greene applies for a $15,000 loan from First National Bank to purchase equipment for her business. The bank grants the loan request on September 15. On that day, Greene signs a note and security agreement describing the equipment in exchange for the bank's check for $15,000 made payable to both herself and the equipment supplier. On September 18, Greene uses the check to purchase the equipment. In this situation, First National's security interest attaches on September 18. Although the security agreement was signed and value given on September 15, Greene did not actually acquire rights in the collateral and thus satisfy the last of the three requirements for attachment until September 18.

Case for Discussion

MILLARD V. KELLY

Facts

On January 2, Millard made a loan to Kelly in exchange for a note and security agreement signed by Kelly purporting to give Millard a security interest in Kelly's car. However, Kelly did not own a car on January 2 but did purchase one on January 6.

Subsequently, Kelly defaulted on his loan payments and Millard attempted to repossess the car. Kelly resisted the repossession on the basis that he did not own a car when he signed the security agreement. Millard then commenced an action to recover the car.

1. What value was given by Millard to Kelly? *the loan*
2. Did Millard's security interest attach? If so, when? *Yes on Jan. 6*
3. Who is entitled to possession of the automobile? *Millard*

Security Agreements

Article 9 defines a **security agreement** as one that creates a security interest (U.C.C. § 9–105(1)(l)). Accordingly, a security agreement is simply a contract between the owner of collateral and another person granting the latter a security interest in the collateral.

Oral Versus Written Agreements

The drafters of the UCC were convinced that, unless the creditor possessed the collateral, an oral security agreement presented dangers of misunderstanding and fraud between the parties to the agreement and third parties claiming an interest in the collateral. Consequently, the UCC provides that a security agreement is not enforceable unless the secured party possesses the collateral or the debtor has signed a written security agreement (U.C.C. § 9–203(1)(a)).

EXAMPLES ▪ Lytle loaned $500 to Hilton. To secure the loan, Hilton orally pledged and gave her watch to Lytle. Hilton failed to repay the loan, and Lytle proposed to sell the watch. Hilton disagreed and claimed that the security agreement was unenforceable because it was not in writing. In this situation, however, the secured party (Lytle) possessed the collateral and this made the security agreement enforceable, even though it was not in writing.

▪ Carpenter loaned $5,000 to Watson in exchange for Watson's oral promise that gave Carpenter a security interest in Watson's inventory. In this situation, the oral security agreement was unenforceable since Carpenter did not possess the collateral.

Contents of Written Agreements

A written security agreement can be very simple. It is sufficient if it

▪ grants a security interest

- includes the debtor's signature

- contains a description of the collateral

SECURITY INTERESTS

By its definition, a security agreement must create a security interest. This is done by including in the security agreement such phrases as "borrower grants lender a security interest in the following described collateral" or "debtor grants to secured party a security interest in the following described inventory."

SIGNATURES

Since most security agreements deal with collateral that will remain in the borrower's possession, a security agreement under the UCC must usually be in writing. Normally, both the debtor and creditor sign the security agreement, but the UCC requires only the debtor's signature (U.C.C. § 9–203(1)(a)). In this respect, the security agreement is similar to any other instrument of conveyance (for example, a deed) in which only the party conveying the property must sign the instrument.

DESCRIPTIONS OF COLLATERAL

When most lenders extend secured credit, they generally use pre-printed security agreements, such as the one shown in figure 7.1. The use of such forms usually makes compliance with the first two requirements of a valid security agreement a matter of filling in blanks. However, one cannot simply fill in blanks to meet the third requirement that the security agreement contain a description of the collateral.

Secured lenders need to provide descriptions of collateral in security agreements that are neither too broad nor too narrow. Otherwise, in either situation, lenders may find themselves without collateral when a default occurs.

A description of collateral is sufficient under the UCC if it permits identification of the property pledged as security (U.C.C. § 9–110). If the collateral cannot be identified, then the security agreement is defective since the parties to the agreement do not know what property could be taken on foreclosure. The collateral classifications under arti-

```
  SECURITY AGREEMENT
                                    September 5, 1982

"The following contains the essentials of a security agreement."

    Paula Schmidt of 542 South Huron Street, Cheboygan, Michigan,
hereinafter called the Debtor, and First State Bank, Cheboygan, Mi-
chigan, hereinafter called the Secured Party, agree as follows:

    1. Creation of security interest. The Debtor hereby grants to the
Secured Party a security interest in the Collateral described in para-
graph 2 to secure the payment of the Debtor's obligation to the
Secured Party described in paragraph 3.

    2. Collateral. The property which is subject to the security interest
created by this agreement consists of equipment, more specifically
described as follows: One Two-Ton Widget, Model 4, Serial #6WYE7,
together with any proceeds from the use of such property.

    3. Debtor's obligation. The Debtor shall pay to the Secured Party
the sum of $9,000 together with interest thereon at the rate of 16%
per annum, as follows: in monthly installments of $1,000, the first
such installment to be paid on November 15, 1994, and each suc-
ceeding installment to be paid on the first day of each month there-
after, until the entire principal sum, together with all accrued interest
thereon, shall have been paid in full.

    4. Default. In the event that the Debtor fails to pay any monthly
installment required to be paid under paragraph 3 of this agreement
on or before the twentieth day of the month in which such installment
is due, all unpaid installments shall, at the Secured Party's option,
become immediately due and payable, and in addition to such right
of acceleration, the Secured Party shall be entitled to any and all
remedies available under the Uniform Commercial Code in force in
the State of Michigan on the date of this agreement.

FIRST STATE BANK


BY: _____        _____
ROBERT CHURCHILL,                    PAULA SCHMIDT, Debtor
Vice-President
```

Figure 7.1   Sample Preprinted Security Agreement

cle 9, such as "consumer goods," "equipment," "inventory," and "documents" generally are insufficient as descriptions to give rise to a valid security agreement.

Thus, to determine whether the description of collateral is sufficient, the lender must ask the following question: Can the particular property pledged as security be identified by the description? If the answer is yes, then the description is sufficient.

In addition to the rights a security agreement gives a secured party in the collateral it describes, the law provides the secured party with a security interest in any **proceeds** from the disposition of the collateral (U.C.C. § 9–203(3)). The UCC defines proceeds to include whatever is received upon the sale, exchange, collection or other disposition of collateral or proceeds. For instance, insurance payable because of loss or damage to the collateral is defined as proceeds, except to the extent that it is payable to a person other than a party to the security agreement (U.C.C. § 9–306).

EXAMPLE ■ Warner sells one of his table saws for $100 the day before the rest of his equipment is destroyed in a fire for which he is insured. He collects $9,000 from his insurance company. First National has a security interest in the table saw and other equipment that was destroyed. In this situation, since both the $100 and insurance money are "proceeds," the bank is entitled to a security interest in them.

Case for Discussion

PRATHER V. SOREL

Facts

In exchange for a loan of $300, Sorel executes a security agreement purporting to convey a security interest in "his air conditioner" to Prather. Sorel signs the agreement, but Prather does not. Later, Sorel defaults on the loan. When Prather initiates foreclosure proceedings, he finds that Sorel has always owned three air conditioners.

Questions for Discussion

1. Did Prather's failure to sign the security agreement affect its validity?

No

2. Which, if any, of the air conditioners may Prather take on foreclosure? Why?

Prather cannot take any b/c his ac is not a sufficient description.

Any of the other air conditioners may be taken b/c the description read "his air conditioner."

Optional Provisions of Security Agreements

Besides the minimum requirements that a security agreement be a written document signed by the debtor and describe the collateral in which a security interest is granted, it may also contain other terms, such as a **future-advances provision**. Under this type of provision, the debtor agrees that the collateral secures repayment of both the original loan and any future loans made to the debtor. Provided both parties contemplated a future-advances provision when they signed the security agreement, this provision is enforceable (U.C.C. § 9–204(3)).

EXAMPLE ■ First National grants a $10,000 loan, secured by equipment, to McFee. One year later, the bank advances an additional $5,000 to McFee, according to the terms of the original loan agreement. The security agreement executed at the time of the first loan provides that "the debtor grants the lender a security interest in the described collateral to secure the debt represented by the promissory note of even date with this security agreement as well as to secure all future advances made by lender to debtor."

In this situation, as a result of the future-advances clause, McFee's equipment secures both the $5,000 and original $10,000 loan.

Like language on future advances, clauses on **after-acquired collateral** are not mandatory in security agreements, but their importance to lenders has made them commonplace (U.C.C. § 9–204(1)). Clauses on after-acquired collateral assure a lender that its secured position in a debtor's property will stay current with the debtor's acquisition of further goods or intangibles of the type originally given as collateral.

EXAMPLE ■ Ross borrowed $15,000 from Third National secured by the equipment used in his home-construction business. The security agreement contained a clause stating that Third National's security interest in Ross's equipment extended to all equipment Ross acquired after the loan date. One year after the loan was granted, Ross paid cash for a new table saw. Upon its acquisition, it became collateral for the balance still due on the $15,000 loan.

Clauses on after-acquired collateral, however, are not effective if the original collateral is consumer goods and the after-acquired consumer goods are obtained more than 10 days after the original loan is made (U.C.C. § 9–204(2)). Again, consumer goods are those used or bought primarily for personal, family, or household purposes (U.C.C. § 9–109(1)). These goods include such items as family automobiles, household furnishings, and appliances.

EXAMPLE ■ Johnson borrows $10,000 from First National to purchase new living room furniture for his family's home. First National takes a security interest in all Johnson's household furnishings, including the newly purchased furniture and all after-acquired household furnishings. Six months later, Johnson pays cash for two new end tables. In this situation, the two end tables— although after-acquired—are not additional collateral for the original loan, since they were purchased more than 10 days after the loan was made. If Johnson had purchased the end tables for his place of business, they would have been equipment and become collateral for the loan made six months before their purchase.

While clauses for future advances and after-acquired collateral are perhaps the two most common "optional" clauses in security agreements, they are certainly not the only ones available. A later section of this chapter discusses other provisions the UCC recognizes as acceptable for inclusion in security agreements.

PERFECTION

A lender who takes a secured interest in collateral wants to ensure that it will be available if the debtor defaults on payment of the loan. If the collateral is available upon default, the lender may sell it and apply the proceeds of the sale to the debt.

To ensure that the collateral is available upon default, the lender must not only attach but also perfect its security interest in the collateral. Perfection is necessary if a lender's security interest in collateral is to take priority over the rights that other creditors may have in the same collateral.

EXAMPLE ■ Arbogast, a debtor, owns a tool and die shop. To obtain a loan from First Bank, he offers the machinery, inventory, and accounts receivable of his business as collateral. However, this is the same collateral that he gave to secure a loan with Second National Bank the year before. In this example, two creditors have a security interest in the same collateral to cover the debts that Arbogast owes them. Which creditor has rights in the collateral and in what order depends upon whether First Bank and Second National Bank have perfected their security interest. The timing of the perfected security interests determines which of the two banks has the first right to use the collateral to satisfy its debts.

The concept of perfection has developed because anyone claiming an interest in an asset belonging to another should notify others of that interest. Only through such action can other creditors realize that their interest in the same collateral is subordinate if acquired at a later time.

Perfection usually means that the secured creditor has taken the appropriate steps to notify interested parties of its security interest in some property owned by the debtor. Normally, to accomplish perfection, a creditor either files a financing statement with a proper public official or takes possession of the collateral.

Perfection becomes critical, however, only when several creditors are vying for the same asset. A single creditor obviously does not need priority, since no other creditors claim an interest in the same collateral. But a single creditor will still want to attach a security interest in some asset owned by the debtor. By doing so, the creditor—without first obtaining a judgment to place a lien on the collateral—can realize upon default some return on the debt through foreclosure.

Financing Statements

To perfect a nonpossessory security interest, the creditor must give notice to third parties of its security interest. The form of notice most often used is the filing of either a security agreement or a financing statement with the proper government authority.

Where perfection can be accomplished by filing either a security agreement or a financing statement, lenders normally file financing statements. This is because filing financing statements in a public office exposes less information about lenders' and borrowers' businesses to the public.

To be effective, a financing statement must

■ be signed by the debtor

■ give the debtor's and secured party's names and addresses

■ describe the collateral that is the subject of the security interest (U.C.C. § 9–402(1)).

A **financing statement** is simply a summary of a security agreement. By providing the lender's and borrower's names and addresses, the statement identifies the parties to the transaction. Its description of collateral provides third parties with a general indication of the property in which the secured party claims a security interest. To clarify the nature and extent of that security interest further, these third parties can then contact the secured party for a copy of the security agreement.

Problems in Identifying Debtors

Although the UCC requirements on the contents of a financing statement are straightforward, lenders should know about certain problems that can arise in the identification of debtors. Since the UCC requires financing statements to be indexed according to the debtor's name (U.C.C. § 9–403(4)), an improperly designated name can lead to disaster.

The effect of improperly identifying or misspelling the debtor's name on a filed financing statement is the same as if the statement had never been filed. Problems with identifying debtors most frequently occur when

■ multiple debtors are involved

■ the debtor operates under a trade name

■ the debtor and the owner of the collateral are not the same person

■ the debtor changes his or her name

MULTIPLE DEBTORS

If more than one debtor is involved, the financing statement must identify all of them. This requirement permits a third party searching the public records to identify any individual debtor on a financing statement.

TRADE NAMES

Trade or assumed names are commonly used in the business world. Accordingly, Heather Martin may operate her sole proprietorship business under the trade name "Floral Display." Martin's lender must then decide whether to file the financing statement with "Martin" or "Floral Design" identified as the debtor.

The UCC resolves this problem as follows:

A financing statement sufficiently shows the name of the debtor if it gives the individual, partnership, or corporate name of the debtor, whether or not it adds other trade names or the name of partners (see U.C.C. § 9–402(7)).

Consequently, Martin's lender can identify the debtor on the financing statement as "Martin" or "Martin doing business as Floral Display" but not simply as "Floral Display." If Martin were incorporated, the lender would identify the debtor as "Floral Display, Inc.," and not "Martin." If Martin were operating as a partnership with Jones under the partnership name of "Floral Display," the lender would properly identify the debtor as "Floral Display" or "Floral Display, Martin and Jones, partners," but not as "Martin and Jones, partners."

DEBTORS AND OWNERS OF COLLATERAL WHO ARE NOT THE SAME

A debtor is not necessarily the owner of the property involved in a security agreement. However, if a borrower does not own the collateral used to secure a debt, the lender must identify the owner of the collateral, rather than the borrower, as the debtor on a financing statement.

EXAMPLE ■ Blake's son Adam wants to borrow $1,000 from First National. Before granting the loan, however, the bank requests collateral. Adam asks Blake to put up the accounts receivable from her business as collateral and she agrees. The financing statement filed by First National must thus identify Blake, not her son, as the debtor.

NAME CHANGES

If a debtor changes his or her name and thus causes a filed financing statement to become seriously misleading, then the financing statement will not perfect an interest in collateral acquired more than four months after the name change, unless the lender files a new financing statement before the end of the four-month period. However, the old financing statement does remain valid for collateral acquired before and up to four months after the name change (U.C.C. § 9–402(7)).

EXAMPLE ■ Valley Corporation borrows funds, secured by its inventory, from First National Bank. The bank files a financing statement that identifies "Valley Corporation" as the debtor. Two years later, Valley Corporation changes its name to "Better Products, Inc." Six months after the name change, Better Products, Inc., acquires more inventory. In this situation, First National has four months after the name change to file a new financing statement showing "Better Products, Inc." as the debtor. If the bank fails to do so, then it will not have a valid security interest in the inventory that Better Products acquired six months after the name change.

Identification of the secured party in a financing statement permits a third party searching the public records to discover the complete details of the debts that a financing statement covers. Typically, the third party searching the public records will be a lender who has received a request for funds from a debtor. Once such a lender locates a financing statement, it can then request the debtor to seek written details of the debt from the secured party identified in the statement (U.C.C. § 9–208). The debtor can in turn provide these details to the third party.

Descriptions of Collateral

Like a security agreement, a financing statement also requires a description of collateral. A secured party may use the description of collateral in its underlying security agreement for the financing statement. However, this may not always be practical, given the space limitations in most financing statements. Thus, to summarize its collateral description in the financing statement, a secured party may simply state the types or items of collateral in which it has a security interest. Article 9 classifications for collateral would seem sufficient for this purpose. However, secured parties should know that some courts have required a more detailed description of collateral than the article 9 classifications.

To determine whether the description of collateral in a financing statement is sufficient, the lender should ask the following question: Does it provide enough information to notify a person that a security interest exists in a particular type of property, so the person can inquire further about the property? If the answer is yes, the description is sufficient.

The UCC does not require a fanatical adherence to its provisions governing financing statements before a security interest is perfected. It merely attempts to simplify the formal requisite and filing requirements leading to perfection. Consequently, minor errors in financing statements, which are not seriously misleading, do not prevent perfection (U.C.C. § 9–402(8)).

Where to File Statements

While a properly drafted financing statement is necessary to ensure perfection of a security interest, the most artfully drafted statement will mean little if it is not filed with the proper public authority. To determine where to file a financing statement, lenders must closely scrutinize the version of UCC section 9–401 adopted by the state in which the statement will be filed. Otherwise, an improper filing may result in an unperfected security interest.

EXAMPLE ■ The state of Franklin requires secured lenders to file financing statements covering farm equipment with the county register of deeds and those covering inventory with the secretary of state. Citizens National Bank of Franklin has a security interest in the inventory of Drake's Farm Equipment Store. The bank properly files its financing statement for that interest with the secretary of state. Meanwhile Drake's sells a tractor to Meadow Farms, the purchase of which is financed by Citizens. Citizens again files its financing statement describing the equipment with the secretary of state. Because of a poor harvest, Meadow Farms defaults on its loan to Citizens. In addition, another party, Julia Claggett, receives a judgment against Meadow Farms that gives rise to a judgment lien on the property of Meadow Farms. Both Claggett and Citizens claim that they are entitled to the tractor.

In this situation, Claggett wins. By filing with the incorrect public authority, the secretary of state, Citizens failed to perfect its security interest in the tractor. Consequently, Citizens' unperfected security interest is subordinate to Claggett's judgment lien.

Since states have adopted variations of UCC section 9–401, no generalization can be made about the proper place to file financing statements for all secured lenders. However, as seen in the preceding example, a secured lender who improperly files a financing statement receives little protection under the UCC against a third party that properly acquires an interest in the same collateral. Accordingly, a lender should carefully review the law of the particular state governing the proper place of filing.

Perfection Without Financing Statements

Filing a financing statement is not the only way to perfect a security interest. Two other methods of perfection alert third parties to a lender's interest in collateral:

- physical possession of the collateral
- certificates of title

Possession

Instead of filing a financing statement a lender may take physical possession of most collateral. In fact, when the collateral is money or instruments, a security interest may be perfected only by possession. When the collateral is chattel paper, negotiable documents, goods, and letters of credit, a security interest may be perfected by either filing a financing statement or physical possession. When the collateral consists of accounts or general intangibles, a security interest may be perfected only by filing a financing statement (U.C.C. §§ 9–304 and 9–305).

A lender who perfects its security interest by physical possession does not need to attach its interest under a written security agreement, since an oral security agreement will suffice under the UCC (section 9–302). However, relying on an oral security agreement is not recommended.

Certificates of Title

Certain types of goods are titled according to state laws outside the scope of the UCC. This is particularly true of motor vehicles, but in some states it is also true of mobile homes, boats, and farm equipment. Certificate-of-title statutes provide for the issuance of certificates to owners of the goods to which the statutes apply. Also, physical control of the certificates normally follows ownership of the goods. Generally, a lender claiming a security interest in titled goods must note such interest on the title itself.

Depending on the particular state law, noting a security interest on a **certificate of title** may or may not be sufficient to perfect the security interest. Some states require lenders not only to note their security interest on a certificate of title but also to file a financing statement in order to perfect their security interest. This type of perfection is commonly called **dual filing** (U.C.C. § 9–302(4)).

Automatic Perfection

In certain situations, neither the filing of a financing statement, nor physical possession, nor notation of a security interest on a certificate of title is needed for a lender to perfect a security interest. In these situations, perfection—at least for a limited time—will occur when the lender's security interest attaches to the collateral.

The most common situation in which attachment alone leads to perfection is with the purchase of consumer goods. A lender who loans money for the purchase of consumer goods, pledged as collateral under a written security agreement, automatically acquires a perfected security interest in the goods without the lender's having to file a financing statement (U.C.C. §§ 9–107 and 9–302(1)(d)).

EXAMPLE ■ Meyer goes to First National Bank and borrows money to purchase a personal computer for her home. At the bank, she executes a security agreement in which the computer is described as collateral. Once Meyer purchases the computer with the loan proceeds, the bank acquires a perfected "purchase-money" security interest in the computer without having to file a financing statement. However, if Meyer had purchased the computer for her business, First National would have had to file a financing statement to perfect its security interest. This is because the UCC would classify a computer used in Meyer's business as equipment instead of consumer goods.

Case for Discussion

MARINA BOATING V. LITTLE

Facts

In anticipation of the summer boating season, Marina Boating, Inc., purchased 28 16-foot Sport Runabouts from a major boat manufacturer. The company arranged financing for this inventory through Citizens Bank of Manchester.

To stimulate preseason sales, Marina advertised a "no money down" special offer for all customers who purchased a runabout during April. Not long after the shipment arrived, Charles Little purchased one of the boats. Little signed a standard conditional sales contract (purchase-money security-interest agreement) for the full retail price of the boat. Under the conditions of the special April sale, Little made no down payment. Also, under Oregon law, titles are not required for pleasure craft of this size, so Little did not obtain a title.

Not long after purchasing the boat, Little decided that it did not meet his family's needs. So, he placed an advertisement in the newspaper and sold the boat to Cecil Walker for a price only slightly below the original purchase price. After selling the boat, Little made no further payments to Marina Boating and the company took immediate action to repossess the craft. However, Walker resisted their efforts and claimed that he had paid Little the full price and thus owned the boat outright. Marina Boating sued for repossession of the craft.

Decision

In this case, the court ruled in favor of Walker. Because an automatic perfection of security interest exists in all consumer goods, Marina Boating, Inc., did not file a financing statement. However, according to the court, Walker was "a consumer purchaser for personal use" and therefore came under a legal exception to the rule of automatic perfection. Thus, Marina Boating was without recourse in this case and could not repossess the boat. (See U.C.C. §§ 9–301 and 9–302.)

Questions for Discussion

1. Did Marina Boating, Inc., have any recourse in this matter in relation to Little?
2. How should Marina Boating, Inc., have perfected its security interest in the property? *By filing a financing statemnt*

CONCLUSION

Article 9 of the UCC, entitled "Secured Transactions," governs the acquisition of security interest in personal property. As a general rule, for a creditor to obtain a valid and enforceable security interest, it must not only attach but also perfect its interest in the property. Attachment occurs when (1) value has been given, (2) the debtor has rights in the collateral, and (3) the secured party possesses the collateral pursuant to an oral or written agreement or a signed security agreement describes the collateral.

Perfection occurs when a creditor gives notice to third parties of its security interest. To give this notice, the creditor usually files either a security agreement or financing statement with the appropriate public officials.

Questions for Review and Discussion

1. Name the two categories of article 9 collateral.

2. What items does the definition of goods include?

3. What items does the definition of intangibles include?

4. Davis borrows $3,000 from Crane and executes a security agreement giving Crane a security interest in a car that Davis promises to buy with the proceeds of the loan. What events must occur before Crane's security interest attaches?

5. What is the basic purpose for taking security in a sale or lending transaction?

6. Define the following terms: secured party, debtor, collateral, security agreement, financing statement, right of redemption, and foreclosure.

7. How does the concept of attachment differ from the concept of perfection?

8. What are the essential ingredients and function of a security agreement?

9. Why would a lender want to include an after-acquired collateral provision in a security agreement?

10. In consideration for a $5,000 loan, Goldberg grants First National a security interest in his family's car and all after-acquired property. Six months after the loan is made, Goldberg pays cash for a personal computer. Does First National have a security interest in the computer? Why or why not?

11. What is the function of a financing statement?

12. Heather Kinney borrows money to purchase equipment for her floral shop. She trades under the name "Floral Display." Since the equipment secures the loan, the lender needs to file a financing statement. Which name should be identified in the statement—"Heather Kinney" or "Floral Display"?

13. Under what circumstances can a lender, without filing a financing statement, perfect a security interest?

Secured Transactions: Priorities in Collateral and Default

After studying this chapter, you will be able to

- accurately state the "first to file or perfect" rule and explain the technical implications of this rule for lending institutions

- discuss the various types of liens outside the scope of article 9 of the UCC, including possessory, judgment, and federal tax liens

- give a legally correct explanation of the phrase "buyer in the ordinary course of business"

- describe the basic legal rights of bankruptcy trustees in collateral owned by a debtor who has filed a bankruptcy petition

- define the term "fixture"

- discuss the concept of self-help repossession

- explain the secured party's right to take possession of collateral, sell it, and apply the sales proceeds to the debt when default occurs

PRIORITIES IN COLLATERAL

Attachment, perfection, security agreements, financing statements, and collateral are just empty words unless they actually benefit lenders. In complying with article 9 of the Uniform Commercial Code (UCC), all secured lenders seek to obtain the highest possible priority in the collateral. Then if a loan default occurs, the lender can take possession of the collateral and sell it.

Otherwise, upon a default, a secured lender seeking collateral may compete with as many as five different competitors:

- the debtor or owner of the collateral

- other secured creditors

- unsecured creditors

- purchasers of the collateral

- bankruptcy trustees

Confronted with this potential competition, a bank can readily understand the importance of strictly following the requirements of article 9 for perfecting security interests.

Owner of the Collateral

Whether he or she is the borrower or a third party who pledged property to secure the borrower's loan, the owner of collateral often resists a bank's effort to take (**repossess**) the property upon default. If the bank can demonstrate that its security interest is attached to the collateral, it can overcome this resistance. In other words, the bank must prove that a written security agreement exists (or that it possesses the collateral), that it gave the borrower value, and that the borrower or third party has rights in the collateral. If the bank can do this, its security interest is enforceable against the owner of the property (U.C.C. § 9–203). Perfection is unnecessary to enforce a security interest against the owner of collateral.

EXAMPLE ■ James Stanton borrowed $10,000 from First National Bank, due December 31, and pledged the equipment in his business as collateral. On October 1, Stanton signed a security agreement and financing statement, but First National neglected to file the financing statement. On December 31, Stanton did not pay the debt and First National demanded his equipment. He refused to turn it over because First National had failed to perfect its interest in the equipment. However, even though the bank failed to perfect its security interest, its interest attached on October 1 and could be enforced against Stanton's equipment. Attachment occurred on that date because Stanton received value, signed a security agreement, and had rights in the collateral.

Other Secured Creditors

While attachment alone gives a secured lender priority in collateral over a defaulting borrower, it may not afford such priority when a bank is competing with another secured creditor for the collateral.

Failure to File

A secured lender who only attaches its security interest to collateral will not have priority over a secured party who has perfected its security interest.

EXAMPLE ■ In exchange for a $20,000 loan also due on December 31, Stanton of the previous example gave Citizens National Bank a security interest in the same equipment pledged to First National. Furthermore, Citizens perfected its security interest on November 1. Subsequently, Stanton defaulted on his loans, and both banks claimed a prior interest in the equipment. In this situation, Citizens National won since it was first to perfect its security interest in the equipment.

The preceding examples illustrate the importance of priority in collateral. If the equipment was worth $25,000, the proceeds from its sale would fully pay the loan extended by Citizens National. First National, however, would realize only $5,000 of the $10,000 loan it had given Stanton. Whether Citizens National actually knew of First National's security interest when it perfected its own security interest is irrelevant, since such knowledge plays no part in deciding priorities under article 9. If First National had perfected its security interest before November 1, its interest would have had priority over that of Citizens National.

First to File or Perfect

The secured lender who files a financing statement first generally has a first right to the collateral. This rule holds true even though another party first obtains a signed security agreement and disburses funds (U.C.C. § 9–312).

EXAMPLE ■ On August 1, in contemplation of making a $20,000 loan, Acme State Bank filed a financing statement covering machinery belonging to Churchill. The loan was scheduled to close on October 1. On September 1, First National Bank filed a financing statement covering the same machinery and disbursed $30,000 to Churchill on that same day. On October 1, Acme State Bank closed its secured loan to Churchill and disbursed $20,000 to him. On December 1, Churchill defaulted on his obligations, and both banks sought the machinery. In this situation, because the UCC gives priority to the first secured lender to file its financing statement, Acme State Bank had priority in Churchill's machinery over First National (U.C.C. § 9–312). This was true even though First National was first to attach its security interest to the collateral and give value to Churchill.

The code's justification for the outcome of the preceding example is that public filing gives subsequent lenders notice of prior interest. Thus, lenders should file financing statements as soon as they think that they will probably make a loan.

Purchase-Money Security Interest

A purchase-money security interest is an exception to the first-to-file-or-perfect rule. A security interest becomes a **purchase-money security interest** when a borrower uses the loan money to purchase property that secures the loan. Either the seller of the property may directly, or a bank or other lender may indirectly, make such a loan.

EXAMPLE ■ Acme State Bank has a security interest in equipment owned by Widget, Inc., including all after-acquired property. The security interest is perfected on March 1. On July 1, Widget purchases from ABC Tools a new piece of equipment for $10,000, $9,000 of which will be paid to ABC on an installment plan secured by the equipment Widget is purchasing. Since Acme State Bank has a continuing security interest or **floating lien** in all of Widget's equipment acquired before, at the time of, or after its perfection on March 1, the bank's security interest would seem to have priority over that of ABC. Under the UCC, however, a purchase-money security interest in collateral other than inventory has priority over a conflicting security interest in the same collateral, as long as the purchase-money security interest is perfected within 10 days after the debtor receives possession of the collateral (U.C.C. § 9–312(4)).

Thus, if ABC Tools perfects its security interest in the equipment that it sells to Widget, Inc., by July 11, its security interest in that equipment will be superior to that of Acme State Bank. However, if ABC Tools fails to file its financing statement or does so after July 11, its priority in the collateral would be determined without regard to its purchase-money security interest. Accordingly, in that situation, its security interest would be subordinate to that of Acme State Bank.

Inventory acquired with purchase-money loans is also an exception to the first-to-file-or-perfect rule. To obtain a security interest superior to that of a secured party who has previously perfected its interest in inventory, a purchase-money lender who takes a security interest in that inventory must comply with the provisions of section 9–312(3) of the UCC. This section states in part as follows:

A perfected purchase-money security interest in inventory has priority over a conflicting security interest in the same inventory and also has priority in identifiable cash proceeds received on or before the delivery of the inventory to a buyer if

(a) the purchase-money security interest is perfected at the time the debtor receives possession of the inventory; and

(b) the purchase-money secured party gives notification in writing to the holder of the conflicting security interest if the holder had filed a financing statement covering the same types of inventory (i) before the date of the filing made by the purchase-money secured party, or (ii) before the beginning of the 21-day period where the purchase-money security interest is temporarily perfected without filing or possession; and

(c) the holder of the conflicting security interest receives the notification within five years before the debtor receives possession of the inventory; and

(d) the notification states that the person giving the notice has or expects to acquire a purchase-money security interest in inventory of the debtor, describing such inventory by item or type.

Case for Discussion   **ACME STATE BANK AND XYZ COMPANY V. HORROCKS**

Facts

Acme State Bank loaned $80,000 to Horrocks on July 15, secured by the present and after-acquired inventory of Horrock's appliance store. On August 1, Horrocks ordered 25 refrigerators from XYZ Company, which agreed to sell them to Horrocks on an installment plan. On the same date, XYZ Company gave notice to Acme State Bank of its conflicting security interest. On August 15, XYZ Company filed a financing statement describing the 25 refrigerators, which were delivered to Horrocks on August 16. On October 1, Horrocks defaulted on his obligations to both Acme State Bank and XYZ Company. Both creditors sued Horrocks for the inventory.

Decision

The court ruled that since XYZ Company complied with the requirements of UCC section 9–312(3), its security interest in the 25 refrigerators had priority over that of Acme State Bank.

Questions for Discussion

1. If XYZ Company had arranged for delivery of the 25 refrigerators over a three-year period, would its initial notice to Acme State Bank still

protect its priority position? Why?

2. If any of the refrigerators had been delivered to Horrocks more than five years after notice of the conflicting security interest was given to Acme State Bank, would XYZ Company's priority in any of the refrigerators have changed? How?

3. Does the bank have any recourse in this situation?

Unsecured Creditors

A secured lender with a defaulting borrower does not need to worry about unsecured creditors, as long as those creditors have not acquired liens outside the scope of article 9.

EXAMPLE ■ On February 10, Helen Rose purchased a used car from Al's New and Used Autos for $3,000. She initially put $1,000 down and began to pay the balance under a time-payment plan. However, Al's did not take a security interest in the car. On March 15, Rose borrowed $2,000 from First National Bank and used the car as collateral. The bank perfected its security interest in the car. Rose then defaulted on her loans from both Al's and First National Bank. In this situation, the bank was the only creditor with a secured interest in the car and, as such, could repossess the collateral. As an unsecured creditor, Al's had no claim to the collateral.

Liens Arising Outside Article 9

Non-article 9 liens—other than those obtained through bankruptcy proceedings or federal tax liens—result from state statutory or common law. State liens that may affect personal property include those for services or materials that people provide in the ordinary course of their businesses while the goods for which the services or materials are provided remain in their possession. Such liens include, for example, storage, innkeepers', garagemen's, and stablemen's liens. These liens are commonly called "possessory liens."

POSSESSORY LIENS

Unless a contrary state law exists, **possessory liens** are superior to article 9 security interests (U.C.C. § 9–310).

EXAMPLE ■ On July 1, Joel McKinley purchased a new car from Rivertown Ford for $9,000 under a retail installment sales contract, which resulted in a perfected security interest. On August 1, the car was in an accident, and Joe's Garage repaired it for $2,000. However, Joe's refused to release the car until McKinley paid the repair bill. In this situation, Joe's Garage had a possessory garageman's lien that took priority over Rivertown Ford's security interest. In most states, if Joe's Garage released the car before McKinley paid the repair bill, the garage would lose its lienor status and become an unsecured creditor.

LIEN CREDITORS

Statutory law outside the scope of article 9 governs a lien creditor's interest in a debtor's property. A **lien creditor** is typically an unsecured creditor who obtains a judgment against a debtor (U.C.C. § 9–301(3)). In some states, a judgment creditor's lien automatically arises upon judgment. In other states, to obtain an interest in the debtor's property, a judgment creditor must also secure a writ of execution following judgment. Normally, a **writ of execution** permits a sheriff to seize and sell the debtor's property to satisfy the judgment.

Under the UCC, a lien creditor has a special priority status. For example, an attached but unperfected security interest is subordinate to a lien creditor's rights. However, if a person becomes a lien creditor after a security interest is perfected, then the perfected security interest prevails to the extent that it secures advances made before and for 45 days after the creditor's lien (U.C.C. § 9–301(4)).

EXAMPLE ■ Citizens National Bank attaches its security interest to the equipment of XYZ, Inc., on February 1 and files a financing statement to perfect that interest on May 1. Jenna Kim receives a judgment against XYZ, Inc., and becomes a lien creditor on March 1. In this situation, since Citizens National Bank had an unperfected security interest when Kim became a lien creditor, its interest is subordinate to Kim's judgment. Under the UCC (sections 9–301(1)(a) and (b)), whether Kim knew of the bank's security interest when she received her judgment is irrelevant to her priority position. Also, the bank's subsequent perfection of its security interest does not affect Kim's priority status as a lien creditor. However, if Citizens National Bank had perfected its security interest before March 1, its priority in the collateral would have been superior to that of Kim.

Suppose instead that Citizens National Bank perfects its security interest on February 1 and then advances funds to XYZ, Inc., on May 1. Subsequently, XYZ, Inc., defaults on its loan obligation, and both Citizens National Bank and Kim claim a prior right to the equipment. In this situation, Kim still wins, even though the bank perfected its security interest before Kim received the judgment on March 1. This is because Citizens National advanced funds to XYZ, Inc., more than 45 days after Kim became a lien creditor.

There is an exception to the lien creditor's priority position over an unperfected security interest. This occurs when the lien creditor's status arises within 10 days of a debtor's taking possession of collateral in which a purchase-money lender has an unperfected interest. If the lender files a financing statement to perfect its security interest within that 10-day period, it will have priority over the lien creditor (U.C.C. § 9–301(2)).

EXAMPLE ■ On April 15, ABC Furniture sells and delivers office furniture to Churchill's business. Churchill purchases the furniture pursuant to a time-payment plan in which ABC retains a purchase-money security interest. On April 17, Small Loan Finance Company obtains a judgment against Churchill, which makes it a lien creditor on that day under applicable state law. On April 24, ABC Furniture files a financing statement covering its collateral.

In this situation, ABC Furniture's priority in the collateral is superior to Small Loan Finance Company's judgment lien.

FEDERAL TAX LIENS

Federal tax liens also arise outside the scope of both article 9 and other state laws. The **Federal Tax Lien Act** provides methods for the federal government to collect delinquent taxes, including the seizure and sale of taxpayers' real and personal property. Such real or personal property may also serve as collateral for secured lenders and thus may give rise to competing claims to the property.

The Federal Tax Lien Act governs the resolution of conflicts between federal taxing authorities and secured creditors. The act provides that a delinquent federal tax becomes a lien once the tax is assessed. However, the lien does not affect the rights of third parties, such as purchasers, secured creditors, or lien creditors, until the government properly files a notice of tax lien. For a secured creditor to obtain a priority in collateral superior to a federal tax lien, the secured party must perfect its interest before the federal government files a notice of tax lien. If a security interest is not perfected when the federal government files such a notice, the secured party's position will be subordinate to that of the federal government.

Purchasers of Collateral

So commerce may flow as smoothly as possible, the UCC (section 9–307) permits a person to purchase goods free from the claims of third parties, as long as the purchase is made

- from a person or entity who is in the business of selling such goods
- in good faith
- without knowledge that the sale violates any third party's ownership rights or security interest in the goods

Buyers in the Ordinary Course of Business

A **buyer in the ordinary course of business** is similar to a holder in due course. Like a holder in due course taking negotiable instruments, this buyer purchases goods free from the claims of third parties.

EXAMPLE ■ Dent walks into Acme Appliance and purchases a refrigerator that is part of Acme's inventory, all of which is collateral for a loan Acme owes First National Bank. Dent is aware of the loan when he purchases the refrigerator. In this situation, Dent is a buyer in the ordinary course of business and thus takes the refrigerator free of First National's security interest in Acme's inventory. Dent's knowledge of First National Bank's security interest does not affect either his status as a buyer in the ordinary course of business or his ability to take the refrigerator free of the bank's security interest. However, if Dent knew the sale of the refrigerator violated the terms of the security agreement between the bank and Acme Appliance, he would not be a buyer in the ordinary course of business and his purchase would be subject to the bank's security interest.

The manner in which a buyer in the ordinary course of business uses the goods purchased also does not affect his or her priority in them. For instance, in the previous example, without impairing his priority over First National's previously perfected security interest, Dent may use the refrigerator either as equipment in his business or as consumer goods in his home.

Consumer Buyers and Sellers

To be classified as a buyer in the ordinary course of business, the buyer must purchase the goods from someone who is in the business of selling such goods. Consequently, if the purchase is a casual sale of consumer goods from one consumer to another, then the use and priority rules are different from those that apply to a buyer in the ordinary course of business. For instance, purchasers of consumer goods take them free from prior security interests only if they will be used for personal, family, or household purposes (U.C.C. § 9-307(2)). Thus, in the previous example, if Dent had purchased the refrigerator from Smith instead of Acme Appliances and they both used the appliance for personal purposes, then again Dent would take the refrigerator free of First National's security interest.

The "consumer buyer and seller" exception to the first-to-file-or-perfect rule is unavailable if a secured party has filed a financing statement before the sale. Thus, in the preceding example, if First National had filed a financing statement covering the refrigerator before Smith's sale, Dent would have purchased the refrigerator subject to the bank's security interest. As discussed in chapter 7, a purchase-money lender's security interest in consumer goods is automatically perfected without the need to file a financing statement. However, this automatic perfection does not protect the lender's security interest in the goods if a consumer subsequently sells them to another consumer for personal use.

EXAMPLES ■ The facts are the same as in the previous example, except that, without filing a financing statement, Acme Appliance takes a purchase-money security interest in the refrigerator to secure an installment note signed by Dent. Since the refrigerator is a consumer good, Acme Appliance's security interest in it is automatically perfected without the need to file a financing statement. Although Acme Appliance has a perfected security interest in the refrigerator, its priority will be subordinate to a buyer subsequently purchasing the refrigerator from Dent for personal, family, or household purposes (U.C.C. § 9–307(2)). If Acme Appliance had not relied on automatic perfection and instead had filed a financing statement to perfect its security interest, its priority would be superior to that of the individual purchasing the refrigerator from Dent (U.C.C. § 9–307(2)).

■ Ryan purchases an oven from Acme Appliance under an installment plan that involves a purchase-money security interest. Again, Acme does not file a financing statement. Subsequently, Ryan sells the oven to Diaz, who is unaware of Acme Appliance's security interest. In this situation, Diaz takes the oven free from Acme Appliance's security interest, as long as she is unaware of Acme's security interest. If Acme Appliance had filed a financing statement, however, it would have preserved the priority of its interests over those of Diaz, whether or not she actually knew of Acme Appliance's security interest (U.C.C. § 9–307(2)).

Bankruptcy Trustees

In addition to other secured parties, a secured lender often competes with a bankruptcy trustee for the rights to collateral. A federal bankruptcy court appoints a **bankruptcy trustee** to represent the interests of unsecured creditors of a debtor who has filed for bankruptcy. To serve those interests, trustees usually try to wrest from secured creditors as much collateral as possible, which the former can then use to pay unsecured debts. Trustees are given three tools to accomplish their duty to unsecured creditors. They may become hypothetical lien creditors, they may set aside any transfer of a debtor's property to a creditor as a preference, and they may place themselves in the position of any lien creditor.

Hypothetical Lien Creditors

First, on the date the debtor files the bankruptcy petition, trustees become **hypothetical lien creditors.** The UCC (section 9–301(1)(b)) sets forth lien creditors' rights in such situations, and the following example illustrates what the status of hypothetical lien creditor can do for a trustee.

EXAMPLE ■ On July 1, Grant borrows $10,000 from Acme State Bank. To collateralize its loan, Acme takes a security interest in Grant's equipment. On July 15, Grant files a petition for bankruptcy. On July 20, Acme State Bank files its financing statement. In this situation, Acme's security interest is junior to the bankruptcy trustee's rights as a lien creditor, because under the UCC (section 9–301(1)(b)) an unperfected security interest is subordinate to the rights of a lien creditor.

Preferences

Second, a bankruptcy trustee seeking collateral from a secured lender can also set aside any transfer of the debtor's property to a creditor as a "preference." A debtor's transfer is considered a **preference** if

■ the property secures a previously existing (antecedent) debt

■ the debtor is insolvent when the transfer is made

■ the transfer is made within 90 days before the debtor files the bankruptcy petition

■ the transfer increases the amount the creditor would otherwise have received from the bankrupt estate without such a transfer

---

EXAMPLE ■ On January 15, First National Bank lends Churchill $20,000 on an unsecured basis, which is due on May 1. On maturity of the loan, Churchill cannot pay the principal and seeks to renew the debt. First National renews the debt but takes a security interest in the inventory of Churchill's business. On June 1, Churchill files a petition for bankruptcy. In this situation, since First National's security interest was perfected before the bankruptcy filing, the bankruptcy trustee cannot use his or her status as a hypothetical lien creditor to take a position in Churchill's inventory prior to that of First National (U.C.C. §§ 9–301 and 9–312(5)(a)). However, because First National's security interest meets all the criteria for a "preference," the trustee can set it aside and make Churchill's inventory available to all his unsecured creditors. Although First National Bank is among those unsecured creditors, instead of receiving all the inventory's value, the bank must share that value with Churchill's other unsecured creditors.

Actual Lien Creditors From section 551 of the **Bankruptcy Reform Act,** a bankruptcy trustee derives a third significant power that can affect a secured creditor's status in collateral. This section enables a trustee to place him- or herself in the position of any **actual lien creditor** whose lien the trustee has voided and who has priority over any secured creditors who have not perfected their security interest.

EXAMPLE ■ On February 1, Welles borrows $50,000, which is secured by inventory, from Acme State Bank. The bank does not perfect its security interest until September 1. Meanwhile, on August 15, Berg obtains a judgment against Welles for $40,000 and, due to applicable state law, Berg becomes a lien creditor on that same day. However, Welles files a petition for bankruptcy on October 15. In this situation, the bankruptcy trustee can set aside Berg's status as lien creditor, because it is a voidable preference under section 547 of the Bankruptcy Reform Act. The trustee may then assume Berg's status as lien creditor and thereby obtain a prior position in the collateral to that held by Acme State Bank on August 15, since at that time the bank's security interest was unperfected. Assuming the collateral is worth $50,000, the trustee will take $40,000 for Welles's unsecured creditors and leave Acme State Bank with only $10,000 to apply to its debt.

Thus, bankruptcy trustees are formidable adversaries for secured creditors seeking collateral from a debtor who has filed for bankruptcy.

FIXTURES

Goods become **fixtures** when they are so related to a particular parcel of real estate that an interest arises in them under real estate law (U.C.C. § 9–313). Items of personal property that may become fixtures include lights, vents and ducts, furnaces, boilers, shelving, and air conditioners.

EXAMPLE ■ Acme Lighting Company agrees to install lights in Brian Wilson's shop. To that end, the company permanently attaches the lights to the walls and ceilings and connects them to the shop's wiring system. While the lights are in Acme's possession, they are goods or, more precisely, inventory (U.C.C. § 9–109). However, once Acme attaches the lights to the shop's walls and ceilings, they become real property, just as the walls and ceilings are real property.

Since the laws governing the use of personal and real property as collateral differ greatly from state to state, creditors wishing to secure debt with fixtures are faced with the problems of perfecting their security interests and maintaining the perfection after the property becomes part of real property.

EXAMPLE ■ Wilson's purchase of lights from Acme in the preceding example amounts to $10,000, $5,000 of which he wants to pay over 36 months. Acme agrees but wants to use the lights to secure the debt. In this situation, as long as the lights remain unattached to the shop building, Acme can enter into a security agreement with Wilson and file a financing statement to perfect its security interest.

However, a problem arises in this example if the lights are attached to the building and are no longer considered personal property. This is particularly troublesome when a mortgage attaches its lien to additions made to buildings on the mortgaged property.

EXAMPLE ■ The facts are the same as in the previous two examples, except Second National Bank holds a mortgage on Wilson's shop. If Wilson defaults under the terms of his mortgage, Second National Bank and Acme both will claim the lights in the shop as collateral.

The UCC resolves the conflict of priorities between those creditors securing debts with goods before they are attached to real property and those securing debts with real property to which goods are attached. Generally, the first creditor to file a financing statement or security agreement in the former situation or to record a mortgage in the latter situation has priority in fixtures (U.C.C. § 9–313(4)(b)).

EXAMPLE ■ Doman owns a home that has a central air conditioning system. He borrows $1,000 from Center State Bank, which is secured by a security interest in the air conditioning system. The bank makes a "fixture filing" with the proper public official. Six months later, Doman mortgages his home with Third Federal Savings and Loan, which properly records its mortgage. In this situation, the bank's security interest in Doman's air conditioning system is superior to that of the savings and loan. However, if the savings and loan had recorded its mortgage before the bank had made its fixture filing, the savings and loan would have had the prior interest.

The principal exception to the first-to-file-or-record rule for fixtures involves purchase-money security interests.

EXAMPLE ■ Independent State Bank holds a mortgage on Hackett's retail shop. Hackett gets a loan from Union National Bank to purchase shelving that he attaches to the walls of his shop. Union National in turn makes a fixture filing that covers its purchase-money security interest in the shelving. In this situation, as long as Union National's security interest in the shelving arises before it becomes a fixture (that is, before Hackett installs it) and the fixture filing occurs before or within 10 days after that time, Union National will have the prior security interest (U.C.C. § 9–313(4)(a)).

The purchase-money priority rule illustrated in the preceding example also has an exception. When a prior recorded mortgage is a construction mortgage, it will have a superior priority to any subsequent fixture filing, whether it is a purchase-money filing or not.

EXAMPLE ■ Morgan State Bank agrees to make a $1 million construction mortgage to Ferrelli to build an apartment unit. The bank records the mortgage with the proper public official. By June 1, Ferrelli has borrowed $500,000 of the committed funds. On that date, he purchases lighting for the apartment unit, financed by the supplier, Britelight Company, which records its fixture filing before Ferrelli installs the lights. Thereafter, Ferrelli borrows the remaining $500,000 from the bank. In this situation, since the mortgage is a construction mortgage, Britelight's purchase-money security interest in the lights is subordinate to Morgan State Bank's mortgage of $1 million (U.C.C. § 9–313(6)).

The procedure used to file a security interest in fixtures differs from that used for goods. To make a **fixture filing,** a creditor files either a financing statement or mortgage in the real estate records of the appropriate public office. The financing statement or mortgage must describe the collateral, state that it is to be filed in the real estate records, and contain a description of the real estate to which the fixtures are attached (U.C.C. §§ 9–402(5) and 9–402(6)).

DEFAULT

Banks and other creditors demand security as additional protection against nonpayment of their loans. If the debtor defaults, the secured party has the right to foreclose on the security interest. This means that the secured party has the right to take possession of the collateral, to sell or otherwise dispose of it, and to use the proceeds to repay the secured creditors according to their respective priorities.

Default is any failure to comply with the terms of a security agreement or the promissory note it secures. The most common default is failure to make agreed payments. However, failure to maintain or properly insure collateral may also be grounds for default if a security agreement includes those requirements. A debtor's failure to provide financial statements or sale of the collateral to a third party may also be defaults, depending on the security agreement's requirements. In other words, a debtor's breach of any terms in a security agreement can constitute a default.

EXAMPLE ■ A security agreement between Kent and Acme State Bank requires him to provide the bank with yearly financial statements prepared by a certified public accountant. Although Kent is current on all payments due to the bank under the agreement, he fails to provide the required financial statements. In this situation, even though he is not behind in his payments, Kent is in default under the security agreement with Acme State Bank.

Declaring a debtor in default does little in itself to solve the lender's problem. The lender's real clout is in the acceleration of the debt upon default. **Acceleration** is the act of demanding that the debtor pay the entire balance due on a debt immediately. However, lenders cannot accelerate payment of a debt unless permitted to do so by language in a loan document, such as a promissory note or security agreement. For instance, language similar to the following would permit acceleration of the debt upon default:

If Borrower is in default, Lender may declare to be immediately due and payable the total of all of the monthly payments remaining to be paid by Borrower under the promissory note.

EXAMPLE ■ Suppose Kent in the previous example owed Acme State Bank a balance of $12,000 when he failed to provide the bank with financial statements. If the bank then declared a default and accelerated the debt, the entire $12,000 would be due at that time. Once the acceleration occurred, Kent could no longer make monthly payments.

Upon acceleration, the debtor can pay the balance due on the debt or face the remedies provided to the creditor under both the UCC (sections 9-501 to 505) and the security agreement. These remedies are cumulative and a creditor may use any combination of them to obtain payment (U.C.C. § 9–501).

Self-Help Repossession

Upon default and acceleration, a secured creditor who cannot obtain full repayment of a debtor's obligation may take possession of the collateral (U.C.C. § 9–503). However, a creditor must accomplish a

self-help repossession of collateral without breach of the peace (U.C.C. § 9–503). Secured creditors breaching the peace in repossession expose themselves to monetary damages for conversion, trespass, assault and battery, and violation of the various states' statutes on fair debt collection practices.

The UCC has not defined exactly what constitutes a breach of the peace, nor have the courts uniformly defined it. Some courts have found that repossession must at least involve a threat of violence to constitute a breach of the peace, while others have found a breach to occur when a lender uses deceit to obtain the collateral.

EXAMPLE ■ Halley is four months behind in his car payments when First National Bank accelerates the debt and asks Halley to come to its office to discuss the problem. While Halley is talking to First National's vice-president about a loan extension, the bank repossesses his car, which is parked outside the bank. Halley sues First National and alleges that in repossessing his car, it breached the peace. In this situation, the court's decision could go either way, although most courts would probably find that no breach of the peace had occurred, since the repossession involved no violence or threat of violence.

The courts are also divided on the issue of whether entering a debtor's property to repossess collateral is a breach of the peace. Most courts find no breach of the peace occurred if the collateral is not behind closed doors when it is repossessed and if the debtor does not confront and order the creditor off the property. If a creditor in the act of repossession is confronted by a debtor (whether on the debtor's property or not), the creditor should temporarily abandon the effort to avoid breaching the peace through threat of violence. Use of law enforcement officers in a respossession constitutes a breach of the peace. The officers' presence constitutes a threat of violence since the debtor could resist the repossession.

Secured lenders should become thoroughly familiar with the definitions for a breach of the peace adopted by their states' courts. While self-help repossessions are legal and secured creditors undertake them regularly, such actions do call for restraint and strict compliance with applicable law.

Replevin   If a secured creditor cannot repossess collateral peacefully, its only alternative is court-imposed relief. Under such circumstances, a creditor may seek a **writ of replevin** or restitution. In most states, to assure that debtors receive due process under the law, courts can grant this writ only after a hearing. At the hearing, the creditor must prove that the debt exists and is in default and that the creditor has a secured interest in the collateral. If a court issues a writ, it will order a sheriff or other law enforcement officer to take possession of the collateral for the creditor.

Assembling Collateral   If a security agreement so provides, a secured lender may require a defaulting debtor to assemble the collateral at a location convenient for both parties, so that the secured party may take possession of it (U.C.C. § 9–503). If the debtor refuses, a court may issue an order to compel the assembly of the collateral.

If collateral is equipment, a secured creditor may take possession of it on the debtor's premises, render it unusable, and dispose of it on those premises. This provision is useful when heavy equipment is involved and its removal is difficult.

Disposing of Collateral   Once a secured creditor possesses collateral, its responsibilities to the debtor do not end. If anything, they increase. The UCC permits secured creditors who possess collateral either to sell or retain it. However, secured creditors selling collateral must ensure that every aspect of the disposition, including its method, manner, time, place, and terms, is performed in a "commercially reasonable" manner (U.C.C. § 9–504(3)).

Preparing Collateral   Collateral may be in disrepair or a work in process. Therefore, before selling it, a secured creditor may first need to decide whether to prepare or process it for sale.

EXAMPLES ■ First National Bank repossesses Dole's car, which lacks a battery and right front tire. In this situation, the bank may purchase a battery and tire for the car and, in fact, may be required to do so, since some courts have found such repairs necessary to meet the standard of commercial reasonableness.

■ Citizens National Bank repossesses the inventory of River Corporation, which includes the parts to make 3,000 toys. The parts are valued at $10,000. However, the value of the toys is expected to be $20,000, with $2,000 in assembly costs. The balance of the debt due Citizens National Bank is $11,000. To receive a higher price at sale, the bank may pay the assembly costs.

Sale Procedures

The UCC strictly controls the method of selling repossessed collateral and, like all other facets of repossession, it must be done in a commercially reasonable manner.

NOTICE OF SALE

A secured creditor who intends to sell repossessed collateral must first give reasonable notice to the debtor of the time and place of any public sale of the collateral or, if the sale is to be private, notice of the date after which the sale will be made. The purpose of the notice is to enable the debtor to exercise his or her redemption rights. Any time before a secured creditor has disposed of repossessed collateral or entered into a contract for its disposition, the debtor (or any other secured party) may pay the secured creditor all amounts owed it, including the underlying debt and expenses incurred in the repossession, and thus redeem the collateral (U.C.C. § 9–506).

The only exceptions to the requirement for reasonable notification of sale are when the collateral is perishable, when it threatens to decline rapidly in value, or when it is customarily sold on a recognized market (U.C.C. § 9–504(3)). If repossessed collateral includes foodstuffs that require immediate sale to avoid spoilage, reasonable notification of sale to a debtor is not required. At least one court has found corporate stock to be the type of collateral whose value may decline so rapidly as to justify sale without reasonable notice to the debtor. Publicly traded securities and commodities are sold in recognized markets and thus the creditor need not strictly adhere to the notice requirement with such collateral. The courts have not generally recognized any other type of collateral as sold in a recognized market and have consistently rejected automobiles as falling within this exception to the notice requirement.

PUBLIC OR PRIVATE SALE?

The content of a notice of sale is determined by whether the sale will be public or private. A notice of public sale must state the time and place of sale. A notice of private sale requires only a time after which the sale will be made (U.C.C. § 9–504(3)).

Depending on what type of sale is most commercially reasonable under the circumstances, the secured party, not the debtor, decides whether a sale of collateral will be public or private. The secured party should base that decision on what type of sale will produce the highest price for the collateral. While public sales will generally result in the best prices for automobiles, this may not be true for specialized equipment or inventory, which are best sold through normal commercial channels.

If a secured party elects to sell collateral by public sale, then it must truly be open to the public through proper publicity. While the UCC itself has no requirements for publicizing a public sale, the courts require adequate information describing the collateral in a public notice of sale. The notice should also include the terms of the sale and a location where potential purchasers can inspect the collateral before the sale. The secured party needs to publish the notice in a newspaper with a general circulation often and far enough before the sale to assure reasonable competition for the collateral.

The only time requirement for the sale of collateral applies to repossessed consumer goods when the debtor has paid 60 percent of their purchase price or 60 percent of the purchase-money loan used to acquire the consumer goods. The secured party must sell this type of collateral within 90 days of its repossession, unless the debtor waives the requirement after repossession (U.C.C. § 9–505).

PRICE

The requirement that all aspects of a repossession sale be commercially reasonable does not mandate that a sale produce the best possible price for the collateral. On this issue, the UCC provides as follows:

The fact that a better price could have been obtained by a sale at a different time or in a different method from that selected by the secured party is not of itself sufficient to establish that the sale was not made in a commercially reasonable manner. If the secured party either sells the collateral in the usual manner in any recognized market thereof or if he sells it at the price current in such market at the time of his sale or if he has otherwise sold it in conformity with reasonable commercial practices among dealers in the type of property sold, he has sold the collateral in a commercially reasonable manner. The principles stated in the two preceding sentences with respect to sales also apply as may be appropriate to the other types of disposition. A disposition which has been approved in any judicial proceeding or by any bona fide creditor's committee or representative of creditors shall conclusively be deemed to be commercially reasonable, but this should not be construed to indicate that any such approval must be obtained in any case or that any disposition not so approved is not commercially reasonable (U.C.C. § 9–507(2)).

Sale Proceeds   Upon the sale of repossessed collateral, a secured creditor can recover any expenses incurred in preparing and processing the collateral for sale. The UCC is specific about distribution of such sale proceeds. Under the UCC (section 9–504(1)), the sale proceeds shall be applied in the following order:

(a) the reasonable expenses of retaking, holding, preparing for sale or lease, selling, leasing and the like and, to the extent provided for in the agreement and not prohibited by law, the reasonable attorneys' fees and legal expenses incurred by the secured party;

(b) the satisfaction of indebtedness secured by the security interest under which the disposition is made; and

(c) the satisfaction of indebtedness secured by any subordinate security interest in the collateral if written notification of demand therefor is received before distribution of the proceeds is completed. If requested by the secured party, the holder of a subordinate security interest must seasonably furnish reasonable proof of his interest, and unless he does so, the secured party need not comply with his demand.

However, under the UCC, a creditor can recover from collateral sale proceeds attorneys' fees and other legal expenses incurred in repossessing collateral only if a security agreement so provides.

EXAMPLE ■ The facts are the same as in the previous example, except in
addition to the $2,000 cost of assembling the toys, Citizens
National Bank pays Speedy Trucking $500 to remove the
inventory from River Corporation's plant to another location.
The bank also pays $200 for a month's storage of the toys, $700
to Stanley Nye to sell the toys, and $800 to its attorney for legal
services rendered regarding the repossession. The bank's security
agreement contains no reference to legal expenses. If the toys sell
for $20,000, Citizens National Bank is entitled to the following
amounts from the sale proceeds:

$20,000	Proceeds from toy sales
− 2,000	Assembly costs
− 500	Moving costs
− 200	Storage costs
− 700	Nye's commission
− 11,000	Balance of debt due Citizens National Bank
$5,600	Surplus

However, because its security agreement contained no reference to
legal expenses, Citizen's National Bank cannot recover its attorneys'
fees of $800.

Note that state laws may prohibit the recovery of attorney's fees and
other legal expenses, particularly if the collateral is consumer goods,
even if such expenses are allowed by the security agreement.

In this example, Citizens National Bank must give the $5,600
surplus resulting from the sale to the River Corporation. Thus, unless
collateral is accounts or chattel paper, the secured party must turn over
any surplus resulting from a repossession sale to the debtor. If the
collateral is accounts or chattel paper, no surplus need be given the
debtor unless the underlying security agreement so provides (U.C.C.
§ 9–504(1)(c)). However, if the sale of collateral does not produce
sufficient funds to cover a secured creditor's allowable expenses and the
debt due it, the debtor is personally liable for any deficiency.

Retention of Repossessed Collateral

A secured creditor may retain repossessed collateral for its own use in one of two ways. First, it may purchase the collateral at any public or private sale. However, if the sale is private, then the collateral must either be customarily sold in a recognized market or the subject of widely distributed standard price quotations, such as stocks sold on the New York Stock Exchange (U.C.C. § 9–504(3)). Second, unless the collateral is consumer goods falling within the 60-percent-payment rule, a secured party may retain the collateral in full satisfaction of the debtor's obligation.

To retain the collateral, the secured party must first notify the debtor of the proposed retention. If the debtor objects to the retention proposal within 21 days of its being sent, the secured party must then sell the collateral. Other secured parties who have given notice of their interests to the secured party holding the collateral also have a right to receive notice of a retention proposal and to object to it within 21 days (U.C.C. § 9–505).

Penalties for Failure to Comply with Repossession Rules

A secured party who fails to comply with the U.C.C. provisions regarding the repossession and sale of collateral is liable for damages to injured debtors or other secured parties. On this issue, the UCC states the following:

If it is established that the secured party is not proceeding in accordance with the provisions of this Part, disposition may be ordered or restrained on appropriate terms and conditions. If the disposition has occurred, the debtor or any person entitled to notification or whose security interest has been made known to the secured party prior to the disposition has a right to recover from the secured party any loss caused by a failure to comply with the provisions of this Part. (See U.C.C. § 9–507(1).)

This provision is not an idle threat to secured creditors who violate the requirements of the UCC regarding the repossession and sale of collateral. Secured creditors violating these provisions often lose the ability to recover deficiencies.

Case for Discussion

ACME STATE BANK V. ALLEN

Facts

Acme State Bank repossesses equipment owned by Allen upon default of his loan agreement. However, the bank fails to notify Allen of the sale of collateral, which results in proceeds that are $5,000 less than the balance owed the bank. After the sale, the bank sues Allen for the deficiency of $5,000. Allen bases his defense on the bank's failure to give him notice of the sale of collateral.

Decision

In this case, the courts are divided. Most courts would require Allen to prove that the bank's lack of notice caused him damages. If Allen could demonstrate his readiness and ability to redeem the equipment but for the lack of notice, he would meet his burden to prove damages. The amount of his damages would then equal his loss of business caused by lack of the equipment. Thus, if Allen could prove damages of $5,000, he would not be liable for the $5,000 deficiency. However, to find Allen not liable for the deficiency, a minority of the courts would require him to prove only that the bank gave no notice of sale.

Questions for Discussion

1. What specific evidence could Allen provide the court to prove that the bank's lack of notice caused him damages? What response could the bank make to each piece of evidence?
2. What procedures should banks take upon a debtor's default to ensure that they give proper notice of the sale of collateral?

In repossessing and disposing of collateral that is consumer goods, a secured lender who fails to comply with UCC requirements is subject to a severe penalty, whether or not the debtor suffers actual damages. The penalty is an amount no less than the finance charge plus 10 percent of the principal amount of the debt, or the time-price differential plus 10 percent of the cash price of the goods (U.C.C. § 9–507(1)).

EXAMPLE ■ Lyons borrowed $10,000 from Citizens National Bank to purchase a car for his personal use. His total finance charge for the loan was $2,500. Later, Lyons defaulted on the loan. The bank then repossessed and sold the car with a notice to Lyons that contained an erroneous date of sale. The bank repeated the error in the public notice of the sale. Lyons sued Citizens National Bank. In this situation, Lyons won. By simply alleging and proving the bank's violations of the UCC and without showing any specific damages, he received a judgment for $3,500. As required by the UCC, the judgment equaled Lyons's finance charge plus 10 percent of the amount financed (U.C.C. § 9–507(1)).

CONCLUSION

Only a secured lender who has obtained a perfected interest in the collateral that is superior to competing claims can accrue benefits upon a debtor's default. Generally, the secured party who is first to file a financing statement has first rights to the collateral. The principal exception to this rule arises when a competing lender claims a purchase-money security interest in the collateral. Under the UCC, a purchase-money security interest in collateral other than inventory takes priority over a previously perfected security interest. If the purchase-money security interest is in inventory, then such interest takes priority over a conflicting interest in the same inventory if (1) the purchase-money security interest is perfected when the borrower receives the inventory; (2) the purchase-money secured party gives written notice to the holder of a previously perfected security interest that the former has or expects to acquire a purchase-money security interest in the inventory, which the notice describes by type or item; and (3) the holder of the previously perfected security interest receives the notice within five years before the borrower receives possession of the inventory.

If a debtor defaults on an obligation, then the secured party has the right to take possession of the collateral, sell it, and apply the sale proceeds to the debt due. However, when secured creditors prepare to sell the collateral, they must perform every aspect of the sale, including its method, manner, time, place, and terms, in a "commercially reasonable" manner. Otherwise, if the sale proceeds are insufficient to cover the debt, the creditor may be unable to recover the deficiency from the debtor.

Questions for Review and Discussion

1. On October 1, Jackson signs a security agreement granting Third National Bank a security interest in her equipment in exchange for a $50,000 loan. On November 1, First State Bank files a financing statement covering Jackson's equipment in exchange for a $30,000 loan. Which bank has priority in the equipment? Why?

2. Define a purchase-money security interest.

3. On January 1, Basil executes a security agreement in favor of Spark giving him a security interest in Basil's diamond ring. Spark files a financing statement properly describing the ring on January 30. On January 15, Basil executes a second security agreement covering the same ring and conveying a security interest to Rogers. Rogers files a proper financing statement the next day. On January 20, Basil delivers the ring to Cooper to secure a loan that Cooper made in December. On February 1, Basil announces that he cannot pay any of his creditors. What is the order of priority in the collateral among Spark, Rogers, and Cooper?

4. If a retail television dealer—without filing a financing statement or taking possession of the collateral—can obtain a perfected security interest in purchase-money consumer goods, when, if ever, would such a dealer feel the need to file a financing statement?

5. If a buyer in the ordinary course of business purchases an item free of a perfected security interest in inventory, why should a bank be interested in perfecting such an interest?

6. Daniels borrows $1,000 on an unsecured basis from First National Bank. Later, Daniels defaults on the loan. The bank proposes to repossess her car and personal computer and sell them to realize its claim. May it do so? If so, under what circumstances? How would the situation differ if the bank had taken a security interest?

7. Describe the surplus and deficiency rules that attend secured transactions and become important in a foreclosure.

8. Under what circumstances may repossessed collateral be sold at a private rather than public sale?

9. When may a creditor forgo notifying the debtor of the time and place for the sale of collateral?

10. Under what circumstances can a creditor recover from the collateral sale proceeds attorney's fees and other legal expenses incurred in repossession?

ANSWERS TO QUESTIONS FOR REVIEW AND DISCUSSION

Chapter 1

1. The four types of negotiable instruments are drafts, checks, notes, and certificates of deposit.

2. An order instrument principally serves as a payment device and thus functions as a substitute for money. A promissory instrument principally serves as a credit device.

3. Checks and drafts are classified as order instruments. Notes and certificates of deposit are classified as promissory instruments.

4. The three parties to a draft are the drawer, the drawee, and the payee.

5. The two parties to a promissory instrument are the maker and the payee.

6. A negotiable instrument may be written on any tangible medium including a napkin.

7. An illiterate person can sign a negotiable instrument by making a mark that he or she intends to operate as his or her signature.

8. An instrument is not negotiable if its payment is conditioned upon the occurrence of some event.

9. A promise or order to pay must be payable in money.

10. If a holder cannot determine from the face of an instrument when payment is due, then the instrument is nonnegotiable.

11. A bearer instrument does not designate a specific payee and thus is payable to anyone who holds it.

12. No. When payees' names are joined by the word "and," the check must be endorsed by both parties.

13. A check made payable to the order of "Tom Wit, President, Allied Shoelace Co." must be deposited to the company's account.

14. If a discrepancy exists between the amount expressed in words and the

amount expressed in figures, the words control. If, however, the words are ambiguous, the figures control the words.

15. If handwritten terms conflict with typewritten or printed terms, the handwritten terms control the typewritten or printed terms.

Chapter 2

1. "Negotiable" refers to an instrument that contains all the elements of negotiability and thus refers to the form of the instrument. "Negotiation" refers to the method by which a negotiable instrument is transferred.

2. The law of contracts governs the transfer of nonnegotiable instruments. Nonnegotiable instruments are transferred by assignment.

3. Order instruments are transferred by endorsement *and* delivery. Bearer instruments are transferred by delivery alone.

4. A holder in due course takes an instrument free from all claims to it by any other person and most defenses of any party to the instrument with whom the holder has not dealt.

5. A person gives value for an instrument when he or she gives money or performs a service for instance in exchange for the instrument.

6. The UCC relies on the subjective test of good faith rather than the objective test. The subjective test accepts the honesty of the holder in taking the instrument as the sole measure of good faith. The objective test uses the standard of honesty of a reasonably knowledgeable and careful person.

7. A person is not a holder in due course if he or she has reason to know that the note was purchased after its maturity date.

8. The shelter doctrine permits a person to become a holder in due course although he or she may not have fulfilled the ordinary requirements of such status. This doctrine applies only when the person who does not meet holder-in-due course status receives the instrument from a transferor who is a holder in due course.

9. A holder in due course is free from any other person's claim of title to an instrument.

10. A party may assert "real" and "personal" defenses against a holder in due course. A holder in due course is only susceptive to real defenses such as infancy, incapacity, and fraud in the factum.

Chapter 3

1. A person's authorized signature obligates him or her to pay an instrument.

2. An individual, called an agent, may sign an instrument at another's request.

3. The two types of liability that may be incurred on an instrument are contractual liability and warranty liability.

4. The parties primarily responsible to a holder for payment of an instrument are makers and acceptors. The parties secondarily responsible to a holder for payment are drawers and endorsers.

5. Drawers or endorsers may write the phrase "without recourse" after their signatures on instruments to escape a contractual obligation to pay them. Payees can, however, pursue drawers or endorsers who have disclaimed their contractual liability to pay instruments on the underlying obligation.

6. Three types of endorsements are special, blank, and restrictive. A special endorsement specifies the person to whom or to whose order an instrument is payable. A blank endorsement specifies no particular endorsee. A restrictive endorsement seeks to prevent further transfers or negotiation of an instrument.

7. A payor whose name is badly misspelled may endorse a check in the misspelled or wrong name, in his or her proper name, or both the wrong and proper names.

8. A transferor's warranty on an instrument is a promise to subsequent holders that certain statements of fact about the instrument are true.

9. The three presentment warranties a transferor makes to a payor are (1) that he or she has good title to the instrument; (2) that he or she has no knowledge that the maker's or drawer's signature is unauthorized (a holder in due course does not give this warranty); and (3) that the

instrument has not been materially altered.

10. If the transferor endorses the instrument, transfer warranties are given to any subsequent holder of the instrument.

11. All parties to an instrument are discharged from liability when no party is left with the right of recourse for payment of the instrument.

12. For a discharge from liability to occur, payment in full must be made to the holder of the instrument. Unless the holder objects, any person may pay an instrument, including a person who is not a party to the instrument.

13. Certification of a check discharges the drawer and all other parties who endorsed the check before the certification.

Chapter 4
1. Article 4 ensures the rapid circulation of negotiable instruments.

2. Cash is available for withdrawal at any time during the next business day after the banking day the deposit was made.

3. An item is considered a local check if it is deposited in a bank located in the same check-processing region as the paying bank.

4. Under the permanent availability schedule, a local check is available for withdrawal at any time on the opening of the second business day following the banking day the deposit was made.

5. An item is considered a nonlocal check if it is drawn on a paying bank that is not located in the same check-processing region as the depositary bank.

6. Under the permanent availability schedule, a nonlocal check is available for withdrawal at any time on the opening of the fifth business day following the banking day the deposit was made.

7. Regulation CC permits depository institutions to extend the hold periods under the following circumstances:

■ when a new account is opened

■ when large deposits are made to an account

- when a check is redeposited to an account

- when a deposit is repeatedly overdrawn

- when a bank has reasonable cause to doubt the collectibility of a check

- when certain emergency conditions arise

8. Depositary, intermediary, and presenting banks are classified as collecting banks.

9. The midnight deadline for an item deposited on Tuesday is midnight Wednesday. The midnight deadline for an item deposited on Friday is midnight Monday.

10. A paying bank is deemed to have returned a check in an expeditious manner if it meets the requirements of either the two-day/four-day test or the forward collection test.

Chapter 5
1. Under the UCC, an unauthorized signature does not operate as that of the person whose name is signed. However, an unauthorized signature would be considered genuine if the person whose signature is forged or unauthorized decides to adopt it as his or her own. Such adoption is called ratification.

2. If a bank pays a check that bears the drawer's forged signature, then, as a general rule, the drawee-payor bank is responsible for the loss.

3. Under the UCC, a customer must exercise reasonable care in inspecting his or her statement and report any forgery to the bank within a reasonable period, not to exceed 14 days after the receipt of the statement. If a year has elapsed before a customer discovers a forged check, he or she is precluded from asserting such forgery against the drawee-payor bank.

4. As a general rule, a bank has a fundamental responsibility to pay its depositor's checks that are drawn on sufficient funds. However, a bank may still dishonor a check, although there are sufficient funds on deposit to pay it, when the customer has placed a stop-payment order on the item.

5. Since the paycheck is stale dated, the bank should not pay it unless the bank knows that the drawer wants the check paid.

6. In order for an altered check to be properly payable in the amount originally drawn, the drawee bank must pay the check in good faith. A customer, however, will be liable for the altered amount if his or her own negligence substantially contributed to the alteration.

7. Once a bank receives a stop-payment order, its sole duty is to obey it.

8. When a wrongful dishonor of a check occurs through a mistake, then the payor bank is liable to its customer only for those damages actually sustained and clearly resulting from the wrongful dishonor.

9. After a payor bank decides to dishonor a check, it must return it within its midnight deadline; otherwise, it becomes accountable for the full amount of the item.

10. The amount of damages that may be recovered against a collecting bank that fails to exercise ordinary care in handling an item is the actual amount of the item in question reduced by any amount that the collecting bank can demonstrate would not have been collected even if it had exercised ordinary care.

11. The following actions constitute final payment of a check by a payor bank: payment in cash, final settlement, or completion of posting the check to the drawer's account.

12. The following events are referred to as the four legals: (1) when the payor bank receives notice that a drawer has filed a petition in bankruptcy, (2) when the payor bank receives a stop-payment order, (3) when the payor bank receives a court order attaching an account, or (4) when the payor bank exercises its right to use funds on deposit in the account to repay a debt its customer owes.

    A person who asserts one of the legals is not always automatically entitled to get paid first from the funds on deposit in the drawer's account. Under the UCC, a payor bank must have a reasonable period of time to act on a legal before it takes priority over the payment of a check. For example, if a bank is served with a restraining order at 10:00 A.M. and then cashes a check drawn on the restrained account at 10:15 A.M., the cashing of the check would probably take priority since the bank did not have a reasonable period of time to act on the restraining order.

As a general rule, the test to determine whether the owner of a check or the person asserting a legal is entitled to the proceeds on deposit in the drawer's account is "first come, first served."

Chapter 6

1. The account party is the customer who requests that a letter of credit be established. The bank that establishes the letter of credit is called the issuer. The person who is entitled to demand payment of a letter of credit is called the beneficiary.

   An advising bank is one that notifies the beneficiary that another bank has issued a letter of credit in his or her favor, and a confirming bank is one that agrees to become liable under the terms of a letter of credit to the same extent as the issuer.

2. A letter of credit is established for an account party when it is sent to the account party or when a written advice of its issuance is sent to the beneficiary. A letter of credit is established for a beneficiary when the beneficiary receives the letter of credit or a written advice of its issuance.

3. Upon establishment of an irrevocable letter of credit, the issuer is precluded from either unilaterally canceling or modifying the credit.

4. A commercial letter of credit supports the sale of goods. A standby letter of credit backs up the performance of an obligation normally owed by the account party to the beneficiary.

5. Once a letter of credit has been established, an issuer is obligated to honor payment of any draft presented as long as the accompanying documents, if any, conform to the terms of the credit.

6. A clean letter of credit is defined as a credit payable upon presentation of a draft for payment.

7. The doctrine of strict compliance provides that payment under the terms of a letter of credit cannot be made unless the documents presented thereunder conform exactly to the terms of the credit. Under the doctrine of substantial compliance, payment may be made under

the credit as long as the documents presented thereunder do not interfere with the substantive terms of the credit even though they do not technically conform exactly to the terms of the credit. The majority of courts adhere to the doctrine of strict compliance.

8. Once an issuer has been presented with documents under a letter of credit, the issuer may defer payment without dishonor until the close of the third banking day after receipt of the documents. A payor bank, however, has only until its midnight deadline to decide whether to pay or dishonor a draft drawn on its customer's checking account.

9. The beneficiary is entitled to recover the face amount of the draft together with any incidental damages and interest.

10. The payment of a letter of credit should only be enjoined based upon a fraud or forgery in the documents themselves or a fraud in the letter-of-credit transaction.

Chapter 7

1. The two categories of article 9 collateral are goods and intangibles.

2. Goods include equipment, farm products, and inventory.

3. Intangibles include instruments, documents, chattel paper, accounts (including contract rights), and general intangibles.

4. Before Crane's security interest in the car attaches, Davis, the debtor, must actually buy the car thereby obtaining rights to the collateral.

5. The basic purpose for taking security in a sale or lending transaction is as an added protection against nonpayment of the debt.

6. A lender or seller who possesses a security interest is called a secured party. The person who owes payment or other performance is called a debtor. The property taken as security is called collateral. A security agreement is one that creates a security interest. A financing statement is a summary of a security agreement which provides third parties with notice of a creditor's interest in collateral. The right to pay a debt and discharge a security interest is known as the right of redemption. The procedure by which a secured party sells collateral upon the debtor's default is called foreclosure.

7. Attachment refers to the creation of a security interest in collateral. Perfection means that the secured party has taken the appropriate steps to notify interested parties of its security interest in the collateral.

8. A security agreement creates a security interest in collateral. The essential ingredients of a security agreement are a grant of a security interest, the debtor's signature, and a description of the collateral.

9. Clauses on after-acquired collateral assure a lender that its secured position in a debtor's property will stay current with the debtor's acquisition of further goods or intangibles of the type originally given as collateral.

10. First National does not have a security interest in the computer since the original collateral, the car, is a consumer good and the computer was acquired more than 10 days after the original loan was made.

11. A financing statement is a summary of a security agreement filed with a proper public official for the purpose of notifying third parties of a creditor's interest in collateral described in the security agreement.

12. The name Heather Kinney should be identified in the financing statement.

13. A lender can perfect a security interest without filing a financing statement if it takes physical possession of the collateral or if state law permits the notation of its security interest on a certificate of title.

Chapter 8

1. First State Bank has priority in the equipment since it perfected its security interest before Third National Bank.

2. A security interest becomes a purchase-money security interest when a borrower uses the loan proceeds to purchase property that secures the loan.

3. The order of priority in the collateral is first Cooper (because he has possession), then Rogers (because he filed his financing statement on January 15), and finally Spark (because he filed his financing statement on January 30).

4. In the event that the dealer had filed a financing statement, he would have been protected if the original purchaser of the television subse-

quently sold it to another consumer for personal use.

5. By filing a financing statement, the bank protects itself against any subsequent sale of the goods by the original purchaser.

6. The bank may not repossess the collateral since it did not obtain a security interest. In order to obtain possession of the collateral, it must first become a judgment creditor whose judgment lien takes priority over other interests in the property. If the bank had taken a security interest in the collateral, it would have been able to accomplish a self-help repossession without the necessity of first obtaining a judgment.

7. Under the UCC, the sale proceeds shall be applied in the following order:

   (a) the reasonable expenses of retaking, holding, preparing for sale or lease, selling, leasing and the like and, to the extent provided for in the agreement and not prohibited by law, the reasonable attorneys' fees and legal expenses incurred by the secured party;

   (b) the satisfaction of indebtedness secured by the security interest under which the disposition is made; and

   (c) the satisfaction of indebtedness secured by any subordinate security interest in the collateral if written notification of demand therefor is received before distribution of the proceeds is completed. If requested by the secured party, the holder of a subordinate security interest must seasonably furnish reasonable proof of his interest, and unless he does so, the secured party need not comply with his demand.

8. The choice as to whether the collateral will be sold at a public or private sale is that of the creditor. The creditor's decision as to the type of sale should be based upon which is most commercially reasonable under the circumstances. This decision should be based upon what type of sale will produce the highest price for the collateral.

9. The only exceptions to the requirement for reasonable notification of sale are when the collateral is perishable, threatens to decline rapidly in value, or is customarily sold in a recognized market.

10. Fees and legal expenses may be recovered from the collateral sale proceeds only if a security agreement so provides and if state law does not prohibit recovery of such expenses.

GLOSSARY

abandonment Absolute, voluntary, and intentional relinquishment of property—total desertion by its owner.

acceleration clause A clause in a loan contract stating that the entire loan balance will become due immediately if a breach of certain conditions stated in the contract occurs.

acceptance Occurs in a contractual situation when conditions in the offer have been satisfied.

acceptor A person who accepts a bill of exchange.

access device A card, code, or other means of access to a consumer's account, which may be used for initiating electronic fund transfers.

accession Installation or affixing of one type of personal property item into another, resulting in a new item of personal property.

account (1) The credit established under a particular name, usually by deposit, against which withdrawals may be made. (2) A record of the financial transactions affecting the assets, liabilities, income, expenditures, or net worth of an individual or business entity. (3) In the Electronic Fund Transfer Act, a demand deposit, savings deposit, or other asset account established primarily for personal, family, or household purposes.

account party A buyer or other person who causes an issuer to open a letter of credit.

administrator An individual or trust institution appointed by a court to settle the estate of a person who has died (a) without leaving a valid will, (b) without naming an executor, or (c) leaving an executor who will not serve. (A female is called an administratrix.)

adverse action Under the Equal Credit Opportunity Act (ECOA), a creditor who denies a consumer's request for credit is a creditor who takes "adverse action" and must advise the applicant of the reason for denial of the credit.

adverse possession An occupation of land inconsistent with the right of the true owner.

advising bank A bank that notifies the beneficiary that another bank has issued a letter of credit.

after-acquired property Property a debtor acquires as security, after the execution of a mortgage or other form of indebtedness, that additionally secures the indebtedness.

agency The relationship between an agent who acts on behalf of another person and the principal on whose behalf the agent acts. *See* fiduciary.

agent A person who acts for another person by the latter's authority. The distinguishing characteristics of an agent are (a) that he or she acts on behalf, and subject to the control, of his or her principal; (b) that he or she does not have title to the property of his or her principal; and (c) that he or she owes the duty of obedience to the orders given by his or her principal.

allonge Paper attached to a negotiable instrument, used for endorsements when there is no room for them on the instrument itself.

antedated item An item bearing a past date.

appellate court A court with jurisdiction to hear appeals from trial courts.

articles of partnership (partnership agreement) A written agreement between business partners that outlines the provisions of their business arrangement.

assignment The transfer by one person to another of the title to property, rights, or other interests.

attachment A concept designed to grant a security interest in a debtor's property. It usually occurs when a debtor signs a security agreement or surrenders possession of the property to the creditor.

bailment The delivery of personal property by one person, the *bailor*, to another, the *bailee*, for a limited period and for some specific purpose, such as use, repairs, or safekeeping, but without passing title to the property.

bank holding companies Companies that own or control banks. Holding companies are permitted to engage in nonbank activities to the extent that those activities relate to providing services to banks, including acting as investment advisers, leasing personal and real property, providing data-processing services, operating insurance agencies, and providing management consulting advice and advertising services.

bankruptcy The legal proceedings by which the affairs of an entity unable to meet financial obligations are turned over to a trustee or receiver for administration, in accordance with bankruptcy laws.

bankruptcy trustee A person or trust institution that holds the legal title to property for the benefit of someone else. A trustee is responsible for preserving and managing the assets of a trust.

bearer A person or company that has physical possession of a check, security, or any negotiable financial instrument with no name entered on it as payee. Any bearer can present such an instrument for payment.

beneficiary (1) The person for whose benefit a trust is created. (2) The person to whom the amount of an insurance policy, annuity, or bequest is payable. (3) The ultimate party to be credited or paid as a result of a transfer. (4) The person in whose favor a letter of credit is issued.

bilateral offer Offer conditioned upon a promise to be made by an offeree.

bill of exchange A draft. A negotiable and unconditional written order, such as a check or trade acceptance, signed and addressed by one person to another. The person who receives a bill of exchange must pay a specified sum on demand or at a specific future time.

bill of lading A document in one or more parts, issued by a transportation company, that acknowledges receipt of specified goods for transporting to a specific location and sets forth the contract between the shipper and carrier.

billing error An error made by a creditor in the billing of an open-end credit account, the allegation of which by a consumer triggers procedures set forth in the Fair Credit Billing Act.

blue-sky laws State laws concerning the registration and issuance of securities. These laws may be different from federal laws and regulations and must be obeyed if a security is to be sold in that state.

bona fide purchaser One who, without having received notice of any defect in the title, purchases property in good faith and pays a valuable consideration for the property.

branch (as defined in the McFadden Act and applicable only to national banks) Any branch bank, branch office, branch agency, additional office, or any branch place of business located in any state or territory of the United States or District of Columbia at which deposits are received, checks paid, or money lent.

bribery The giving or receiving of any undue reward to influence the behavior of the person receiving such award in the discharge of his or her official duty.

certificate of deposit (1) A formal receipt for funds left with a bank as a special deposit. Such deposits may bear interest, in which case they are payable at a definite date in the future or after a specified minimum notice of withdrawal; or they may be noninterest bearing, in which case they may be payable on demand or at a future date. These deposits are payable only upon surrender of the formal receipt, properly endorsed. (2) A certificate issued to the owners of bonds or stocks as evidence of the deposit of a stated number of shares or bonds when a corporation is reorganized.

certificate of incorporation A certificate issued by a state acknowledging corporate existence.

certificate of title A certificate that represents ownership of property, titled according to state or federal law outside the scope of article 9 of the Uniform Commercial Code.

certified check A customer's check that has been presented to a bank for authentication and guarantee. By its certification, the bank guarantees that sufficient funds have been set aside from the customer's account to cover the amount of the check when payment is demanded. Legally, with the certification of a check, payment becomes the bank's responsibility.

check A commercial demand deposit instrument (a draft) signed by the maker and payable to a person named or to a bearer upon presentation to the bank on which it is drawn.

clean payment A payment unencumbered by documents.

clearing house (1) An establishment maintained by financial institutions for settling clearing claims. (2) A place where representatives of the banks in the same locality meet daily at an agreed time to exchange checks, drafts, and similar items drawn on each other and to settle the resulting balances. (3) An adjunct to a futures exchange through which transactions executed on the floor of the exchange are settled by matching purchases and sales. A clearing organization is also charged with the proper conduct of delivery procedures.

close corporation A corporation whose outstanding stock is held by a few people, often members of a single family. The stock is not available for sale and thus is not traded publicly.

closed-end credit A type of credit, usually installment credit, that involves an agreement with a customer specifying the total amount involved, the number of payments, and the due date for each payment.

collateral Specific property, securities, or other assets pledged by a borrower to a lender as a backup source of loan repayment.

collecting bank Any bank handling an item for collection, except the payor bank.

commercial letter of credit An instrument, issued by a bank, that substitutes the bank's credit for that of the buyer of goods. It authorizes the seller to draw drafts on the bank and guarantees payment of those drafts if the stated terms have all been met.

common law Body of law originating in medieval England and derived solely from usage, habits, and customs. Decisions in common law became the basis for subsequent decisions.

common stock *See* stock.

community property Property in which a husband and wife both have an undivided one-half interest by reason of their marital status.

compensatory damages Damages that place the injured party in the economic position that he or she would have enjoyed if the breach had not occurred.

Competitive Equality Banking Act (CEBA) Legislation enacted by Congress in 1987 significantly affecting the operations of nonbank banks, the powers granted to commercial banks and bank holding companies, and the timeframe during which banks of deposit must make checks available to customers.

Comptroller of the Currency An officer of the U.S. Treasury that regulates national banks.

confirmed letter of credit A letter of credit issued by the local bank of an importer and confirmed by another bank, usually located in the exporter's country. The second bank's obligation is added to the obligation of the issuing bank to honor drafts and documents presented according to the terms of credit.

consequential (special) damages Damages that accrue because of some special or unusual circumstance of the particular contractual relationship of the parties, such as loss of employment, business credit, or customers.

consideration Something of value given by one party to another in exchange for a promise or act by another party.

constitutions Fundamental laws of states or nations. In the United States, constitutions are created by conventions called for that purpose and ratified by voters, rather than enacted by legislative bodies.

consumer reports Information supplied by consumer-reporting agencies regarding consumers' creditworthiness, credit capacity, character, and personal lifestyle.

contract An agreement between two or more people to perform, or to refrain from performing, certain acts.

Consumer Leasing Act (1976) An act requiring lessors to disclose specified information about payment, trade-in allowances, and estimated value of property at the end of the lease.

corporate borrowing resolution A resolution passed by a corporation's board of directors specifying who may sign loan documents on behalf of the corporation. This resolution is then kept in the corporation's loan files at the various lending institutions with which it does business.

corporation A business organization that is treated as a single legal entity and is owned by its stockholders, whose liability is generally limited to the extent of their investment. The ownership of a corporation is represented by shares of stock that are issued to people or other companies in exchange for cash, physical assets, services, and good will. The stockholders elect the board of directors, which then directs the management of the corporation's affairs.

cosigner A person who signs an instrument along with another and becomes responsible for the obligation.

court of general jurisdiction A court having power to entertain any action on the trial level, regardless of the amount, subject matter, or type of relief demanded.

court of limited jurisdiction A court that is limited by state constitution or statute to entertain only certain actions. Those limitations are usually stated in terms of subject matter, amount, or type of relief sought.

cram down A confirmation of a reorganization plan gained by the court's forcing the plan on dissenting classes of creditors, as long as at least one impaired class consents to the plan and the plan does not discriminate unfairly.

credit A right granted by a creditor to defer payment of a debt, to incur debt and defer its payment, or to purchase property or services and defer payment on them. *See* open-end credit and closed-end credit.

credit card Any card, plate, coupon book, or other single credit device used, upon presentation, to obtain money, property, labor, or services on credit.

credit union A type of financial institution formed on the basis of a common bond. This institution must be a nonprofit corporation and all profits are distributed among members in proportion to their deposits.

cumulative voting One vote for each share of stock owned, multiplied by the number of directors to be elected. Board members of national banks must be elected by cumulative voting.

curtesy The life estate of a widower in the real property of his wife. Most states have abolished this estate. *See* dower.

damages A pecuniary compensation or indemnity that may be recovered in the courts by any person who has suffered loss, detriment, or injury, whether to his or her person, property, or rights, through the unlawful act, omission, or negligence of another. *See* compensatory damages, consequential (special) damages, punitive (exemplary) damages, incidental damages, and liquidated damages.

debt A sum of money owed to another person.

deceit *See* fraud.

deed, quit claim A deed that transfers only such interest, title, or right a grantor may have in real estate when the conveyance is executed.

deed, warranty A deed that guarantees the seller's right to convey clear title to a piece of property and that guarantees the property is free from debts not specifically disclosed.

defamation The invasion of the interest in one's reputation by the communication of derogatory information to a third person. Oral communication is *slander*; if it is in writing or a permanent embodiment, it is *libel*.

default (1) The failure of a borrower to make a payment of principal or interest when due. (2) The state that exists when a borrower cannot or does not pay bond- and noteholders the interest or principal due. (3) A breach or nonperformance of any of the terms of a note or the convenants of a mortgage. (4) The failure to meet a financial obligation.

deferred posting A method of posting bank transactions to accounts after the day of receipt.

demand deposit Funds that a customer, usually by writing checks or using an automated teller machine, may withdraw from a bank with no advance notice. Checking accounts are the most common form of demand deposits.

depositary bank The first bank to which an item is transferred for collection (including the paying bank).

discharge Legal termination of an individual's responsibility for repayment of a debt.

disaffirmation Action by a party lacking capacity to enter into a contract to relieve him- or herself from a contractual obligation.

disclosures Data that federal or state law require to be given to cardholders regarding the terms of the credit extended. Disclosures must appear on cardholder agreements, monthly (periodic) billing statements, or any documents in which the rates for finance charges are mentioned.

dividend A payment made periodically, usually quarterly, by a corporation to its stockholders as a return on investment. Dividends can be paid in cash, stock, or property.

doctrine of avoidable consequence *See* mitigation of damages.

donor, donee *See* gift.

dower The life estate of a widow in the real property of her husband. At common law, a wife had a life estate in one-third (in value) of the real property of her husband if he died without leaving a valid will or she dissented from that will. Many states do not recognize common-law dower. *See* curtesy.

dragnet clause Language in a mortgage expressing open indebtedness.

drawee The party on whom a draft is drawn and who is directed to pay the sum specified.

drawer The party who instructs the drawee to pay funds to the payee.

easement An acquired right of use or enjoyment, falling short of ownership, which a person may have in the land of another (for example, one person's right-of-way over another's land).

electronic fund transfer Any transfer of funds, other than a transaction originated by check, draft, or a similar paper instrument, which is initiated through an electronic terminal, telephonic instrument, computer, or magnetic tape so as to order, instruct, or authorize a financial institution to debit or credit an account. Such a transfer includes, but is not limited to, point-of-sale transfers, automated teller machine transactions, direct deposits or withdrawals of funds, and transfers initiated by telephone. *See* Regulation E.

embezzlement (misappropriation of funds) The fraudulent appropriation to one's own use of funds or other property entrusted to one's care by another.

empirically derived credit system A credit-scoring system that evaluates an applicant's creditworthiness. This system primarily allocates points or weights to key characteristics that describe the applicant or various aspects of the transaction.

endorsement (1) The signature, placed on the back of a negotiable instrument or in an accompanying power, that transfers the instrument to another party and legally implies that the endorser has the right to transfer the instrument. (2) The placement of an endorsement stamp on bank card sales and credit slips to identify the originating bank and the date processed.

Equal Credit Opportunity Act (ECOA) A federal law passed in 1974 requiring lenders and other creditors to make credit equally available without discrimination based on race, color, religion, national origin, sex, age, marital status, receipt of income from public assistance programs, or past exercising of rights under the Consumer Credit Protection Act. The ECOA specifies actions and questions that are prohibited when one is obtaining information on credit applicants.

estate The right, title, or interest that a person has in any property, to be distinguished from the property itself. The term is often used to describe decedent's property.

estate at sufferance The interest of a tenant who rightfully has possessed land by the permission of the owner but continues to occupy the land after the period for which he or she is entitled.

estate at will A lease that continues at the will of the lessor.

estate for years A lease that continues for a definite period.

estoppel The preclusion of a person from alleging in his or her action what is contrary to his or her previous action or omission.

executor A party, frequently a trust company, named in a will to carry out its terms. The executor gathers the assets of the creator of the will; pays all taxes, debts, and expenses; and distributes the net estate as ordered in the will. (A female executor is called an executrix.)

executory interest A future estate or interest running in favor of a third person instead of a grantor.

Expedited Funds Availability Act (EFAA) A law passed by Congress in 1987 that requires financial institutions to make deposited items available for withdrawal on an expedited basis. Implemented by Regulation CC issued by the Federal Reserve Board, the act also requires lobby notices and special notices to a customer if funds will not be made available on the scheduled basis.

Fair Credit Billing Act of 1974 An amendment to the Truth in Lending Act, this federal law requires that creditors resolve billing errors in a prescribed manner within a specified period. Lenders must furnish customers a detailed description of their rights and the procedures they must follow to make complaints about billing errors. *See* Regulation Z.

Fair Debt Collection Practices Act The federal act that prohibits abusive debt collection practices by those collecting debts for parties other than themselves.

federal box A document, or an area within a document of a closed-end credit transaction, where all applicable transaction disclosures are grouped together.

Federal Deposit Insurance Corporation (FDIC) The federal regulatory agency for state banks that are not members of the Federal Reserve System. The FDIC insures the savings of bank customers.

Federal Reserve Board The federal regulator of state banks that are members of the Federal Reserve System.

Federal Reserve System A system created by enactment of the Federal Reserve Act in 1913 to encourage cooperation among all banks, whether state or federal.

federal system A system, such as that found in the United States, in which federal and state governments share power.

fee simple (absolute) The broadest form and most common kind of real property interest. With this kind of interest, the owner may use, abuse, and exclusively possess the real property; take its profits; and dispose of it by deed or will without restriction. Fee simple absolute provides the safest interest for mortgage purposes.

fee simple subject to condition subsequent (conditional) An estate that terminates once a stated event occurs and the owner acts to reenter and repossess the estate.

fee tail An estate limited to a person and the heirs of that person's body. Most states have abolished fee tail estates and generally converted them into fee simple estates.

fiduciary A person or trust institution charged with the duty of acting for the benefit of another party on matters coming within the scope of the relationship between them. A fiduciary relationship between two parties with regard to a business, contract, or piece of property requires that each party place trust and confidence in the other and exercise a corresponding degree of fairness and good faith. Examples of fiduciary relationships are those between guardian and ward, agent and principal, attorney and client, trustee and beneficiary, and one partner and another.

financing statement A statement, filed with the appropriate public official by a creditor, recording a security interest or lien on the debtor's assets.

fixture Any personal property so affixed to the land as to become part of the realty.

float (1) The difference between deposits credited to an account and the amount of those deposits that has been collected. (2) The difference between amounts credited by the Federal Reserve to depositary institutions and the amount of those items collected by the Federal Reserve. (3) The amount of deposited cash items in the process of collection from drawee banks. (4) The time interval between the creation of a check and its ultimate payment by the bank on which it is drawn. Float is simply a means of quantifying the efficiencies or inefficiencies of the "cash in-cash out" cycle and focusing on the associated opportunities and costs. By minimizing the float associated with collection of accounts receivable and extending the float on the accounts payable side, corporations can increase cash flow and improve their working capital position.

floating lien An ongoing security interest in all property, whether acquired before, at the time of, or after perfection.

forbearance Refraining from proceeding against a delinquent debtor or in exacting the enforcement of a right.

foreclosure A legal procedure undertaken to permit a creditor to take possession of and to sell property that is collateral for a defaulted loan.

fraud (deceit) Acts, omissions, or concealments intentionally meant to deprive another of his or her rights.

freehold estate A legal estate in land, commonly referred to as an estate of inheritance. The three freehold estates are fee simple, fee tail, and life estate.

future interest Any fixed interest except a reversion, with the right of possession and enjoyment postponed until some future date or event occurs.

gift voluntary transfer of property by one person (*donor*) to another person (*donee*), who gives no consideration for it.

gift causa mortis A gift of personal property made by a person in expectation of, and contingent on, death, completed by actual delivery of the property and effective only if the owner dies of the expected cause. *Distinguish from* gift inter vivos.

gift inter vivos A gift of property by one living person to another. Actual delivery of the property must be made during the lifetime of the donor and without reference to his or her death. *Distinguish from* gift causa mortis.

good faith A standard of conduct between parties, meaning honesty in fact, in the conduct of a transaction. As an element of a defense to violations under several statutes, a good faith effort to comply means that the defendant did not know about the violation and took reasonable steps to avoid it.

good faith estimate of settlement services A disclosure statement required for loans coming within the Real Estate Settlement Procedures Act (RESPA), giving estimates of an applicant's settlement costs.

goods Any item of merchandise, commodity, etc., having value.

grantee *See* grantor.

grantor A person conveying an interest in real property to another person, the *grantee*.

guarantor A person or legal entity that undertakes responsibility for another party's debt or obligation to perform some specific act or duty. Although the original debtor is responsible for the debt, the guarantor becomes liable in the event of default. The liability of the guarantor is secondary and collateral since it is based on a second, independent undertaking and is not part of the original contract as in *surety*.

guardian A person or trust institution appointed by a court to care for the property, person, or both of a minor or incompetent person. When the guardian's duties are limited to the property, he or she is called a guardian of the property. When the guardian's duties are limited to the person, he or she is called a guardian of the person. If the duties apply to both property and person, he or she is simply called a guardian. *See* ward.

guardianship by nature The relationship of a parent and child. For a guardianship by nature, no court appointment is necessary during the child's minority.

holding company A company that owns stock in other corporations and influences the managerial decisions of those companies.

holder in due course Under the Uniform Commercial Code, a party who accepts an instrument in good faith, for value, and without notice that it has been dishonored, is overdue, or has any claim against it.

imputed knowledge Knowledge charged to a person because the facts in question were open to his or her discovery and it was his or her duty to inform him- or herself about them.

incidental damages Damages that include expenses incurred as a result of a breach.

indemnify To agree to compensate or reimburse an individual or other legal entity in the event of a potential loss.

infant (minor) A person not of legal age, which at common law was 21 years but has been changed in some states.

insider *See* preference.

insolvent Unable to pay one's debt obligations when they become due.

interest Money charged as compensation for the loan of money or compensation for forbearance from collecting money owed.

intermediary bank A bank between the receiving bank and the beneficiary's bank through which a transfer must pass if specified by the sending bank. In such cases, this is the receiving bank's credit party.

intestate Refers to a person who has died without having made and left a valid will.

issuer A bank or other person that issues a letter of credit.

joint tenancy Ownership of a piece of property shared equally by two or more people, each having full right of usage. If one owner dies, the survivor takes full ownership. *Distinguish from* tenancy in common and tenancy by the entirety.

junior mortgage A lien that is subordinate to the claims of the holder of a prior, senior lien.

larceny Taking the property of another, without his or her consent and against his or her will, with intent to convert it to the taker's use.

lessee (tenant) The party who holds the exclusive right of possession under a valid lease.

lessor (landlord) A party who leases property to a tenant.

letter of administration A certificate of authority to settle a particular estate issued to an administrator by the appointing court. *Distinguish from* letter testamentary.

letter testamentary A certificate of authority to settle a particular estate issued by the appointing court to the executor named in the will. *Distinguish from* letter of administration.

liability (1) An amount owed to someone else. (2) A legal obligation to make good some loss or damage that results from an action or transaction.

libel *See* defamation.

license Temporary authority to do one or more acts on the land of another, without possessing any estate or interest therein.

lien A legal claim or attachment filed on record against property, as security for the payment of an obligation. A lien is the guaranteed right of a lender or investor to specific property in case of default.

life estate An estate that can never be inherited and ends upon death—either the death of the life tenant or the death of another on whose life the estate is based.

limited partnership A type of partnership in which individuals may invest in business without exposure to unlimited liability for the partnership's debts. Limited partners cannot participate in control of the business.

liquidated damages Those damages recovered under an advance agreement as to the amount recoverable in case of breach of contract. A contract liquidating damages is enforceable if the amount is reasonable. Otherwise, courts will ignore it and award damages as if the liquidation clause did not exist.

liquidation The complex procedure in which a corporation's assets are sold and the net proceeds after all expenses are passed along to creditors, bondholders, and shareholders. Payments are made in accordance with the laws and contracts protecting each class of creditor.

living (inter vivos) trust A living, personal trust that becomes operative during the maker's lifetime. *Distinguish from* testamentary trust.

maker The party who executes an instrument, such as a check, draft, or note. *Also called* drawer.

material alteration An alteration that changes the contract of a party to an instrument.

mechanic's lien A lien filed against real property as a result of nonpayment for work performed or materials delivered.

misappropriation of funds *See* embezzlement.

mitigation of damages (Doctrine of Avoidable Consequence) The obligation of an injured party in a breach-of-contract action to attempt to limit his or her own damages.

mortgage An instrument whereby the borrower (*mortgagor*) gives the lender (*mortgagee*) a lien on property as security for the payment of an obligation. The borrower continues to use the property and, when the obligation is fully extinguished, the lien is removed.

most-favored-lender doctrine Under the National Banking Act, the ability of national banks to charge the maximum rate of interest allowed to any other state lender located in the same state.

National Credit Union Administration (NCUA) An agency of the federal government that regulates federal credit unions and acts as an insuring agency for all deposits in federal credit unions and for deposits in those state-chartered credit unions that opt to join NCUA.

negligence Failure to use reasonable care under the circumstances.

negotiability The extent to which a financial instrument can be transferred by endorsement.

negotiable Transferable by endorsement. Title to a negotiable instrument can be transferred by delivery, without need for further certification. Negotiable instruments must be safeguarded as if they were cash. Bearer securities are automatically negotiable by nature, whereas registered securities can only be rendered negotiable by the completion of a power of assignment.

negotiable instrument A written instrument (such as a check, promissory note, draft, or bill of exchange), payable to order or to the bearer. A negotiable instrument is transferred by endorsement and delivery or by delivery alone. It must meet all the requirements of article 3 of the Uniform Commercial Code.

negotiation (1) Dealings between parties with the goal of reaching an agreement as to the amount, price, quantity, quality, and other terms of an agreement. (2) The transfer of negotiable instruments.

note Written evidence of a debt. A note is an unconditional promise to pay a specified amount to a certain entity on a specified date. (2) A medium-term (1 to 5 or 10 years' maturity) security. (3) Currency.

novation The substitution of a new debt or obligation for an existing one.

offer A promise conditioned upon a thing to be done by the offeree.

Office of Thrift Supervision An arm of the Department of Treasury created under the Financial Institutions Reform, Recovery and Enforcement Act of 1989 to regulate federally chartered savings and loan associations.

on-us check A check deposited or otherwise negotiated at the bank on which it is drawn.

open-end credit The extension of credit, through bank credit cards or personal lines of credit, that allows customers to continue to add purchases or cash advances to their credit accounts.

order instrument An instrument that is payable to a specific person's order.

overdraft (1) The amount by which a debit or charge against an account exceeds the balance of the trust account. (2) A negative balance in a depositor's account that results from paying checks for an amount larger than the depositor's collected balance. (3) A check that overdraws an account. Banks are not legally obligated to pay an overdraft.

parol evidence rule The rule that states that, where parties have entered into a written contract that reflects their complete statement of the contract, no written or oral evidence of prior understandings or negotiations is admissible to contradict or vary the terms of the written contract.

partnership A legal entity composed of two or more people to enable them to carry on business as co-owners for profit.

partnership agreement *See* articles of partnership.

payee The person named in the instrument as the recipient of the sum shown. Thus, the payee is the party who receives the payment of an instrument.

payment A transfer of funds in any form between two parties.

payor The party that delivers funds.

perfected lien A security interest in an asset that has been properly documented and filed with the appropriate legal authority to protect the claim of the creditor.

piercing the corporate veil An action in which shareholders become personally liable for corporate debts, usually arising when a corporate entity has been used to perpetrate a fraud or commit an injustice.

postdated check A check bearing a future date.

power of attorney (1) A document, witnessed and acknowledged, authorizing the person named in it to act as attorney-in-fact for the person signing the document. (2) The authority to act as an attorney-in-fact. A general power of attorney allows action for the principal in all matters; a special power of attorney limits authority to specified matters.

preference (1) An insolvent debtor's transfer of property satisfying debts owed to one or more creditors to the disadvantage of the rest. (2) Under the Bankruptcy Code, a term describing a voluntary or involuntary transfer of an insolvent debtor's interest in property to benefit one creditor over other creditors, the transfer dating within 90 days before the date of filing of the bankruptcy petition. If the transfer occurs between 90 days and one year of that date, the recipient creditor is an "insider."

preferred stock *See* stock.

presenting bank The bank that forwards an item to another bank for payment.

principal (1) A party who appoints another to act on his or her behalf. (2) The actual amount of a deposit, loan, or investment, exclusive of interest charges. (3) The primary borrower on a loan, as opposed to the guarantor. (4) The original amount of an estate or fund together with accretions, which may include income. (5) The individual with primary ownership or managerial control of a business.

proceeds The total amount received from the sale, exchange, collection, or other disposition of collateral.

profit a prendre A right to take something from the land of another (for example, soil, minerals, or timber).

promissory estoppel A doctrine (for the most part, limited in actual application to cases of charitable subscriptions, gratuitous bailments, and parol gifts of land) that states that when a person has changed his or her position in good faith, relying on a promise upon which a reasonable person might be expected to rely, the promisor should be prevented (estopped) from using as a defense the absence of consideration for his or her promise.

promissory note A written promise made by one person (the *maker*) to pay a certain sum of money to another person (the *payee*), on demand or at a determinable future date.

property Assets subject to ownership. *Real property* is fixed or immovable, while *personal property* is movable.

prospectus An official document that must be given to buyers of new issues registered with the Securities and Exchange Commission (SEC). A prospectus is an abstract of the lengthy registration statement filed with the SEC and describes the issuer's products and business, the industries in which it competes, its physical facilities, and its management background. It presents historical financial statements and describes the issue and intended use of the funds to be received. The SEC neither approves nor disapproves the prospectus.

publicly held corporation A corporation whose stock is traded in the securities markets and is subject to both federal and/or state securities laws and regulations.

punitive (exemplary) damages Damages in excess of compensation, awarded to console the plaintiff and punish the defendant.

purchase-money security interest A security interest when the money loaned to the borrower is used to purchase the property that secures the loan.

quasi contrast A legal obligation arising out of the receipt of a benefit for which there has been no actual promise to pay, but the retention of which without giving consideration would be unjust.

quiet enjoyment A covenant in a warranty deed that gives the right of possession without disturbance caused by defects in title.

quit claim deed *See* deed, quit claim.

ratification Conduct by a person consistent with the existence of a contract, which could have been avoided. This act must be performed with full knowledge of its ratifying what is known to be voidable.

Real Estate Settlement Procedures Act (RESPA) A 1974 federal law requiring lenders to provide home mortgage borrowers with information of known or estimated settlement costs. This act is administered by the Department of Housing and Urban Development and establishes guidelines for escrow account balances and the disclosure of settlement costs.

recording statutes State laws governing the registration of all conveyances of all real property.

redemption (1) A statutory or contractual right to repurchase or repossess pledged, sold, or mortgaged property within the time and according to statutory or contractual conditions. (2) The right of a party under a disability to redeem or recover property taken from him or her, under color of right during the period of his or her disability. (3) The repaying of principal and interest to retire a security.

redemption period The time in which a mortgagor, by paying the amount owed in a foreclosed mortgage, may buy back property. The specific time is subject to estate law.

regulation A written rule usually issued by agencies of the executive branch of state and federal governments to implement statutes.

Regulation B A Federal Reserve regulation that prohibits creditors from discriminating against credit applicants, establishes guidelines for gathering and evaluating credit information, and requires written notification when credit is denied.

Regulation CC A Federal Reserve regulation that covers the availability of funds deposited by customers, disclosures of a bank's policy on availability, and the standards that must be used in endorsing checks.

Regulation E A Federal Reserve regulation that establishes the rights, liabilities, and responsibilities of parties in electronic fund transfers, and protects consumers using electronic fund transfer systems.

Regulation M A Federal Reserve regulation that implements the consumer-leasing provisions of the Truth in Lending Act.

Regulation X A Department of Housing and Urban Development regulation applicable to all federally related mortgage loans.

Regulation Z A Federal Reserve regulation that prescribes uniform methods of computing the cost of credit, disclosure of credit terms, and procedures for resolving billing errors on certain credit accounts.

remainder A future estate or interest in property that will become an estate or interest in possession, upon the termination of the prior estate or interest created at the same time and by the same instrument as the future estate. *Distinguish from* reversion, which remains in the grantor, while the remainder goes to a grantee.

rescission Cancellation of a contract without penalty. Under the Truth in Lending Act, the ability of a consumer to unilaterally terminate a credit transaction, that is, without the creditor's consent.

restrictive covenants Limitations imposed on the use of a tract of property to benefit the entire parcel.

reversion The interest in an estate remaining in the grantor after a particular interest, less than the whole estate, has been granted by the owner to another person.

reverter The interest that the grantor retains in property for which he or she has conveyed an interest less than the whole to another party. If the grantor makes the conveyance subject to a condition that may or may not be broken sometime in the future, he or she retains a *possibility of reverter*.

right of offset The common-law right of a lender to use the balances in any of the customer's accounts as payment for the loan in the event of default.

Right to Financial Privacy Act A federal act limiting the ability of the federal government to gain access to the records of bank customers.

Rule against Perpetuities A rule of common law that makes void any estate or interest in property so limited that it will not take effect or vest within a period measured by a life or lives in being at the time of the creation of the estate, plus 21 years and the period of gestation.

savings and loan association A type of financial institution that traditionally, before passage of the Depository Institutions Deregulation and Monetary Control Act of 1980, limited its activities to the areas of savings deposit accounts and residential mortgages.

secured creditor A creditor whose claim against another person is protected by collateral that he or she holds to ensure the settlement of the claim.

Securities and Exchange Commission (SEC) A government agency that regulates the sale of securities in interstate commerce and through the mail.

security agreement An agreement between a seller and buyer which states that the seller will have a security interest in the goods being traded.

security interest (1) Under Federal Reserve Regulation Z, any interest in property that secures performance of a consumer credit obligation and is recognized by state or federal law. (2) Any interest in property that secures as collateral the payment or performance of an obligation.

settlor A creator of a living trust.

severalty Ownership by one person.

shareholder derivative suit A suit brought by shareholders in the name of a bank against board members and/or officers as individuals.

sight draft A draft that is payable on sight (demand) when presented to the drawee.

slander *See* defamation.

small loan finance company A company chartered exclusively under state law, with no ability to accept deposit accounts. The interest rates charged by a small loan finance company are traditionally higher than those charged by other financial institutions.

sole proprietorship The simplest form of business organization, owned and operated by an individual person.

sovereign immunity A doctrine that a state cannot be sued against its will.

special information booklet A pamphlet given applicants for loans coming within the Real Estate Settlement Procedures Act (RESPA). This pamphlet describes the procedures used when a residential real estate buyer enters into a purchase agreement, obtains financing, and completes settlement.

specific performance The actual accomplishment of a contract by the party bound to fulfill it. An action to compel the performance of a contract according to its terms is usually brought when the payment of damages would not adequately compensate the aggrieved party.

stale check Any check dated more than a reasonable time (a few months) before presentation. According to the Uniform Commercial Code, a bank is not required to pay on a check (other than a certified check) that is presented more than six months after its date. When a bank receives a stale check, it may call the writer for permission to pay the check or it may return the check.

standby letter of credit A letter of credit against which funds can be drawn only if another business transaction is not performed.

Statute of Frauds A statute, first enacted in England in 1677, designed to prevent many fraudulent practices by requiring proof of a specific kind, usually in writing, of the important transactions of business.

statute of limitations A statute that bars suits upon valid claims after the expiration of a specific period. In most states, there is a 20-year limitation on judgments, a 6-year limitation on contract claims, and a shorter period for tort claims (injuries to people or property).

statutory law (statutes) Laws enacted by state legislatures and the U.S. Congress.

stock A certificate evidencing ownership in a corporation. The stock of a corporation is usually divided into two classes, common and preferred. *Common stock* represents the basic ownership, usually with a voting privilege, but subordinate to claims of bondholders, creditors, and preferred stock-holders. The holder of *preferred stock* enjoys priority as to income and generally as to assets.

strict liability Automatic responsibility for certain torts.

subordination agreement An agreement between two creditors of a particular borrower whereby one party grants to the other a priority claim to the borrower's assets if default occurs.

surety A person or company that, at the request of another, usually called the principal, agrees to be responsible for the performance of some act in favor of a third person if the principal fails to perform as agreed. In suretyship, there is only one contract, making the surety's liability original, primary, and direct. *Distinguish from* guarantor.

tax lien A claim against real property for unpaid taxes. Property tax liens usually take precedence over a first mortgage, while other tax liens (income, etc.) do not.

tenancy by the entirety A tenancy by a husband and wife in which, except in concert with the other, neither the husband nor the wife has a disposable interest in the property during the other's lifetime. When either dies, the property goes to the survivor. *Distinguish from* joint tenancy and tenancy in common.

tenancy in common The joint ownership of property without the right of survivorship, in which each person's interest in a property can be distinguished from the others' interests. *Distinguish from* joint tenancy and tenancy by the entirety.

tenancy in partnership The holding of property in a partnership's name.

testamentary trust A trust established by the terms of a will to manage assets for a beneficiary. This trust becomes active after the maker's death and settlement of the estate. *Distinguish from* living trust.

testate Refers to a person who has died after having made and left a valid will. *Compare with* intestate.

time draft A draft that is payable at a fixed or determinable future time.

tort A private injury proximately caused by breach of a legal duty arising by operation of law. It can include, but is not limited to, assault; battery; intentional infliction of emotional distress; false imprisonment; trespass to land or goods of another; conversion; injuries by animals or extra-hazardous activities; causing a nuisance, fraud, or misrepresentation; defamation; invasion of privacy; false advertising; and negligent manufacturing of goods. Some torts are also criminal offenses and may be prosecuted.

transit item A check drawn on an out-of-town bank.

trust A fiduciary relationship in which a person or corporation, the *trustee*, holds the legal title to property, the *trust property*. The trustee is subject to an obligation, enforceable in a court of equity, to keep or use the property for the benefit of another person, the *beneficiary*. *See* living trust and testamentary trust.

trust property *See* trust.

trustee A person or trust institution that holds the legal title to property for the benefit of someone else. A trustee is responsible for preserving and managing the assets of a trust.

Truth in Lending Act The popular name for the Consumer Credit Protection Act of 1969, which applies to all lenders that extend credit to consumers. The act requires disclosure of credit terms (for example, the annual percentage rate and total finance charges) using a standard format. *See* Regulation Z.

ultra vires act An act by a corporation's agents, officers, or directors that exceeds the rights of its charter and is thus void.

unauthorized use The use of a credit card by a person other than the cardholder—a person who does not have actual, implied, or apparent authority to use the card—and a use from which the cardholder receives no benefit.

Uniform Commercial Code (UCC) A coordinated code of laws governing the legal aspects of business and financial transactions in the United States. It regulates such topics as the sale of goods, commercial paper, bank deposits and collections, letters of credit, bulk transfers, and documents of title.

usury (1) A higher rate of interest than is allowed by law. (2) The act of charging a higher rate of interest for the use of funds than is legally allowed by a state.

ward A person who by reason of minority, mental incompetence, or other incapacity is under a court's protection, either directly or through a guardian. *See* guardian.

warranty A guarantee made by a seller for the quality or suitability of the product or service for sale.

warranty deed *See* deed, warranty.

wrongful dishonor The failure to pay a properly payable item.

zoning A government specification for the type of use and density of development for a given piece of property.

INDEX

Additional Publications of Interest from ABA

To order copies, contact your local AIB chapter or call ABA Order Processing at (202) 663-5087.

Personnel and the Law

A must for anyone who supervises others, this seminar covers every aspect of the employment process from recruitment to discharge. Included are actual legal cases, application exercises, and situation analyses that simulate real-life employment situations.

	Order Number	Price	ABA Member Price*
Handbook	623202	$ 24.00	$ 18.00
Leader's Guide	623203	$ 38.00	$ 28.00

Law & Banking: Principles 1990

A banker's guide to law and legal issues with special emphasis on the Uniform Commercial Code, this textbook includes up-to-date summaries of laws pertaining to contracts, real estate, and bankruptcy. Also included is a complete chapter that summarizes the numerous regulations involved in consumer lending. A glossary of legal terminology related to banking and commercial transactions and an index round out this comprehensive text.

	Order Number	Price	ABA Member Price*
Textbook	050241	$ 51.00	$ 38.00
Instructor's Manual	250240	$ 24.00	$ 18.00
Workbook	050242	$ 20.00	$ 15.00

Banking Terminology

This comprehensive, authoritative dictionary unlocks the language of "bankspeak" and makes it comprehensible to all. It defines clearly and concisely over 5,000 terms and almost 200 acronyms used in the banking and financial services industry.

	Order Number	Price	ABA Member Price*
Text			
(1-4 copies)	629600	$ 34.00	$ 25.00
(5-19 copies)		$ 30.00	$ 23.00
(20 or more)		$ 27.00	$ 20.00

A Legal Guide to Employee Relations

This comprehensive guide covers the legal aspects of the entire employment process from pre-employment tests to termination. Designed for practical application, the text is organized by types of employee-related decisions and problems that a supervisor might encounter. Also addressed are such timely issues as drug testing and layoffs, nondiscrimination laws, affirmative action plans, union and nonunion employee relations, the consequences of litigation, and the effects of decisions on employee morale, productivity, and employer-employee relations.

	Order Number	Price	ABA Member Price*
Text	050250	$120.00	$ 90.00

*The discounted prices are available to ABA member banks and AIB chapters. All prices are subject to change without notice.